What Is God Like?

Children's Bible Studies
Volume Two

R. B. THIEME, JR., BIBLE MINISTRIES
HOUSTON, TEXAS

> FINANCIAL POLICY
>
> There is no charge for any material from R. B. Thieme, Jr., Bible Ministries. Anyone who desires Bible teaching can receive our books, MP3 CDs, and tapes without obligation. God provides Bible doctrine. We wish to reflect His grace.
>
> R. B. Thieme, Jr., Bible Ministries is a grace ministry and operates entirely on voluntary contributions. There is no price list for any of our materials. No money is requested. When gratitude for the Word of God motivates a believer to give, he has the privilege of contributing to the dissemination of Bible doctrine.

A catalogue of available audio recordings and publications will be provided upon request.

R. B. Thieme, Jr., Bible Ministries
P. O. Box 460829, Houston, Texas 77056-8829
www.rbthieme.org

© 2004 by R. B. Thieme, Jr. All rights reserved

No part of this publication may be reproduced or transmitted in any form or by any means, electronic or mechanical, including photocopy, recording, or any information storage and retrieval system, without permission in writing from the publisher, with the exception of the visual aids.

The visual aids illustrations in this book, the copyright of which belongs to R. B. Thieme, Jr., may be reproduced in part or in whole by any means without written permission provided the materials are distributed at no charge and are not distributed or published on the internet or by any other means of mass publication and distribution.

Unless otherwise indicated, all Scripture taken from the New American Standard Bible,
© 1960, 1962, 1963, 1968, 1971, 1972, 1973, 1975, 1977
by The Lockman Foundation. Used by permission.

Printed in the United States of America

ISBN 1-55764-403-9

Contents

Preface xi

History of *Children's Bible Studies* xiii

To the Parents xv

How to Use This Book xvii

Chapter One—How God's Word Came to Us 1
    Overview 1
    Lesson One: The Bible—The Word of God 2
        Tablets of Stone 2
        What God Wants Me to Know 3
        Lesson Review 3
        Memory Verse 3
    Lesson Two: God Again Gives Moses the Law 3
        Exodus 34 3
        What God Wants Me to Know 4
        Lesson Review 4
        Memory Verse 4

Chapter Two—How Do We Know the Bible Is the Word of God? 5
    Overview 5
    Lesson One: God Breathed His Words into Men 6
        Words Given by God 6
        What God Wants Me to Know 6
        Lesson Review 7
        Memory Verse 7
    Lesson Two: God Inspired Daniel 7
        What God Wants Me to Know 8
        Lesson Review 8
        Memory Verse 9

Chapter Three—The Word of God, Its Message and Power 10
    Overview 10
    Lesson One: In the Mirror of the Bible 11
        The Bible Is Your Lamp 11
        What God Wants Me to Know 12
        Memory Verse 12
    Lesson Two: Conversion by Reading the Word of God 12
        The Good News of the Gospel 12
        What God Wants Me to Know 13
        Lesson Review 13
        Memory Verse 14

Chapter Four—How Jesus Used God's Word to Overcome Temptation 15
   Overview 15
   Lesson One: The Word of God—The Sword of the Spirit 16
      The Enemy of the Lord Jesus—Satan 17
      What God Wants Me to Know 17
      Memory Verse 17
   Lesson Two: Victory over Temptation 18
      The Temptation to Act Apart from the Father's Provision, Matthew 4:3–4 18
      The Temptation to Go against God's Word, Matthew 4:5–7 18
      The Temptation to Bypass the Father's Plan, Matthew 4:8–11 19
      What God Wants Me to Know 19
      Lesson Review 20
      Memory Verse 20

Chapter Five—The Word of God Lives Forever 21
   Overview 21
   Lesson One: The Blessings of Remembering the Word 22
      Young King Josiah 22
      What God Wants Me to Know 23
      Lesson Review 24
      Memory Verse 24
   Lesson Two: Dire Results of Forsaking the Word 24
      Jehoiakim Did Not Love God's Word 24
      What God Wants Me to Know 25
      Lesson Review 25
      Memory Verse 25

Chapter Six—Hearing and Doing God's Word 26
   Overview 26
   Lesson One: Four Kinds of Hearers and Listeners 27
      The Word of God Is Planted in the Soul 27
      The Wayside (Hard) Soil, Luke 8:5, 12 28
      The Rocky Soil, Luke 8:6, 13 28
      The Thorny Soil, Luke 8:7, 14 28
      The Good Soil, Luke 8:8, 15 28
      What God Wants Me to Know 28
      Lesson Review 28
      Memory Verse 29
   Lesson Two: Fruit-Bearers for the Lord 29
      Pharaoh—The Hard Heart, Exodus 5 29
      Peter—The Rocky Heart-Soil, Matthew 26:69–75 29
      Demas—The Sticker-Weed Heart-Soil, 2 Timothy 4:10 30
      Timothy—The Good Heart-Soil, Acts 16:1–5; 2 Timothy 1:5; 3:15 30
      What God Wants Me to Know 31
      Memory Verse 31

Teaching the Essence of God 32

Chapter Seven—The Sovereignty of God 33
   Overview 33
   Lesson One: Nebuchadnezzar's Dream 34
      A Mighty King 34
      The King's Dream 34
      Nebuchadnezzar's Dream Interpreted 35
      What God Wants Me to Know 35
      Lesson Review 36
      Memory Verse 36

Table of Contents

Lesson Two: The Mightiest King of All ... 36
    The Dream Comes True ... 36
    Nebuchadnezzar Realizes God Is Sovereign ... 36
    Nebuchadnezzar Believes in the Lord ... 37
    Nebuchadnezzar's Restoration ... 37
    Nebuchadnezzar's Declaration ... 37
    What God Wants Me to Know ... 37
    Lesson Review ... 37
    Memory Verse ... 38

Chapter Eight—Sovereignty and Serving the Heavenly King ... 39
  Overview ... 39
  Lesson One: Saul Meets the Heavenly King ... 40
    Saul, the Enemy of Christ and Christians ... 40
    Saul Meets the Risen Lord ... 40
    Saul's Conversion ... 40
    Saul Receives His Sight Back ... 41
    God's Plans for Saul's Life ... 41
    Saul's Enemies and New Friends ... 41
    What God Wants Me to Know ... 41
    Lesson Review ... 41
    Memory Verse ... 41
  Lesson Two: Paul Serves His Sovereign ... 42
    God Protects Paul ... 42
    God's Plan Made Known to Paul ... 42
    God Works Out His Plan ... 42
    Paul Serves the Heavenly King ... 43
    A Dangerous Journey ... 43
    To Rome, At Last ... 43
    What God Wants Me to Know ... 43
    Lesson Review ... 43
    Memory Verse ... 44

Chapter Nine—The Righteousness of God ... 45
  Overview ... 45
  Lesson One: God's Righteousness and Man's ... 46
    The Righteousness of Man as Seen by God ... 46
    The Righteousness of Man as Seen by Man ... 46
    Not Good Enough ... 46
    The Righteousness of God ... 47
    Christ Was Punished for Our Sins ... 47
    Made Righteous in Christ ... 47
    What God Wants Me to Know ... 47
    Lesson Review ... 47
    Memory Verse ... 48
  Lesson Two: The Pharisee and the Publican ... 48
    The Pharisee and the Publican ... 48
    What God Wants Me to Know ... 49
    Lesson Review ... 49
    Memory Verse ... 49
  Lesson Three: The Test in the Garden ... 50
    The Creation ... 50
    Adam and Eve in Eden ... 50
    The Test Declared ... 50
    The Temptation ... 50
    The Fall of Man ... 51

  What God Wants Me to Know 51
  Lesson Review 51
  Memory Verse 51

Chapter Ten—The Justice of God 52
 Overview 52
 Lesson One: The Fall and Judgment of Man 53
  Adam and Eve before the Fall 53
  The Wages of Sin 53
  Operation Coverup 53
  Sin Discovered 54
  God Judges 54
  What God Wants Me to Know 54
  Lesson Review 55
  Memory Verse 55
 Lesson Two: The Great White Throne Judgment 55
  Two Teams 55
  Two Places 55
  The Qualifying Rule 56
  The Teams Separated and Judged 56
  The Book of Life 56
  The Last Judgment 56
  The Deciding Factor 56
  What God Wants Me to Know 57
  Lesson Review 57
  Memory Verse 57

Chapter Eleven—The Love of God 58
 Overview 58
 Lesson One: The Grace of God 59
  God's Love and the Sin Barrier 59
  John 3:16 59
  What God Wants Me to Know 60
  Lesson Review 60
  Memory Verse 60
 Lesson Two: The Good Shepherd 61
  Watching the Sheep and Shepherds, John 10:1–6 61
  The Good Shepherd, John 10:7–19 61
   The Door to Heaven 61
   His Life for the Sheep, John 10:14–15 61
   His Love and Care of the Sheep, John 10:12–13 62
   The Shepherd Psalm 62
  What God Wants Me to Know 62
  Memory Verse 63

Chapter Twelve—Eternal Life, the Great I AM 64
 Overview 64
 Lesson One: Moses Learns That God Is Eternal Life 65
  A Question You May Have Asked 65
  How God Counts Time 65
  Moses Sees a Strange Sight 65
  God Speaks to Moses out of the Burning Bush 66
  The Great I AM 66
  Moses Tells Us of the Great I AM 66
  What God Wants Me to Know 66
  Lesson Review 67
  Memory Verse 67

Lesson Two: The Great I AM 67
    The Eternal Word 67
    God Cannot Die 67
    Before Abraham Was Born, I AM 68
    Rejection of the Son of God 68
    What God Wants Me to Know 68
    Lesson Review 69
    Memory Verse 69

Chapter Thirteen—Omniscience: How God Looks at Man 70
  Overview 70
  Lesson One: The Story of David 71
    God Knows Israel's Next King 71
    God Knew a Prophet 71
    God Sends Samuel to Anoint David 71
    How God Looks at Man 71
    What God Wants Me to Know 72
    Lesson Review 72
    Memory Verse 73
  Lesson Two: God Reveals a Secret 73
    Jesse Sent for David 73
    What God Saw in David 73
    David Anointed 73
    David Trusts in God's Omniscience 74
    What God Knew about David 74
    What God Wants Me to Know 74
    Lesson Review 74
    Memory Verse 75

Chapter Fourteen—Omniscience: The Plan of the All-Wise God 76
  Overview 76
  Lesson One: The Story of Joseph 77
    God Knows the Love, Envy, and Hatred in Jacob's Family 77
    The First Dream, a Message and Promise from God 77
    The Second Dream 78
    The Brothers' Wicked Plan 78
    What God Wants Me to Know 78
    Lesson Review 78
    Memory Verse 78
  Lesson Two: What God Always Knew Would Happen to Joseph 79
    The Oldest Son's Selfish Plan 79
    Joseph Thrown into the Dry Well 79
    Joseph Sold as a Slave 79
    The Brothers Tell a Lie 79
    God Knows All Things 80
    What God Wants Me to Know 80
    Lesson Review 80
    Memory Verse 80
  Lesson Three: God Knows 81
    God Knows Why Jacob Wept 81
    God Knows How Joseph Was Sold to Potiphar 81
    God Knows Joseph Is in Prison 81
    Pharaoh's Dream 81
    God Knows All Dreams and Their Meanings 82
    Joseph Promoted 82
    What God Wants Me to Know 82

  Lesson Review 83
  Memory Verse 83
 Lesson Four: How "All Things" Worked "Together for Good" 83
  God Knows How to Keep Them Alive in Famine 83
  A Dream Comes True 84
  Joseph's Nobility—He Rewards Evil with Good 84
  Joseph Makes Himself Known to His Brothers 84
  All Things Work Together for Good 85
  What God Wants Me to Know 85
  Lesson Review 85
  Memory Verse 85

Chapter Fifteen—Omnipresence: The Ever-Present God 86
 Overview 86
 Lesson One: Jacob Learns of God's Omnipresence 87
  Background to Genesis 28 87
  Jacob Leaves Home 87
  Alone in the Dark? 87
  The Ever-Present God 87
  Jacob Has Learned His Lesson 88
  What God Wants Me to Know 88
  Lesson Review 88
  Memory Verse 88
 Lesson Two: A Lesson for Jonah 89
  God Sends Jonah to Nineveh 89
  Jonah Flees 89
  A Lesson for Jonah 89
  The Storm 89
  The Fish 90
  What God Wants Me to Know 90
  Lesson Review 91
  Memory Verse 91
 Lesson Three: God's Loving Care 91
  God Delivers Jonah 91
  God Speaks Again to Jonah 91
  Nineveh Spared 92
  Jonah Sulks 92
  Jonah's Last Lesson on What God Is Like 92
  What God Wants Me to Know 92
  Memory Verse 93

Chapter Sixteen—Omnipotence: The Greatness of God's Power 94
 Overview 94
 Lesson One: God's Power to Help 95
  How the Israelites Came to Egypt 95
  A Family Becomes a Nation, Exodus 1:7a 95
  God's Power to Deliver, Exodus 14 96
  The Trap 96
  What God Wants Me to Know 96
  Lesson Review 96
  Memory Verse 96
 Lesson Two: God's Power over the Sea 97
  God Fights a Battle 97
  The Egyptians Defeated 97
  What God Wants Me to Know 98
  Lesson Review 98
  Memory Verse 98

Table of Contents

Chapter Seventeen—Omnipotence: Letting God Fight Our Battles 99
  Overview 99
    Lesson One: The Walls of Jericho 100
      Joshua, Israel's New Leader 100
      A Walled City 100
      Joshua Believed It 100
      The "Battle" of Jericho 101
      God's Victory at Jericho 101
      What God Wants Me to Know 101
      Lesson Review 101
      Memory Verse 102
    Lesson Two: God Fights a Battle 102
      God Repeats His Promise 102
      The Longest Day and the Shortest War 102
      What God Wants Me to Know 103
      Lesson Review 103
      Memory Verse 104

Chapter Eighteen—Immutability: God Keeps His Promises 105
  Overview 105
    Lesson One: God Never Changes 106
      God Keeps His Promises 106
      What God Wants Me to Know 107
      Lesson Review 107
      Memory Verse 107
    Lesson Two: Noah and the Flood 108
      The Coming of the Flood, Genesis 6:8–22 108
      The Rains Came, Genesis 7 108
      A New Beginning, Genesis 8 109
      What God Wants Me to Know 109
      Lesson Review 110
      Memory Verse 110

Chapter Nineteen—Veracity: God Is Truth 111
  Overview 111
    Lesson One: God's Word, Ways, and Works Are Truth 112
      God Is Truth 112
      The Father of Lies 113
      What God Wants Me to Know 113
      Lesson Review 113
      Memory Verse 114
    Lesson Two: God's Truth and Satan's Lies 114
      God's Truth and Satan's First Lie 114
      How God's Truth Overcame 114
      What God Wants Me to Know 115
      Lesson Review 116
      Memory Verse 116

Chapter Twenty—Divine Essence Understood and Applied 117
  Overview 117
    Lesson One: The Golden Image 118
      The Golden Idol, Daniel 3:1–7 118
      God's Essence and the Events on Earth, Psalm 33:13–14 118
      The Crisis, Daniel 3:8–15 119
      The Decision, Daniel 3:16–18 119
      What God Wants Me to Know 119

- Lesson Review ... 120
- Memory Verse ... 120
- Lesson Two: The Fiery Furnace ... 120
  - Nebuchadnezzar's Command, Daniel 3:19–23 ... 120
  - God Is Able, Daniel 3:24–28 ... 121
  - With God Nothing Shall Be Impossible, Daniel 3:28 ... 121
  - What God Wants Me to Know ... 122
  - Lesson Review ... 122
  - Memory Verse ... 122

Chapter Twenty-One—Promotion ... 123
- Overview ... 123
- Lesson: Samuel's Promotion ... 124
  - Samuel Is Born, 1 Samuel 1:1–23 ... 124
  - Samuel Comes to the Tabernacle, 1 Samuel 1:24—2:11, 18–26 ... 124
  - Samuel Promoted, 1 Samuel 3 ... 124
  - How Samuel Got His Promotion ... 125
  - What God Wants Me to Know ... 125
  - Memory Verse ... 125

Chapter Twenty-Two—Thanksgiving Holiday Lesson ... 126
- Overview ... 126
- Lesson: Daniel Thanks the Lord ... 127
  - False Thanksgiving ... 127
  - True Thanksgiving ... 127
  - What God Wants Me to Know ... 128
  - Memory Verse ... 128

Chapter Twenty-Three—Christmas Holiday Lesson ... 129
- Overview ... 129
- Lesson: The Christmas Star Gives Light and Life ... 130
  - Christmas Is a Person ... 130
  - Lights in the Darkness ... 130
  - The Promised Savior ... 130
  - Wise Men Seek the God Who Made the Stars ... 130
  - The Star Appears ... 131
  - The Journey of the Magi ... 131
  - Herod's Question ... 131
  - The Wise Men Find Jesus ... 131
  - The Wise Men Warned ... 131
  - What God Wants Me to Know ... 131
  - Memory Verse ... 132

Chapter Twenty-Four—Easter Holiday Lesson ... 133
- Overview ... 133
- Lesson: The Risen Savior ... 134
  - The Resurrection ... 134
  - The Women at the Tomb ... 135
  - The Race between Peter and John ... 135
  - A Surprise for Mary Magdalene ... 135
  - What God Wants Me to Know ... 135
  - Memory Verse ... 135

Visual Aids ... 137

Preface

Before you begin your Bible study, if you are a believer in the Lord Jesus Christ, be sure you have named your sins privately to God the Father.

> If we confess our [known] sins, He is faithful and righteous to forgive us our [known] sins and to cleanse us from all [unknown, or forgotten sins] unrighteousness. (1 John 1:9)

You will then be in fellowship with God, filled with the Holy Spirit, and ready to learn Bible doctrine from the Word of God.

> "God is spirit, and those who worship Him must worship in [the filling of the] spirit and [biblical] truth." (John 4:24)

If you have never personally believed in the Lord Jesus Christ as your Savior, the issue is not naming your sins. The issue is faith alone in Christ alone.

> "He who believes in the Son has eternal life; but he who does not obey [the command to believe in] the Son shall not see life, but the wrath of God abides on him." (John 3:36)

THE WORD OF GOD is alive and powerful, sharper than any two-edged sword, piercing even to the dividing asunder of the soul and the spirit, and of the joints and the marrow, and is a critic of thoughts and intents of the heart. (Heb. 4:12)

All Scripture is God-breathed, and is profitable for doctrine, for reproof, for correction, for instruction in righteousness; that the man of God might be mature, thoroughly furnished unto all good works. (2 Tim. 3:16–17)

Study to show thyself approved unto God, a workman that needeth not to be ashamed, rightly dividing the word of truth. (2 Tim. 2:15)

History of *Children's Bible Studies*

Children's Bible Studies were originally published in the 1960s as the *Doctrinal Bible Studies*, a compilation of Bible lessons taught to children in Berachah Church Sunday School. Affectionately referred to as "The Quarterlies," the series comprised thirty-two books addressing eight age levels. Each level was divided into the Quarterlies: Fall, Winter, Spring, and Summer. The series begins with basic doctrines for the very young child and progresses toward more advanced doctrines for the older child.

In 1972, Pastor R. B. Thieme, Jr., replaced Berachah Church Sunday School with Prep School and a new system of teaching. From the Bible doctrine resident in their souls, teachers would prepare their own Bible lessons to teach the children. However, the Quarterlies have remained a treasure-trove of ideas for parents and teachers looking for ways to communicate Bible doctrine at a child's level of understanding. When complete, *Children's Bible Studies* will contain all of the original material in eight volumes: *What God Wants Me to Know*; *What Is God Like?*; *The Persons of the Godhead*; *God's Plan of Salvation*; *The Christian Way of Life*; *The Life of Moses*; *The Mental Attitudes*; and *The Dispensations*.

Children's Bible Studies complement the lesson formats and research guide from *Train Up a Child...Children's Bible Studies Source Book*. The lessons are organized into chapters with an overview outlining the subject, titles of the lessons, story objective, vocabulary and doctrinal concepts, *Source Book* keywords, and activities. New visual aids pertinent to the lessons are included in the back of the book for use in making training aids. The lessons in the *Children's Bible Studies* are easily incorporated into the extensive curriculum found in the *Source Book* enabling parents and teachers to master lesson preparation while providing creative ways to teach Bible doctrine.

What Is God Like?, the second volume in the series, covers two main subjects: the authenticity of the canon of Scripture and the essence of God. The first lessons establish in the child's mind that the Bible is the very Word of God. The child is challenged to believe God's Word, and to love and desire divine truth above everything else in life. The following lessons explain what God is like through the Doctrine of Divine Essence. Each divine attribute—sovereignty, righteousness, justice, love, eternal life, omniscience, omnipresence, omnipotence, immutability, and veracity—is presented emphasizing the essence and oneness of the Godhead. The child will come to know that the very essence of God stands behind His every Word and is the basis of his own security and well-being. With confidence in the Word of God and the Doctrine of Divine Essence firmly established in his soul, the child will learn to both respect and love God, and to live his Christian life in a way that both honors and glorifies God.

To the Parents

God mandates you, the parent, to study and learn Bible doctrine. With Bible doctrine in your soul, you are the best teacher in the world for your children. From your own doctrinal frame of reference, personality, and approach, you can then fulfill your responsibility to God to teach your children the Word of God.

> "And these words, which I am commanding you today, shall be on your heart; and you shall teach them diligently to your sons and shall talk of them when you sit in your house and when you walk by the way and when you lie down and when you rise up." (Deut. 6:6–7)

Teach your children Bible doctrine the way you teach them to play ball, to make a bed, to wash their hands, to use table manners. Teach them over and over. Then, check them. Repeat and repeat, until they know Bible doctrine as readily as they know their own name. When the time comes for them to leave home, you can rest confidently in God's promise:

> Train up a child in the way he should go,
> Even when he is old he will not depart from it.
> (Prov. 22:6)

Consider how much time you already spend training your children how to live as well-mannered, responsible citizens. How much more time are you willing to spend to insure that they know how to live as believers in the Lord Jesus Christ who reflect the glory of God? You have the privilege of teaching your children that learning and applying Bible doctrine is the most wonderful blessing in life. In fact, Bible doctrine is the most valuable heritage you can give your children.

> I was very glad to find *some* of your children walking in truth, just as we have received commandment *to do* from the Father. (2 John 4)

How to Use This Book

Teaching the Word of God requires careful preparation. You cannot teach what you do not know. To facilitate your preparation, each chapter of the *Children's Bible Studies* begins with an Overview, the plan for developing the subject of that particular chapter. The Overview provides a solid foundation on which you can build your own lesson plans, tailored to your setting, teaching style, and the children's age levels.

THE CHAPTER OVERVIEW:

Subject: The chapter title summarizes the primary doctrinal emphasis and the biblical reference upon which each story is based.

Lesson Titles: The lesson titles reflect a further delineation of the doctrinal concepts taught in each story.

Story Objective: The story objective is a synopsis, from an adult frame of reference, of the doctrines to be taught in each chapter. Each primary doctrine is documented with Scripture references. The story objective includes teaching pointers regarding specifics for presentation of the doctrine in that particular chapter.

Vocabulary and Doctrinal Concepts: Each chapter has a list of specific, technical vocabulary words that are used in the stories. It is important that the child understand the definitions of these words as the story progresses. The list of doctrinal concepts extrapolated from the stories is provided with Scripture references for preparation.

Source Book **Keywords:** Keywords provide a link to the corresponding subject in the Research Guide in *Train Up a Child...Children's Bible Studies Source Book*. The Research Guide provides Scripture references, book titles, and audio recordings on keyword subjects taught by R. B. Thieme, Jr. These resources are available upon request at no charge from R. B. Thieme, Jr., Bible Ministries, 5139 West Alabama, Houston, Texas 77056, USA.

Activities: A list of suggested activities is provided to enhance and reinforce the biblical concepts of the lesson. For a comprehensive list of teaching aids and resources, consult the *Source Book*.

Suggested Visuals: Most of the lessons have diagrams that illustrate the doctrinal concepts in the story as it unfolds. These diagrams may be used in any number of applications, including: flannel boards, worksheets, craft projects. The visuals used in assembling these diagrams are located in the back of this book. They may be copied, traced, or scanned and are intended to be colored, glued, glittered, used for models, mobiles, or backed with flannel fabric for use on a flannel board (a piece of board covered with flannel fabric).

Games, Songs, Worksheets: Any or all of these activities can be utilized to enhance the doctrinal concepts in the lessons. Many memory type games can be modified to challenge recall of doctrinal principles and vocabulary. Singing doctrinal lyrics fitted to familiar tunes reinforces biblical concepts. Worksheets provide an effective way to review the key points of each lesson.

Memory Verse: A Scripture verse pertinent to the subject is woven throughout the entire chapter and is for review at the end of each lesson.

Opening and Closing Prayer: Each lesson must begin with the private confession of sin (1 John 1:9). Opening prayer is time for soul preparation, time to request help from God the Holy Spirit for concentration and understanding of the Bible lesson to be taught. Each lesson should end with closing prayer, thanking God for His Son and His gift of our so-great salvation, thanking Him for the opportunity to learn His Word, and asking Him to challenge us in the application of His Word in our lives.

THE LESSONS:

Learning comes by repetition. Teach these lessons repeatedly, drawing the many different applications for the child from them. The lessons are organized so that doctrine is built upon doctrine, from the basic concepts to the more complex. Each lesson has three sections: The Story, What God Wants Me to Know, and the Lesson Review.

The Story illustrates how Bible doctrine can be learned, stored, and applied. The story is presented for a child's frame of reference and can be adjusted to any age level. Each story incorporates the chapter memory verse, weaving it throughout and tying it to the story objective.

What God Wants Me to Know gives the application of the doctrinal concepts to the child's life. In this section, the Gospel is also presented. That a child is saved cannot be taken for granted. Therefore, the need for and the way of salvation can never be presented too often.

Lesson Reviews are specifically designed for a categorical review of the doctrinal concepts, vocabulary words, and memory verse presented in each story. Utilizing the review not only insures that the key points of the lesson are covered, but leaves the children with something to anticipate in the next lesson.

GENERAL SUGGESTIONS:

Whether you teach in the classroom or in the home, formally or informally, with complex lessons and many activities or with simple, concise presentations, always make learning Bible doctrine enjoyable for the children. Never bore your children with the Word of God. Remember, "The word of God is alive and powerful" (Heb. 4:12)! Captivate their imaginations with God's truth. Hold their attention so that they eagerly look forward to learning more and more Bible doctrine. Let your children have an active part in the lessons. Encourage their natural curiosity, individual thought, expressions, and questions. For the effective communication of God's Word, the following guidance is provided for your consideration.

Reinforce the lesson subject in different ways. Use whatever methods are comfortable for you and effective with your children: sing songs, use puppets, play games, have surprises, use a variety of teaching aids. Many different teaching aids are readily available such as flannel graph stories, coloring books, recordings, CDs, and storybooks found in Bible bookstores and toy stores. Stores that provide materials for public school teachers are also an excellent source of teaching aids. Chalk or dry erase boards, worksheets, puppets, or craft projects for your children to make can all be adapted to enhance any lesson. Do not limit yourself to your classroom; go on a picnic, or to the zoo, or visit a museum.

Begin each lesson with the private confession of sin. Teach the children that the only way to approach the Word of God is after restoration of fellowship with Him through the filling ministry of God the Holy Spirit. Remind them that the Holy Spirit is the real teacher of God's Word (John 14:26).

Devote part of each lesson to learning the memory verse. Then, make reference to it as it applies to the subject. Help the children look up the verse in the Bible and impress on their minds that God's written Word is the source of all truth. For younger children, paraphrase or shorten verses for easier memorization. Most importantly, make memorizing verses a delightful part of the lesson.

Present the Gospel in every lesson. You never want to take the salvation of your children for granted. Even though you may feel certain your children are born again, repeat the Gospel. Find the opportunity to talk to each child individually about his eternal relationship with the Lord. Provide for those who want to believe in the Lord Jesus Christ as their Savior the time and opportunity to make the decision.

Define the vocabulary words. Understanding the doctrinal concepts depends upon understanding the meaning of the technical vocabulary words. Never assume the child already knows the meaning of a word, or is necessarily hearing the word correctly. You need to enunciate the word clearly, and define it in terms of the child's frame of reference.

Review, review, review. The doctrinal concepts, vocabulary words, and memory verse all need to be reviewed, and then reviewed again. When asking questions, provide hints that will help the children to recall the correct answers. Encourage them to express, in their own vocabulary, what they have learned. Make the reviews enjoyable by playing games, singing songs, reviewing teaching aids, and having contests. Always leave your children with Bible doctrine to consider and Bible doctrine to anticipate.

Chapter One

How God's Word Came to Us

OVERVIEW

A. Subject: How God's Word Came to Us—Exodus 24, 32, 34

B. Lesson Titles:
1. Lesson One: The Bible—The Word of God
2. Lesson Two: God Again Gives Moses the Law

C. Story Objective:

The Holy Scriptures or Bible is the inspired Word of God and is authoritative, inerrant, and God-breathed (Matt. 5:18; John 16:12–13; 2 Tim. 3:16–17; 2 Pet. 1:20–21). As such, the Bible is the only criterion concerning spiritual and eternal matters. All that God desired mankind to know is contained in the pages of the Word of God.

The Bible's scope: heaven and hell; God and man; angels and Satan; the Creator and His creatures; things past, present, and future; sin and salvation; carnality and spirituality; God's plan for the human race—all are contained in the Bible and given to us by God to be used "For teaching [doctrine], for reproof, for correction, for training in righteousness; that the man of God may be adequate [mature], equipped [thoroughly furnished] for every good work" (2 Tim. 3:16b–17).

The Bible in the teacher's hand is the only textbook from which our instructions come. Use it; explain it; emphasize the need to bring a Bible to Bible class, even as school books are required in public schools.

D. Vocabulary and Doctrinal Concepts:
1. Vocabulary: covet, deserve, idol, law, pure, scrolls, servant
2. Doctrinal Concepts:
   a. Words of the Lord (Ex. 4:10–12; Prov. 30:5–6; Ps. 119:130; Matt. 24:35)
   b. The Lord's comment on Moses (Deut. 34:10–12; Heb. 3:2, 5)
   c. The Law (Ps. 19:7–11; 119:18, 165)
   d. The Commandments (Ex. 24:12; Ps. 119:10)
   e. The Word (Ps. 119:89, 105, 140; Isa. 55:10–11; 2 Tim. 2:15; Heb. 4:12)
   f. Inspiration of Scripture (Acts 8:35; 2 Tim. 3:16–17)

E. *Source Book* Keywords: Bible, idolatry, Moses, Ten Commandments, volition

F. Activities:
1. Suggested Visuals: none
2. Games, Songs, Worksheets
3. Memory Verse: "The words of the LORD are pure words." (Ps. 12:6a)
4. Opening and Closing Prayer

Lesson One
The Bible—The Word of God

You have been in school just a short while, but already you are learning to read and write, add and subtract. You are learning about the people and animals around you, about our country and the world we live in. As you go on, you will find that there are many books to study—geography, history, science, English, and many more. These books were written by learned men and women. These books will teach you about many different subjects. When you go to school, you take along the school books you need to learn these things.

In church, we also need a Book to show us what we must learn. Do you know what Book that might be? You are right; it is the Bible. When I go to church, I bring my Bible. Do you have your Bible with you? If I came to church without bringing my Bible, I would feel as if I had come without my clothes!

The Bible is a very wonderful Book and it is the most important Book. Have you ever seen a real pearl necklace? Between its clasp, one little pearl is strung upon another, and then another—each one of the pearls perfect in itself and all making up one lovely necklace. Where did these pearls come from? They came from the ocean, where God had caused them to be formed inside of many oysters.

Did you ever take a close look at your Bible? Between its covers, one sentence is followed by another and another, page after page, each word perfect and pure and true and all forming the completed Word of God. Where did the Bible come from? The Bible came from way on High, from the Lord Himself who gave His thoughts and words to the writers of the Bible and promised that His Word will last forever. Because these are God's words, we call the Bible "The Word of God." What are God's words like? The Bible says that "The words of the LORD are pure words" (Ps. 12:6a).

What does the Bible tell us that makes it so important? It tells us all we need to know about God and angels; about man and animals. The Word of God speaks of heaven and hell, of our wonderful Savior—the Lord Jesus, and warns us of Satan our enemy. Every time you hear God's Word read, listen carefully, because through it God speaks to you in His own words. Have you ever wondered just how we got God's Word? Well, I will tell you how God's Word came to us.

Tablets of Stone

From time to time, God spoke to certain men who believed in Him and said, "Write down every word which I shall speak to you." But why write down what God says? So that we may know what God wants us to know. How did these men write? With pencil? Or ink? On a piece of paper? When the Bible was first written there was no paper, so God's words were carved into special blocks of stone. These were called "tablets of stone." Many years later, the words were written on scrolls, but now we have them in our printed Bibles.

One of the men whom God used to write down His words was Moses. Do you remember Moses? Moses was God's faithful servant. God often spoke to Moses face-to-face (Deut. 34:10b), just as I am speaking to you now. There were many things which God wanted Moses to know so that Moses could teach the people of Israel. One day, God said to Moses, "Come up to Me on the mountain and remain there, and I will give you the stone tablets with the law and the commandment which I have written for their [the people] instruction" (Ex. 24:12). Was this the first time that God had sent His words to the people of Israel? No, He had spoken to them many times before, and each time the people had promised to obey the words of the Lord.

Now Moses was climbing up Mount Sinai while the children of Israel waited down below in their tents. For six days a thick cloud covered the mountain. The Lord was in that cloud. Do you know who the Lord is? The Lord is the one true God, but God is also three. We call God Three-in-One. God is God the Father, God the Son, and God the Holy Spirit. Which One of the Three was in the cloud speaking to Moses? It was God the Son. What other name does God the Son have? Yes, the Lord Jesus Christ.

On the seventh day, the Lord called Moses into the midst of the cloud. Do you know how long Moses stayed up on the mountain with God? "Forty days and forty nights" (Ex. 24:18). That was surely a long talk. You and I have never talked that long to anyone. When the Lord had finished saying all He wanted Moses to write down, He gave Moses the two tablets of stone. Just as He had promised, God Himself had written the words of the Ten Commandments on the stones with His own hand (Ex. 31:18).

In the meantime, the people of Israel waited for Moses to come back to them. Ten days passed, twenty days, thirty days, and still there was no sign of Moses. The people grew restless, just like you sometimes get wiggly and forget to pay attention to God's Word and get into trouble. The Israelites surely got into a lot of trouble, too. They did not know what had happened to Moses and decided he would not come back at all. They began to turn away from the Lord God. They forgot about the promise they had made to

God to obey all His words. Instead, they made themselves a false god, an idol of gold in the shape of a calf, and fell down and worshiped it. "This calf," they said, "is our god." Do you think God was pleased? Do you think Moses will praise them for it? Listen!

When the forty days were up, Moses came down from the mountaintop (Ex. 32:15–35). From far away he could hear singing voices and laughter, but when he came close he saw the terrible things the people were doing. They were praying and singing to the idol which they had made. They had turned away from God. Moses became so angry with them that he raised the tablets of stone way above his head and smashed them to pieces against the mountain. Certainly the people did not deserve a message from God which God Himself had written for them.

What God Wants Me to Know

None of us deserve God's message or His salvation. If God gave us what we deserve, He would have left us all to die in our sins. But God loves us. And He loved those Israelites even though they had all sinned. In His love, God the Father sent His Son to be our Savior. The Lord Jesus Christ paid for all the sins of the world on the cross. He just wants you to believe in Him and you will be saved.

What happened to the Israelites and the broken Law? God did not leave them without His Law. If He had, we would have no Bible today and no Word of God.

Lesson Review

We talked about how important it is for you to bring your Bible to church. This is the Book we are to learn about and it is very important that you bring it with you.

Where did our Bible come from? That's right, God gave it to us. Did He write it down for us as we have it today? No, He gave it to us a little bit at a time. Who was the first man to take down God's words? Moses. Did God write any of His words Himself? Yes, He wrote down the Ten Commandments. What did God write them on? Tablets of stone.

Memory Verse
"The words of the LORD are pure words." (Ps. 12:6*a*)

LESSON TWO
GOD AGAIN GIVES MOSES THE LAW

God has given us many promises in the Bible. When we pray to Him, God wants us to remind Him of what He has promised. Do you need something? Then God wants you to tell Him that He has promised to take care of your needs. This shows that you believe He will do what He says.

God was very angry with His people for disobeying Him. He told Moses that they deserved to die for their sin. But Moses reminded the Lord that He had promised to bring His people into the land of Canaan. God was pleased that Moses remembered His promise, so He told Moses that He would not destroy the people. Instead, God did something very wonderful.

Exodus 34

God in His love and goodness again talked to Moses. This time He had special instructions for him. God said, "Cut out two tablets of stone, just like the first ones which I gave to you, and I will write on them the words that I wrote on the first tablets, which you broke." Why did God do such a wonderful thing? Because God had promised that His words would last forever (Matt. 24:35). Every word which God speaks to us is most important, and each word is pure. That means it is true and perfect. Can you say Psalm 12:6*a* with me? "The words of the LORD are pure words."

God also told Moses, "Be ready in the morning, and come up to the top of the mountain to meet me. But come all alone. Let no one, not even the animals, come near the mountain" (Ex. 34:2–4). Moses obeyed. He went up to Mount Sinai in the morning, as the Lord had commanded him. And the Lord came down from heaven in a cloud and spoke to Moses. Moses learned how good the Lord was and how patient and forgiving. Then Moses bowed his head and worshiped and prayed to the Lord.

God gave Moses all the words which he must tell the people. But this time Moses had to write the commandments on the tablets of stone himself (Ex. 34:27–28). Were these words the words of Moses? No, they were God's own words. Again forty days and forty nights passed, and Moses was still on the mountain. He did not eat or drink all that time. Yet he did not feel hungry, for God looked after him. When he came down the mountain, his face shone like a bright light because he had been with the Lord. The more time you and I spend with God in His Word, the more we will shine out for Him, and others will be able to tell we know and love the Lord Jesus (Acts 4:13b). Moses read God's Word many times to the people, and in between times, it was safely kept in a box covered with gold, called the ark (Deut. 10:5).

Would you like to see all the words that Moses wrote? Open your Bible to the first Book. Can you read the name of it? That's right, Genesis. Now, turn over to the second Book. What Book is that? Exodus. Then Leviticus, Numbers, and Deuteronomy. What strange names! But each one tells what the Book is about. Genesis is the Book of Beginnings; Exodus means "going out," and tells about the Israelites going out of Egypt. Later on you will be able to learn more about the books of the Bible. These first five books of the Bible are called the Books of Moses.

Moses also wrote some of the Psalms. But these books do not make up all of our Bible. How did the rest of God's Word come to us? After Moses died, God chose other men to write down His Words. It took many men many years to write all that God wanted us to know. Were these all given on tablets of stone? No, until men learned to print on paper as you see in books today, they wrote by hand on scrolls. It took many, many scrolls to complete the whole Bible. Then the priests of Israel copied God's Word for the leaders of the different tribes, so that all the people would be able to hear it read.

What God Wants Me to Know

Wouldn't it be wonderful if God would speak to us face-to-face as He spoke to Moses? Some day He will, when we are in heaven with Him. But while we are on earth, God speaks to us through His Word. That is why He had His words put down in the pages of the Bible. Men, women, children—everyone needs to hear, learn, trust the Lord, and obey all the words of the Bible (Deut. 31:12).

God tells us in His Word that He loves us, and that we may speak to Him in prayer because we are His children. He says He cares for us always and will never leave us. How happy we are because we know that God's words are pure (Ps. 12:6). And remember, this means they are perfect and true, every one.

God also speaks to those who are not His children through the Bible. What does He say to them? He says that only those who believe on the Lord Jesus Christ belong to God. God gave the Law to Moses to show that all people are sinners and need a Savior. Would you like to see some of the words of the Law (Ex. 20)?

"You shall have no other gods before Me." We are to believe and worship only the true God. "You shall not make for yourself an idol." God said we must not make any idols or images and call them God. "You shall not take the name of the Lord your God in vain." We must not use God's name wrongly, for He is holy. "Remember the sabbath day, to keep it holy." God wanted the people to take a special day to remember Him. "Honor your father and your mother." God says that it is important for you to love and obey your parents. "You shall not murder." "You shall not steal." You are not to take anything that does not belong to you. "You shall not bear false witness against your neighbor." "You shall not covet." You should not want things that don't belong to you or that you should not have.

Do you always do all these things? Do you know anyone who does? Of course not. None of us can always do everything God's Law tells us to do. Every one of us has told a lie, or disobeyed our parents. We have all forgotten the Lord at some time or other. We have all wanted something we should not have. To disobey God's Law is sin. God knew that no one could do all that He said. He gave us His Law to show us that we are sinners, that we do not always obey Him. Sinners need a Savior. We need someone to save us and to bring us to God.

When we read our Bible, God speaks to us about these things. We hear about the Lord Jesus Christ. We learn that He came down from heaven to die for our sins, and that He was buried and rose again from the dead. God says that if we will only trust in the Lord Jesus Christ and receive Him as our Savior, then we will go to heaven and be with Him forever. Trusting is the same as believing. God's Word was written "that you may believe that Jesus is the Christ, the Son of God; and that believing you may have life in His name" (John 20:31). God's Word is true. Will you believe it?

Lesson Review

God called Moses to the top of Mount Sinai. There He talked to His faithful servant and gave him the Law. It was written on tablets of stone. Moses stayed on the mountaintop forty days and forty nights. Meantime, the people turned away from God and made an idol in the shape of a golden calf. When Moses came down from the mountain, he heard loud voices. As he came near, he saw the people worshiping the golden calf. Surely they did not deserve the Law written by God's own Hand. Moses raised the tablets of stone above his head and broke them. Later on God again gave Moses the Law, for He had promised that His Word would last forever. Today, God speaks to us from the pages of our Bible.

Moses wrote down what God told him to write, and that is how we got some of our Bible. But how do we know that *all* the Bible is the Word of God? This is what we will learn next.

Memory Verse

"The words of the Lord are pure words." (Ps. 12:6a)

Chapter Two

How Do We Know the Bible Is the Word of God?

OVERVIEW

A. Subject: How Do We Know the Bible Is the Word of God?—Daniel 10

B. Lesson Titles:
   1. Lesson One: God Breathed His Words into Men
   2. Lesson Two: God Inspired Daniel

C. Story Objective:
   The Bible declares itself to be the Word of God. It is inspired of God, that is, God's thoughts given to man. He not only saw to it that His thoughts went into the writers, but that His thoughts came from their pens correctly to us. "God-breathed" is the correct translation for "inspiration of God." However, God-breathed implies both inspiration and expiration. The Word was spoken by God to prophets, kings, priests, and others, either face-to-face or by angels, dreams, or visions. The Holy Spirit endued the specially chosen men to direct their thoughts as they penned the words they had heard. Yet even though God used men to record His message with perfect accuracy, He allowed them to express His thoughts in their own personality, vernacular, and literary style.
   There are many infallible proofs of inspiration: the witness of the New Testament writers; the testimony of Christ Himself as to the authenticity of the Old Testament; the fulfillment of Scripture; and the belief of thousands of believers, many of whom were willing to suffer and die for it.

D. Vocabulary and Doctrinal Concepts:
   1. Vocabulary: endued, expire, filling of the Holy Spirit, fills, indwells, inspired, Old Testament, theophany
   2. Doctrinal Concepts:
      a. The men who wrote the Bible said it was the Word of God (Ex. 20:1; 2 Sam. 23:2; Jer. 1:9; Hosea 1:1; Hab. 2:2; 1 Cor. 2:9–10, 16; 14:37; Gal. 1:11–12; 1 Thess. 4:2; 2 Tim. 3:16; Heb. 1:1–2).
      b. Many were willing to suffer and die for the Word of God (Jer. 38:6–13; Acts 5:18–40; 14:19).
      c. The Bible tells of the future, and much of it has already come to pass (Isa. 7:14; 9:6; 53:1–12).
      d. Jesus said the Bible was the Word of God (Matt. 24:35; Luke 4:21; John 5:39; 17:17).
      e. Jesus quoted from the Bible (Matt. 12:40; John 3:14).
      f. The Holy Spirit brought God's words to the memories of the writers and guaranteed accuracy (John 14:26; 1 Cor. 2:13; Heb. 3:7; 9:8; 10:15; 1 Pet. 1:12; 2 Pet. 1:19–21).

E. *Source Book* Keywords: Christ (appearances), God the Holy Spirit (enduement of, filling of, indwelling), inspiration

F. Activities:
   1. Suggested Visuals: angels, elect; Daniel praying
   2. Games, Songs, Worksheets
   3. Memory Verse: "All Scripture is inspired by God." (2 Tim. 3:16*a*)
   4. Opening and Closing Prayer

Lesson One
God Breathed His Words into Men

First, we want to find out what we mean by "the Word of God." We can speak words or we can write words. While I am talking, the words I say are my words. When God speaks, the words are God's words. God did not want His words to be forgotten, so He said to the writers of the Bible: "Write down what I will tell you."

If I hold your hand while you write "the Bible is God's Word," whose words are on the chalkboard? Yours or mine? Those are my words, but I made you write them down. This way I can be sure there will be no mistakes. You understand that, don't you? People make mistakes often, but God never makes a single mistake.

Does God speak to us as He spoke to Moses or as we speak to each other? No, He has sent us a letter, a long letter—the Bible. The words we read in the Bible are God's Words and that is why we call our Bible "the Word of God."

Words Given by God

God did not sit down and take a pen and paper and write like we would write. He used forty different men to write down His words in the books of the Bible. To help you remember: How many days was Moses on top of Mount Sinai? Forty. How many nights? Forty. How many writers did God use for the Bible? Forty.

The words of the Bible were given by God to forty "men moved by the Holy Spirit" (2 Pet. 1:21). These men were God's prophets or preachers (Heb. 1:1–2). Some were kings, such as David (2 Sam. 23:2) and Solomon (1 Kings 1:39), and others were people with plain, everyday jobs. A tentmaker, a tax collector, a farmer, a doctor, a fisherman, and a soldier were among the Bible's writers. We are told that God spoke through these men who loved Him and had trusted Jesus Christ for salvation. God did not permit these men to make any mistakes. How do you think God gave His thoughts to the writers of the Bible? How did He show them what He wanted them to write? God *inspired* the men He chose. What do we mean by "inspired"?

"Inspire" means to breathe. God "breathed" His words into men. Try taking a deep breath. Your lungs are all filled up with air, aren't they? Oh, oh, I see you already have to let out the air from your lungs. You can't keep the air in very long, and you can't keep it out very long. You must breathe in and breathe out. We call this "inspire" and "expire." Breathing in and breathing out. Do you think God just blew on the men who were to write His words and they knew what to write? No, "God's breath" is a picture of His power. God is able to put His thoughts into special men in such a way that they write down exactly what He wants them to write. "To inspire" means that God not only put His words in men, but made sure that the words came out exactly right when they were written down.

God allowed no errors when He told men what to write. His words went in and came out without any mistakes. He "inspired" and "expired" the words through men exactly as He wanted them to be. The words came in and went out as God's own thoughts. This is the way we know for sure that the Bible is the message of God to man.

Now, let's imagine for a moment. If I told forty of you to write about something, do you think I could put all of your writings together and make one perfect book without one mistake or a single disagreement? Why, it would never fit together at all! Only God, who has all power, could cause forty different men who lived hundreds of years apart to write a book and make it turn out to be a perfect Book. Everything in the Bible fits together perfectly, though most of the writers never knew the other writers at all. They did not need to know each other for God in His power told them what to write. He made sure their pens wrote down the right words, yet He let them use their own language and way of speaking.

How did God tell men what to write, and how did He make sure they put it down correctly? Sometimes these men would fall asleep and dream special dreams in which an angel or even the Lord Jesus Christ would speak to them. Or, they might see angels who would give them a message. Often the Lord Jesus Christ would appear in a theophany and speak to them face-to-face. Let me tell you about a little boy named Samuel who lived in the Temple-church with Eli the priest. Samuel heard God's voice calling to him, but he did not know whose voice it was. Eli knew God, and he knew who was speaking to Samuel. He told Samuel to tell God that he was listening. Then Samuel listened, just like you should listen when God's Word is taught (1 Sam. 3:1–9). But how could men remember all the things that the Lord Jesus or angels told them? The Holy Spirit helped them to remember it (John 14:26; Heb. 3:7; 9:8; 10:15; 2 Pet. 1:20–21).

What God Wants Me to Know

Who is the Holy Spirit? In our last lesson we talked about "Three-in-One." Do you remember who is the Three-in-One? Yes, God is Three in One. Let's say together who God is: God is the Father, the Son, and the Holy Spirit. The Father is God, the Son is God, and the Holy Spirit is God. The Holy Spirit has the same power as God the Father and God the Son. Though God the Holy Spirit is very real and is called a "Person" in the Bible, He does not have a body. Today, God the Holy Spirit indwells each one of us who believes in Jesus as our Savior. God the Holy Spirit also fills our souls so that He can help us remember the things we have learned from God's Word. He helped the writers of the Bible remember all the things God the Son or angels had told them. In our next lesson, I will tell you the true story of what happened to a man that caused him to write a book in our Bible.

Lesson Review

How did God "breathe in" and "breathe out" His words? Did God make sure that His words went into the writers' minds correctly? Yes. Did He make sure that they came out exactly right when they were written down? Yes.

How did God tell men what to write? Through dreams, angels, and Jesus Christ speaking personally to the writers. How were the writers able to remember all that God said? The Holy Spirit helped them.

Memory Verse
"All Scripture is inspired by God." (2 Tim. 3:16a)

LESSON TWO
GOD INSPIRED DANIEL

Today, I am going to keep my promise and tell you a story from the Old Testament about a prophet whom God used to write down His words. I would like for you to open your Bibles to the Book of Daniel where our story is found. First, open your Bibles to the middle. Did you open to the Book of Psalms? Now keep turning to the right until you come to Daniel, chapter 10.

Long, long ago there lived a man whose name was Daniel. Daniel lived in Persia. He loved the Lord and talked to Him every day in prayer. God wanted to use this man to write a book of the Bible. God had to find a way to make His thoughts known to Daniel. Do you remember the different ways in which He did this? Speaking face-to-face, through dreams or visions, or by angels. What is the big word we learned that tells how God made sure His thoughts were written down correctly? Inspiration. Listen, and I will tell you what happened on the day God inspired Daniel.

One day in the spring of the year, some men walked beside the river Hiddekel. Daniel was with them. Everything looked pretty and new and green, and the water in the stream was cool and clear. Daniel prayed. When he raised his head he saw a most wonderful sight. Right before his eyes stood a man dressed in robes of fine, white linen. He wore a belt of pure gold, and His body sparkled like many jewels. His face was bright as lightning, His eyes like lamps of fire. His arms and feet shone like polished brass, and when He spoke it sounded like the voice of thousands of men talking.

The ground began to quake as in an earthquake. Frightened by the earth shaking, the men who were with Daniel fled in terror and looked for a place to hide. But they could not see this marvelous sight; only Daniel saw Him. Who was He? None other than our Lord Jesus Christ, God the Son Himself. Why could only Daniel see the Lord, and not the others? Why could only Daniel hear the powerful voice? Because Daniel believed in the Lord Jesus Christ. Only believers can understand God's Word (1 Cor. 2:9–10).

What happened to Daniel when he saw the Lord? He first turned pale; then, he became helpless as a little baby. At the sound of the Lord's voice, he fell to the ground face down and sank into a deep sleep, not because he was tired, but because the Lord had a special reason for him to be asleep. God was going to tell Daniel about things which would happen in years to come. He would show him what He wanted written down.

Suddenly a hand touched Daniel's shoulder to wake him up. God had sent the angel Gabriel to strengthen him (cf., Dan. 8:16; 9:21). The angel lifted up Daniel to a kneeling position. Then Gabriel spoke: "Daniel," he said, "God loves you very much." Why does God love Daniel so much? Because Daniel trusted in Jesus. When we believe in Jesus, we, too, are loved by God because God loves Jesus. "God has sent me to you," the angel said, "to make you understand the words that I will tell you. Now, stand up straight." When Daniel heard the angel he began to tremble. Daniel was afraid, but the angel told him not to fear. We who have believed in the Lord Jesus Christ must not fear God, but trust in Him.

What do you think the angel Gabriel told Daniel? He explained to Daniel what would happen in years to come, not only during the time that Daniel would live, but long, long after. When the angel had finished speaking, he asked Daniel to write down all he had told him. If I told you to write down every word of today's lesson, could you do it without leaving out something or making a single mistake? Of course not. But you see, God *inspired* Daniel, so there were no mistakes. Not a word was left out. Daniel could not have done that on his own. Every time God showed the writers of the Bible what they must write, He inspired them, so that every part of the Bible might be just as perfect and true as every other part. God the Holy Spirit guided the minds of the writers of the Bible.

What God Wants Me to Know

Out of all the men who stood by the river when the Lord appeared to Daniel, only Daniel could see and hear Him. If you have not taken Christ to be your Savior, you cannot understand God's inspired message. The only thing you can understand is that you are a sinner. "For all have sinned and fall short of the glory of God" (Rom. 3:23). All people in the world, and that means you and me too, are sinners. Jesus came to earth to pay the penalty for our sins. He said, "I will die for Mary's sins, for Johnny's sins. I will take their place so they will not have to be judged for their sins."

All that Jesus Christ asks of you is that you believe that He died for you (Acts 16:31). As soon as you tell God the Father that you believe Jesus died to save you and give you eternal life, God the Father will give you the Holy Spirit to help you to understand the Bible, just as Daniel understood God's words.

As God, the Lord Jesus Christ spoke to Moses and to Daniel in the Old Testament times. Many times people were afraid because the sight of God was so bright and terrifying. But, when God the Son came to earth as a Man, He covered His brightness and glory with a human body so that He might speak to many people. He told them the Bible was the Word of God. He told them and us that everything that happened in the Old Testament was true. Do you believe in the Lord Jesus Christ? Then you should also believe that all of the Bible is God's Word. Jesus said that the Old Testament tells about Him, and many times He repeated the words of the Old Testament when He taught the people of Israel.

All of the men who wrote the Bible said that God had inspired them to write their words. Indeed, no one but God could have known what would happen long before it ever came to pass. We don't know what is going to happen five minutes from now. The Bible tells the things that will happen many years later on. Daniel was one of the men to whom God told some of the things which would happen. Everything that God told Daniel happened just as He said. Some of the things are still yet to happen, but we know they will come true because God has said so.

So many people have been sure that the Bible is God's inspired, God-breathed Word, that they have been willing to suffer and die for it. Daniel was thrown into the lions' den; Shadrach, Meshach, and Abednego were thrown into the fiery furnace; Jeremiah was put in a dungeon; Isaiah was sawed in two; John the Baptist had his head cut off; James was killed with a sword; Stephen was stoned to death; Paul suffered much, was stoned, put in prison, and finally killed; and John the Apostle was sent off to a lonely island. We, like them, can believe the Bible's message from cover to cover. We should never be afraid to tell people that God's Word is true. We should be glad to tell our friends that it is God's Word, even if they laugh at us or hate us for it.

Do you remember to thank God that all the words of the Bible are true? Just think of it, you have God's own thoughts in God's Word. Everything that God wants you to know is written down. Your Bible is a perfect guidebook for every part of your life (1 Cor. 2:16). If you do not learn God's Word, you will go the wrong way many times as you grow up. But if you learn God's Word, you will have God's thoughts in your mind and will always know the right way.

Lesson Review

Our Bible is called "the Word of God." Do you know why? Because God's words were written down and became the Bible. But who wrote the words? Did you or I? No, "men moved by the Holy Spirit" were chosen by God to write the words God wanted recorded. Sometimes God would speak to these men Himself; at other times He might send an angel with a message, or He would let the writers see in a dream the things which would happen many years later. God would not let the writers of the Bible make a single mistake. To make sure they would not make mistakes, He breathed His message into the writers. What is the new word that tells us how God's Word came down to men? It starts with an "I." Think of your memory verse. "All Scripture is inspired by God" (2 Tim. 3:16*a*). Yes, inspired.

Let's see how much we remember about one man God inspired. God spoke to a great prophet whose name was Daniel. One day as Daniel walked by the river Hidekkel, the Lord Jesus Christ appeared to him. Daniel heard the Lord speak. His voice sounded mighty, like the voice of many people. Only Daniel saw this wonderful vision. The others were frightened and ran away. When Daniel saw the Lord he sank into a deep sleep. He awoke when a hand touched his shoulder. God had sent the angel Gabriel to tell him not to be afraid, and to write down all the words which God would tell him. Daniel obeyed and did not make a single mistake because God inspired him.

This is how the Book of Daniel was written. The Book of Daniel is found in the Old Testament. Let me show it to you, or perhaps you can remember how to find it yourself. Daniel is a wonderful book. Yet it is only one of sixty-six books in the Word of God, and each book is just as important as the next. Bible means "The Book," and indeed it is the Book of books, the most wonderful Book in all the world.

Memory Verse
"All Scripture is inspired by God." (2 Tim. 3:16*a*)

Chapter Three

The Word of God, Its Message and Power

OVERVIEW

A. Subject: The Word of God, Its Message and Power—Acts 8:25–40

B. Lesson Titles:
   1. Lesson One: In the Mirror of the Bible
   2. Lesson Two: Conversion by Reading the Word of God

C. Story Objective:
Preserved through the ages by His divine promise (Matt. 24:35), and in spite of man's attempt to destroy and discredit it, the Word of God is just as applicable today as it was in the days of its writing. Whether educated or uneducated, young or old, all are equally absorbed by its message and stories. However, only the believer can understand the Bible through the revealing ministry of God the Holy Spirit (1 Cor. 2:10).

The term Bible, as such, is not found in the Word of God. It is derived from the Greek word *biblos* or *byblos*, meaning "book" or "papyrus." The Bible has been referred to as the Book of books, and it truly is that: sixty-six books written over a period of fifteen hundred years by forty different writers in three different languages. Yet, every word was divinely inspired to proclaim the same message to all people of all time. The Bible speaks to man about God showing, on the one hand, as in a mirror the glory of God (2 Cor. 3:18) and, on the other hand, the sinfulness of man (Rom. 3:23). God's remedy for sin is plainly given—salvation in the Person of the Lord Jesus Christ (John 14:6; Acts 4:12), and the penalty for sin is also clearly stated—eternal condemnation (Rom. 6:23*a*). In its entirety, "the word of God is living and active and sharper than any two-edged sword, and piercing as far as the division of soul and spirit, of both joints and marrow, and able to judge the thoughts and intentions of the heart" (Heb. 4:12). The Bible is perfect in every way, "restoring the soul . . . making wise the simple" (Ps. 19:7). God's Word shall never "return to Me empty, Without accomplishing what I desire, And without succeeding *in the matter* for which I sent it" (Isa. 55:11).

D. Vocabulary and Doctrinal Concepts:
   1. Vocabulary: Africa, chariot, converted, desert, Ethiopia, lamp, light, New Testament, preachers, prophets, rejoicing, scrolls
   2. Doctrinal Concepts:
      a. Treasured the words of His mouth more than my necessary food (Job 23:12; Matt. 4:4).
      b. Converting the soul (Ps. 19:7).
      c. "The unfolding of Thy words gives light; It gives understanding to the simple" (Ps. 119:130).
      d. "Hear the word of the LORD" (Isa. 1:10*a*).
      e. The Word accomplishes God's pleasure (Isa. 55:11).
      f. Unbeliever convicted of sin, righteousness, and judgment (John 16:8).
      g. "No other name under heaven that has been given among men, by which we must be saved" (Acts 4:12*b*).
      h. "All have sinned and fall short of the glory of God" (Rom. 3:23).
      I. Wages of sin versus gift of God (Rom. 6:23).
      j. The Word revealed to believer by the Holy Spirit (1 Cor. 2:10).
      k. The Bible, a mirror showing the glory of God (2 Cor. 3:18).

1. "The prophetic word *made* more sure" (2 Pet. 1:19).

E. *Source Book* Keywords: the Gospel

F. Activities:
   1. Suggested Visuals: none
   2. Games, Songs, Worksheets
   3. Memory Verse: "But these have been written that you may believe that Jesus is the Christ, the Son of God; and that believing you may have life in His name." (John 20:31)
   4. Opening and Closing Prayer

LESSON ONE
IN THE MIRROR OF THE BIBLE

Do you remember how many men were used by God to write the Bible? Yes, forty. But did you know that it took more than fifteen hundred years to complete? When you bring your Bible to church, you really carry sixty-six books with you. The Bible is divided into two parts, the Old Testament and the New Testament. Now, if we open the Bible right in the middle, we'll find the Book of Psalms. Let's try it, shall we? I want to read to you something which God has to say about His Word right from the middle of the Bible.

Now listen to this verse: "The unfolding of Thy words gives light; It gives understanding to the simple" (Ps. 119:130). If you were looking for something in the dark and someone turned on the light for you, would it not be much easier for you to see? In the same way, when God's words come into our lives, we suddenly see and understand the things of God. But how do you suppose the Word enters into us?

The Lord has made you and me wonderfully well (Ps. 100:3*a*; 139:14). He gave us feet to take us to church, hands to hold our Bibles, eyes to see, and ears to hear. Do you know what the Lord Jesus Christ said about our eyes and ears? "Blessed are your eyes, because they see; and your ears, because they hear" (Matt. 13:16). Do you have seeing eyes? Do you have hearing ears? The Word of God comes in through the ears and eyes. What do your eyes see in the Bible? Words, words, and more words, and all of these words were written for one reason: "But these have been written that you may believe that Jesus is the Christ, the Son of God; and that believing you may have life in His name" (John 20:31).

The Bible Is Your Lamp

Looking into the Bible and reading the Word of God is like looking into a mirror. I am sure every one of you looks into the mirror at least once every day. A mirror can tell you a great many things without speaking out loud. What might those things be? Perhaps it will tell you that your hair needs combing, or that you have a smudge on your face. You see the mirror will always tell you the truth. But one thing is sure, the mirror cannot wash your face for you. You must do that for yourself.

In the mirror of the Bible, God shows us what we are really like—sinners. Because Adam sinned in the Garden of Eden, sin entered into the world (Rom. 5:12). Since then "all have sinned." Yes, you and I were sinners even long before we were old enough to tell lies, or think ugly thoughts, or disobey our parents and teachers, or take things which did not belong to us. Adam passed down to us a sin nature which he received when he disobeyed God; we are born with a sin nature. This sin nature is a sinful way which makes us want to sin. That is why the Bible points at us as if to say, "Look at you, you are one great, big smudge of sin." Then, God shows us the other side of the mirror and lets us see "the glory of the Lord" (2 Cor. 3:18). "Look how great and wonderful God is," the Bible says. Now, if God had only wanted us to see how bad we are and how good He is, we would have only one verse, Romans 3:23, printed in our Bibles. "For all have sinned and fall short of the glory of God." "All right," you say, "I'll get all cleaned up; I'll be good from now on." "No!" says the Bible. "Being good may be your way, but God's way is different" (Isa. 55:8*b*). "There is a way *which seems* right to a man, But its end is the way of death" (Prov. 14:12). No matter how hard you try, being good will never get you into heaven. When you were born, you started on your way. Which way will it be for you, God's way or man's way? So that you might find the right way, God has given you a lamp to guide you. The Bible is your lamp. Now, I don't see any rays of light coming out of my Bible, do you? No, the amount of light you receive depends on how much you read and hear the Word of God.

What God Wants Me to Know

Surely, if God's words are so important, there must be a special message in the Bible. And there is. What do you suppose the message says? That Christ Jesus "came into the world to save sinners" (1 Tim. 1:15). Why do sinners need to be saved? So that we can live with God forever. Now, God has provided a way for us to be saved and that way is through the Lord Jesus Christ. He took our place and paid the penalty for our sin when He died on the cross. We should have died for our own sins, but Jesus took all our sins in His own body so that we could go free (1 Pet. 2:24). Now, if we will only believe in Him, He will give us eternal life.

God's message has never changed. God promised that His words would not pass away (Matt. 24:35); that is why "the word of God is living and active" (Heb. 4:12*a*). What kind of power would that be? Power to change anyone's life! Power to make any boy or girl or grown man or grown woman who believes in the Lord Jesus Christ a child of God (2 Cor. 5:17).

Memory Verse

"But these have been written that you may believe that Jesus is the Christ, the Son of God; and that believing you may have life in His name." (John 20:31)

LESSON TWO
CONVERSION BY READING THE WORD OF GOD

Did you ever have someone run up to you and say, "Oh, I've got something to tell you!" You can almost guess by the look on their face whether it is good news or bad news. None of us likes to hear bad news, do we? The Bible has both good news and bad news. It is bad news to hear that we are sinners and lost from God. It is good news that we can be saved from our sins. The most important message of the Bible is the good news that Christ died for our sins so that we might have eternal life. The Bible calls this good news "the Gospel." Gospel means good news.

It makes people happy to hear good news. Have you ever told anyone the good news of the Gospel and made them happy? I am going to tell you a story about a man who made someone very happy because he told him the good news of the Gospel. You can find this story in the Book of Acts, chapter eight.

The Good News of the Gospel

Long ago before the Bible was printed and bound into one book as we have it today, God's words had been written on scrolls of paper. Only the very rich could own these scrolls, and not too many people could read. And so preachers and prophets, men to whom God spoke, went throughout the land to make known the Word of God. One of these preachers was named Philip. He preached "the gospel to many villages" (Acts 8:25).

Philip would have kept right on telling the people how they might be saved, but all at once he received an order from an angel of the Lord: "'Arise and go south to the road that descends from Jerusalem to Gaza.' (This is a desert *road*.)" (Acts 8:26). What a strange command! Why would the Lord want Philip to leave a place where many people were listening to him preach about Jesus and go to a desert where no one lived? God is very great and He knows all things. He knew all along that someone would come down a certain road just as Philip got there. God was going to show the power of His Word and its wonderful message. Let's find out what happened next.

Philip didn't ask, "Why do I have to?" like we often do. He obeyed the Lord and went right away to the road in the desert which the Lord had shown him. Sure enough, when he got to the place, Philip saw a very fine chariot and a man sitting in it. His clothing was that of a rich man, and indeed this man was rich and mighty. He was chief over all the treasures of the country of Ethiopia in Africa from which he had come. What do you think the rich man was holding in his hands? Yes, a scroll, one of the books in our Bible—the Book of Isaiah.

"Go and talk to the man, Philip," said God the Holy Spirit. Now Philip was close enough to the chariot to hear what this man was saying. Why, he was reading the Scriptures, reading them out loud. Quickly Philip ran up to the chariot. "Do you understand what you are reading?" he asked (Acts 8:30b). The man in the chariot must have had a very puzzled look on his face as he answered, "How could I, unless someone guides me?" (Acts 8:31a). I am going to tell you a secret. The reason this man did not understand the words of God is that he did not know or believe in the Lord Jesus Christ. Only believers can understand the Bible, because God the Holy Spirit teaches them (1 Cor. 2:10). Remember, we learned that the filling of the Holy Spirit gives us understanding. Unbelievers do not have the Holy Spirit. But God the Holy Spirit *does* help unbelievers to understand the Gospel when they hear how to be saved. "Come into my chariot and help me understand," begged the rich man from Ethiopia.

As Philip began to talk, the words entered in through the Ethiopian's ears, and the entrance of the Word gave light to him. Philip explained God's message, saying how Jesus came into the world to save sinners, how He suffered and died to save us and pay the penalty for our sin. After hearing and reading the Word of God, the rich man saw himself as God saw him. The Word was like a mirror, and showed him that he was a poor, lost sinner. Now, he understood how he needed the Lord Jesus Christ. Right then and there, he believed in Jesus Christ and was saved. "I believe that Jesus Christ is the Son of God," he said happily (Acts 8:37b). Soon afterward, he returned to his own country rejoicing. Do you know why he was so happy? The words of the Bible had shown him the way to eternal life. Those words had "converted" his soul (Ps. 19:7). Not only was he saved from the terrible penalty of sin, but God had removed the penalty of his sins from him "as far as the east is from the west" (Ps. 103:12a).

The Ethiopian changed roads right in the middle of his journey. He had been on his way to eternal death and the lake of fire; now, he was on his way to heaven. Hearing the Word of God had made all the difference in his life (Rom. 10:17). God had sent out His message and His Word; once again, He had done what He pleased (Isa. 55:11).

Remember, the Word of God is alive and powerful. It has the power to give life to anyone who will believe it.

What God Wants Me to Know

I am sure that the man in our Bible story loved very much the portion of God's Word which he owned, because it had showed him the way to his Savior. I am also sure that he read and studied as many scrolls as he could afford and that he told others in his own country of God's written message.

Oh, how very important the Bible is in our lives. How thoughtless and careless we often are about it, forgetting to bring it to church, never opening it during the week, and yet we have known about the Bible ever since we were very small. How many times a day do you eat? Three times? Four? How about all the little snacks in between? The Lord Jesus said, "MAN SHALL NOT LIVE ON BREAD ALONE, BUT ON EVERY WORD THAT PROCEEDS OUT OF THE MOUTH OF GOD" (Matt. 4:4).

How often do you take in the Word of God either through the eye-gate or the ear-gate? How many times during the week do you ask your mother or dad to read you something out of the Bible? God wants you to take in His Word every day, to hide it in your hearts that you might not sin against Him (Ps. 119:11). He wants you to use His Word, not just your own words, to tell others about the Lord Jesus Christ. When you use God's words and someone argues with you and says, "Who says so?" then you can tell them, "God says so." Maybe next week you can tell a friend that all the words in the Bible were written "that you may believe that Jesus is the Christ, the Son of God; and that believing you may have life in His name" (John 20:31).

I am sure you did not come in a chariot like the Ethiopian did, but you have heard the message of the Word of God. Will you leave here as happy as the Ethiopian did, knowing that you have believed on the Lord Jesus Christ and that your sins are all forgiven and washed away? Your eyes have seen, your ears have heard, but your volition must decide for you.

Let's be very quiet while we think about the Lord Jesus Christ. Is He already your Savior? Then you need not receive Him again. But if you have not believed in Him as your own Savior, you may do so now. You may pray with me silently: "Father, I now believe that Jesus died for me, in my place, and I thank you for my salvation."

Lesson Review

We have been talking about God's words. Where are God's words written down? Yes, in the Bible. I wonder just how many words there are in the Bible? Well, we don't know—thousands and thousands. But we do know how many books are in our Bible. Sixty-six.

What do we call the two parts that divide the Bible? The Old and New Testaments. You might call them the "Old Promise" and the "New Promise." Many, many years ago God gave promises to His people, the Jews. Now you and I and all those who believe in Jesus are His people, and God has made many new promises to us. One of these promises is the important verse we learned. Who can say it? "But these have been written that you may believe that Jesus is the Christ, the Son of God; and that believing you may have life in His name" (John 20:31).

Does God's Word have power to give eternal life—life that never ends? I should say it does. God's Word is as strong as God because God is behind every word He says. If a boy or girl should say to you, "I'll take you to the beach tomorrow," you would only laugh, wouldn't you? But if he said, "My daddy will take you to the beach tomorrow," you could believe him because his daddy is able to do it. God is able to do what He says He will do.

What man in the Bible had his whole life changed as he read, heard, and believed God's Word while riding in a chariot? Yes, the man from Ethiopia. God sent Philip to help him understand and believe. Have you told anyone God's Words?

> **Memory Verse**
> "But these have been written that you may believe that Jesus is the Christ, the Son of God; and that believing you may have life in His name." (John 20:31)

Chapter Four

How Jesus Used God's Word to Overcome Temptation

OVERVIEW

A. Subject: How Jesus Used God's Word to Overcome Temptation—Matthew 4:1–11

B. Lesson Titles:
1. Lesson One: The Word of God—The Sword of the Spirit
2. Lesson Two: Victory over Temptation

C. Story Objective:

In His earthly ministry, Jesus Christ believed and used the Word of God. He demonstrated the power of the Word to resist temptation in the satanic attack of Matthew 4:1–11. All spiritual victory is related to God's Word. Called the "sword of the Spirit" in Ephesians 6:17, the Word, like a sword, wards off the believer's spiritual enemies and is the means through which the filling of the Holy Spirit teaches and enlightens the believer. It is therefore imperative for the believer to know and study the Word of God.

The temptations of Christ were unique because they involved His divine attributes, yet by application they teach the believer how to overcome the temptations of his enemies, the world, the flesh, and the devil. The emphasis for the student will be on how to use the Word of God in problems and temptations relating to them, rather than the unique problems the Lord Jesus faced in His battle with Satan. However, a basic understanding of Christ's temptations is necessary in order to make proper application to the believer's life.

The plan of God for Christ during His incarnation was for the Holy Spirit to sustain His humanity (Isa. 11:2–3; 61:1; Matt. 4:1; 12:18, 28; John 3:34). Christ voluntarily restricted the use of His divine attributes and depended upon the sustaining ministry of the Holy Spirit for the enabling power to fulfill the Father's plan. This set the pattern for believers in the Church Age who would be indwelt and filled by the Holy Spirit.

In the first temptation of Christ by Satan, this plan was attacked. Jesus was tempted to act independently of the Spirit and use His own deity for sustenance rather than to rely upon the provision of the Father. Jesus' answer demonstrated the importance of the daily intake of the Word over the details of life.

In the second temptation, Satan attacked the source of Christ's resistance, the Word itself. This was an extremely subtle temptation to act independently of the Word of God by quoting it out of context. For a believer to resist being led astray by a subtle distortion of the Word by false teachers, he must know the Word.

The third attack of Satan was a temptation to bypass the cross by accepting the crown, rulership of the world, from Satan at that time, instead of at the time appointed by the Father. Satan's offer was legitimate since he is the "god [ruler] of this world" (2 Cor. 4:4; Eph. 2:2). Again, Jesus counterattacked with "it is written," which delineates all divine power (Matt. 4:10).

Satanic temptation is basically to go contrary to the plan of God. However, Satan works more through systems of religion and human viewpoint than through personal attack on believers. Dependence on God and fulfilling the plan of God depends on knowing, believing, and applying the Word of God.

D. Vocabulary and Doctrinal Concepts:
1. Vocabulary: enemy, serpent, tempts
2. Doctrinal Concepts:

a. The importance of the Word:
     1) "Man does not live by bread alone, but man lives by everything that proceeds out of the mouth of the LORD" (Deut. 8:3).
     2) "I have treasured the words of His mouth more than my necessary food" (Job 23:12).
     3) "Thy word I have treasured in my heart, That I may not sin against Thee" (Ps. 119:11).
     4) "Thou hast magnified Thy word according to all Thy name" (Ps. 138:2).
     5) "The LORD was pleased for His righteousness' sake To make the law great and glorious" (Isa. 42:21).
     6) "So shall My word be which goes forth from My mouth; It shall not return to Me empty, Without accomplishing what I desire" (Isa. 55:11).
     7) "Thy words were found and I ate them" (Jer. 15:16).
  b. Satan:
     1) Prince, god, ruler of this world (John 12:31; Eph. 2:2; 1 John 2:16; 4:4; 5:19).
     2) Satan uses agents, such as false teachers, demons, religion (2 Cor. 11:13–15; Eph. 6:12; 1 Tim. 4:1; Rev. 12:9).
     3) Adversary of believer (1 Pet. 5:8).
  c. Victory over temptation through the Word:
     1) "You are mistaken, not understanding the Scriptures, or the power of God" (Matt. 22:29).
     2) Victory over Satan won at the cross; positional truth; potential for every believer (John 12:31; Col. 1:13; 2:14–15; Heb. 2:14–15).
     3) "God is faithful, who will not allow you to be tempted beyond what you are able, but with the temptation will provide the way of escape" (1 Cor. 10:13).
     4) "In the word of truth, in the power of God" (2 Cor. 6:7a).
     5) Take "the sword of the Spirit, which is the word of God" (Eph. 6:17b).
     6) "The Lord knows how to rescue the godly from temptation" (2 Pet. 2:9a).
     7) "Resist the devil and he will flee from you" (James 4:7).
     8) "Draw near to God and He will draw near to you. Cleanse your hands, you sinners; and purify your hearts" (James 4:8; 1 John 1:9).

E. *Source Book* Keywords: Satan, sword

F. Activities:
  1. Suggested Visuals: Christ on earth, Satan
  2. Games, Songs, Worksheets
  3. Memory Verse: "MAN SHALL NOT LIVE ON BREAD ALONE, BUT ON EVERY WORD THAT PROCEEDS OUT OF THE MOUTH OF GOD." (Matt. 4:4b)
  4. Opening and Closing Prayer

LESSON ONE
THE WORD OF GOD—THE SWORD OF THE SPIRIT

*I*t is very, very important to know God's Word because it tells us how to be saved and go to heaven. However, there is another reason why we must learn God's Word. We have enemies that would like to make us sin and disobey God. Do you know what an enemy is? An enemy is someone who does not like you, and may even try to hurt you. You have an enemy inside of you and an enemy outside. Your inside enemy we call the sin nature or sinful way because it tempts us to sin. Maybe you have heard of this enemy before. The first man, Adam, was created perfect by God without a sin nature, but when he decided to say "No" to God and "Yes" to self, he became a sinner with a sin nature. You, and I, and everyone born into the world since Adam, except the Lord Jesus Christ, has received a sin nature. The sin nature is an enemy that makes us want to sin and disobey God.

Well, now, perhaps you remember who it was that came to Eve in the Garden and made her think it would be all right to disobey God? Yes, Satan himself. Of course, he hid inside the serpent so that he could fool Eve. Satan was the very first sinner. You know that sin is disobeying God. Satan disobeyed God, of all places, right up in heaven where he lived with God. When God created him, Satan was a beautiful, shining angel named Lucifer. God made him to serve and praise Him. But one day, Lucifer didn't want to serve and praise God any longer. He said, "I want to be God, and I want to please myself." What a terrible sin!

God had to punish Satan. He could no longer be the greatest angel in heaven and someday would be thrown into the lake of fire forever. Satan did not like his punishment. He became God's enemy. He hated God and wanted to hurt God. But God was too strong for Satan to hurt, so now, Satan tries to hurt the people that God creates and loves. Satan is our outside enemy. We cannot see our enemies, the sin nature and Satan, but they are real just the same. We know how real they are because they tempt us to sin, even when we try not to.

God's Word tells us we need to know all about our enemies so that we will understand how to fight against them. Our enemies are very clever and have many ways to trick us. How shall we fight them if we cannot see them? God has given us a "sword" with which to fight our enemies, but it does not look like a soldier's sword. The Bible says it is the "sword of the Spirit, which is the word of God" (Eph. 6:17b). One day when Jesus was here on earth, He showed us how to use the sword of the Spirit, and the Word of God to defeat our enemy, Satan.

The Enemy of the Lord Jesus—Satan

The Lord Jesus Christ does not have an enemy sin nature as you and I do. He was born into the world just like we were, but He had no sin nature in Him. Because Jesus did not have a sin nature and never did one wrong thing—not even one sinful thought or act—He could be our Savior. But even though Jesus did not have a sin nature, He did have an enemy. Remember who had become the enemy of God? Satan, the great and mighty angel also called the devil. Since Satan was the enemy of God, he was also the enemy of Jesus, for Jesus is God as well as man.

Satan is ruler of the world and he did not want Jesus to come into the world. The devil knew who Jesus was, and he knew Jesus could take away his power. So Satan tried his best to keep Jesus from coming into the world, and after He came, Satan tried to kill Him many times. Isn't the devil a dangerous and terrible enemy? I wonder who is stronger? Well, we shall see.

Jesus knew what Satan was up to. He was not at all surprised one day when His enemy came to start a fight. Sometimes one boy will come up to another boy and say something like, "I'll bet you I'm stronger than you are." And maybe the second boy answers, "Oh, yeah? I could beat you up any time!" Then, they begin to punch and hit at each other to prove who is stronger. Girls act like this too, though they usually fight with words. The one who thinks of the fewest unkind things to say to the other is the one who goes off crying.

Well, that enemy, Satan, wanted to prove to Jesus that he was stronger. He watched and waited. He very cleverly chose a time when the Lord was weak and hungry. Jesus had been alone in a desert place praying to God the Father and talking about His Word for forty days and nights (Matt. 4:2). He had not taken time to eat during all that time. Forty days and nights is a long time to go without food, isn't it? Did you ever think prayer and the Word of God were more important than eating your food? Jesus did. But Satan didn't know that prayer and the Word of God gave Him more strength than food.

What God Wants Me to Know

You see, Jesus was trusting God the Father for everything. The Holy Spirit was with Him and He was filled with the Spirit (Matt. 4:1). If Jesus is your Savior and all of your sins are confessed, the Holy Spirit fills you and gives you strength, just as He did Jesus. Jesus didn't have any sin to confess; He always obeyed His heavenly Father. The Holy Spirit took care of Him and helped Him, just as He will you. One of the best times to pray and look into the Word is in the morning when you first get up. That way you will have strength to face all the battles that come up in your life. However, these battles are not just fistfights or shouting ugly words back and forth, they are also unseen battles in your soul (Eph. 6:12). In our next lesson we will see just how Jesus faced this kind of a battle and how He won the victory.

Memory Verse

"MAN SHALL NOT LIVE ON BREAD ALONE, BUT ON EVERY WORD THAT PROCEEDS OUT OF THE MOUTH OF GOD." (Matt. 4:4b)

Lesson Two
Victory over Temptation

The Bible says, "the tempter came to Jesus" (Matt. 4:3). A tempter is someone who tries to get you to do wrong. That is exactly what Satan wanted Jesus to do, for if he could get Jesus to disobey His Father even one time, then Jesus would be a sinner and could never be the Savior of the world. Oh, how afraid Satan was for Jesus to go to the cross and die for our sins. If Jesus died for our sins, then Satan would lose his battle against God.

The Temptation to Act Apart from the Father's Provision
Matthew 4:3–4

Remember, Jesus had not eaten for forty days and forty nights. He was weak from hunger, so Satan said, "If [meaning since] You are the Son of God [and he knew Jesus was], command that these stones become bread" (Matt. 4:3). Could Jesus have done this? Oh, yes, for He is God and God can do anything! It was Jesus who had made all things (John 1:3), and He could easily have made bread from a stone. Do you know what Satan really wanted Jesus to do? He wanted Him to quit trusting God the Father and the Holy Spirit and to disobey God. For Jesus to do something that the Father and Holy Spirit did not want Him to do would be sin, wouldn't it?

The Lord Jesus had a "sword," which He quickly used on Satan. It was the sword of the Spirit, which is the Word of God. It was not a written copy of the Bible, but He had it hidden away in His heart or soul (Ps. 119:11). He answered Satan: "It is written [in God's Word], 'MAN SHALL NOT LIVE ON BREAD ALONE, BUT ON EVERY WORD THAT PROCEEDS OUT OF THE MOUTH OF GOD'" (Matt. 4:4b). Satan could not fool Jesus that time. Satan has no answer for the Word of God because he knows it is true.

You won't sin or be fooled by Satan either if you have been "feeding" on God's Word every day. God's Word feeds your new, spiritual life which you receive when you believe in Jesus. Jesus said that feeding your spiritual life is more important than your food. How do you feed on God's Word? You get someone to read it to you, you listen to your parents and teachers teach it, and you remember it in your soul, just as Jesus did.

The Temptation to Go against God's Word
Matthew 4:5–7

Satan was not going to give up easily; he would try another trick to get Jesus to sin. The devil would use Jesus' own sword. You see, Satan knows God's Word too. If Jesus was going to do everything God's Word said, Satan would take a verse and try to make it say something it doesn't really mean. Satan took Jesus up to the great Temple in Jerusalem—up, up, up to the very tiptop of the tower. Anyone falling from there would surely be broken in pieces. Satan said, "If You are the Son of God throw Yourself down; for it is written, 'HE WILL GIVE HIS ANGELS CHARGE CONCERNING YOU'; and 'ON *their* HANDS THEY WILL BEAR YOU UP, LEST YOU STRIKE YOUR FOOT AGAINST A STONE'" (Matt. 4:6).

But, Satan didn't say the verse correctly. He left out some words. Did Jesus know how Satan changed God's Word? I should say He did. Jesus knew that God the Father's plan did not include doing something so senseless as jumping off the Temple tower to the valley floor 450 feet down. He knew Satan was trying to get Him to sin so that He couldn't go to the cross. If He disobeyed His Father and jumped down from the Temple tower, it would be sin. Jesus used His sword again and told Satan that God's Word says, "YOU SHALL NOT PUT THE LORD YOUR GOD TO THE TEST" (Matt. 4:7). Satan lost another battle because his word was not as powerful and sharp as the Lord's.

The Bible says Satan has "fiery missiles," or poison arrows that he throws at believers (Eph. 6:10). These are really thoughts filled with lies. If you don't know what God's Word says, Satan can easily fool you with his lies and get you to sin. Someone might come to you and say, "God only takes good boys and girls to heaven." If you don't know what God's Word really says, you will become worried or afraid and think you can never be good enough to go to heaven. These are Satan's terrible, poisonous lies. Do you know what the Word really says? It says no one is good enough to go to heaven, but if you will believe that the Lord Jesus Christ died for your sins, He will give you His goodness. You must learn God's Word every day so that you will not be fooled by Satan's lies.

The Temptation to Bypass the Father's Plan
Matthew 4:8–11

Well, do you know that Satan was not ready to give up the fight yet? Even though he saw he could not get Jesus to go against His Father to make food for His body or do something God's Word did not say, he had another trick up his sleeve. This time he took Jesus way up on a high mountain. From up on this mountain they saw all the cities of the world and the beauty of them. Then, Satan said to Jesus something like this: "All these belong to me. I have power over them and I rule them, and I can give this power to anyone I choose. If you will kneel down and worship me, I will give it to *you*."

You will not be offered the world to rule, but many times you will be tempted to take something you should not or that would not be pleasing to the Lord. Will you say "no" to these temptations? What did Jesus say? He said "no!" I imagine the cities of the world did look beautiful from way up there, much as they do when you see them from an airplane. But, from high up you cannot see the ugliness and sadness and sin in those cities. Jesus could see all this, and that is why He could say "no." He knew the Father's plan and that He must go to the cross and die for the sins in the world. One day, God the Father will give Jesus the whole world to rule. But before that happens, Jesus must first die to take away the sin of the world. This was what God the Father had planned to do long ago, even before the world was created (Eph. 1:4). Why, if Jesus became ruler of the earth up on that mountaintop, He would have forgotten His Father's plan, and you and I could never have been saved from our sins. If Jesus bowed down to Satan, that would be saying Satan was greater than God!

Jesus did not have a sinful desire to rule the world when it was not the Father's time. Again, Jesus brought out His powerful sword which had won every battle for Him against Satan's temptations: "Begone, Satan! For it is written, 'YOU SHALL WORSHIP THE LORD YOUR GOD, AND SERVE HIM ONLY.'" Jesus knew God's Word and it kept Him from saying yes to something most anybody would want—to have power over all the earth. If you know God's Word, you know that to have everything in the whole world is not worth a thing if you do not have the Lord Jesus. Just to serve and please the Lord can make you happier and richer than anything Satan or the world can give you.

Satan had tried all his tricks and fiery missiles in three great battles with Jesus and lost them all. Jesus had won the victory, and there was nothing more for Satan to do but leave. Then, God the Father sent angels to bring Jesus food and watch over Him as He slept. How tired Jesus was after the long, hard battle with Satan, but it was more important to Him to win the victory over Satan than to eat or sleep.

What God Wants Me to Know

God the Father let His enemy, Satan, try to get Jesus to sin to show us how we may win over our enemies—the sin nature and Satan—and not sin. We have the same wonderful sword Jesus used, but we must learn how to use it.

First of all, you must believe that God's Word is powerful and will win every battle for you. "For the word of God is living and active and sharper than any two-edged sword" (Heb. 4:12). Even though God does not speak out loud so that you can hear Him with your ears, the words written down in your Bible have as much power as if He were right here fighting for you in Person.

Second, you must never think that you can win any battle over your unseen enemies without using the Word of God. Satan and the sin nature are too strong and too smart for you. So this means you must know what God's Word says.

Third, when you want to sin and do something you know is wrong, use your sword. When you think, "Oh, I would rather stay home and play than come to Bible class and hear God's Word," then, oh, the battle is on! Remember, these wrong thoughts are Satan's fiery missiles, or poison arrows, and they are aimed at you to get you to sin. Right away you should say to yourself, "MAN [that's me] SHALL NOT LIVE ON BREAD ALONE, BUT ON EVERY WORD THAT PROCEEDS OUT OF THE MOUTH OF GOD" (Matt. 4:4). Another day, when you don't want to pick up your toys and you think you will run off and play with your friends, quickly get out your sword instead, for this is another fiery missile from your enemy to get you to sin. Do you know Ephesians 6:1? "Children, obey your parents in the Lord, for this is right." Just to remember God's Word in your soul will win the victory over the temptation to sin.

Sometimes your enemies want you to be afraid and worry. Sometimes they want you to tell a lie. But if you know a Bible verse that tells you what God wants you to do, you will not sin like your enemies want you to. There is a Bible verse for every missile and trick Satan has and every sinful desire your sin nature has. But you have to learn the verses and remember them when the temptation comes. When you are filled with the Holy Spirit, He will help you. Don't forget, though, if you do sin, tell God the Father what you did so that He can forgive you and the Holy Spirit can again fill your soul and help you.

Remember, we said that Satan tries to hurt God by hurting the people God created. God loves all people and wants them all to be saved and someday come to heaven to live with Him. That's why Jesus came to die on the cross. But Satan doesn't want anyone to be saved or to love God or serve Him. When you were born into the world, you were born in Satan's world and you belonged to him. He wants to keep you on his side. He doesn't want you to believe in Jesus and be on God's side. Satan tries to make you believe you don't need a Savior. He would like you to think you will get to heaven if you are a good boy or girl, or if you go to church, or pray.

But this is a lie, because that is not what God's Word says. Anyone who tells you something that God's Word does not say is not telling the truth, for God's Word is Truth. What does God's Word say? "All have sinned and fall short of the glory of God" (Rom. 3:23a). "For God so loved the world, that He gave His only begotten Son, that whoever believes in Him should not perish, but have eternal life" (John 3:16). Will you believe Satan's lie or God's truth?

Lesson Review

What is the sin nature? Our inside enemy; the sinful way inside of us. How did we get an inside enemy? We were born with Adam's sin. How did Adam sin? He disobeyed God and ate the fruit from the tree of the knowledge of good and evil. Was it really the serpent who tempted Eve? It was Satan. Who tempted Jesus to sin many years later out in the desert? Satan. What did Satan want Jesus to do about the stones? Turn them to bread. How did Jesus answer him? "MAN SHALL NOT LIVE ON BREAD ALONE, BUT ON EVERY WORD THAT PROCEEDS OUT OF THE MOUTH OF GOD" (Matt. 4:4b).

What "weapon" did Jesus use to win over Satan? The sword of the Spirit which is the Word of God. Satan took Jesus to the top of the Temple tower in Jerusalem and tempted Him to jump off. What did Jesus' sword point out to Satan this time? God's Word says, don't tempt the Lord your God. "YOU SHALL NOT PUT THE LORD YOUR GOD TO THE TEST" (Matt. 4:7b).

How does Satan try to get you to sin? The fiery missiles, or sinful thoughts of worry, fear, lies, etc. Why did Satan show Jesus the cities of the world? Satan would have to make Jesus ruler of them if He would have worshiped Satan. Will Jesus ever be ruler of the world? Yes, at the Father's right time. How can you use God's Word to keep Satan from getting you to sin? Learning God's Word and remembering it when you are tempted to sin.

Memory Verse
"MAN SHALL NOT LIVE ON BREAD ALONE, BUT ON EVERY WORD THAT PROCEEDS OUT OF THE MOUTH OF GOD." (Matt. 4:4b)

Chapter Five

The Word of God Lives Forever

OVERVIEW

A. Subject: The Word of God Lives Forever—2 Kings 22; 2 Chronicles 34; 36:1–7; Jeremiah 36:1–32

B. Lesson Titles:
  1. Lesson One: The Blessings of Remembering the Word
  2. Lesson Two: Dire Results of Forsaking the Word

C. Story Objective:
  From the beginning of time, Satan has motivated men to attempt to destroy or neutralize God's Word. Through neglect, unbelief, ridicule, hatred, and literal destruction of the written Word, he has succeeded in blinding men's eyes to its truth and temporarily neutralizing it (2 Cor. 4:4). But God has said that "THE WORD OF THE LORD ABIDES FOREVER" (1 Pet. 1:25), and "Heaven and earth will pass away, but My words shall not pass away" (Matt. 24:35). In spite of repeated attacks against His Word, the promise has proved true; the Word has stood the test of time.
  Although man's attitude does not change the Word of God, man's attitude does affect himself. Eternal condemnation is the status of those who will not believe God's Word (Prov. 13:13), but everlasting life is the portion of those who will believe (John 3:18; 3:36; 5:24). The name of anyone who does not believe the Word of God will be removed from the Book of Life (Deut. 12:32; Rev. 19, 22). To add anything to the Word of God also invokes a special anathema (Rev. 22:18). Those who declare that we must believe and be baptized, or believe and keep the Ten Commandments, etc., are adding to the Word of God and are liars (Prov. 30:6).

  Children should learn early in life that God's Word is precious and holy and worthy of utmost respect and love. It is God's Word in truth and must be believed if one desires life (John 20:31) and obeyed if one desires happiness (John 13:17). The lesson of Jehoiakim will teach the dire results of forsaking the Word, as well as the blessings of remembering it.

D. Vocabulary and Doctrinal Concepts:
  1. Vocabulary: abides, distort, faith, idols, printing press, prisoner, prophet, punishment, remember, scholars, translate, wrath
  2. Doctrinal Concepts:
    a. The preservation of the Word:
      1) "You shall not add to nor take away from it" (Deut. 12:32).
      2) "Forever, O LORD, Thy word is settled in heaven" (Ps. 119:89).
      3) "Heaven and earth will pass away, but My words shall not pass away" (Matt. 24:35).
      4) "THE WORD OF THE LORD ABIDES FOREVER" (1 Pet. 1:25).
      5) "If anyone takes away from the words of the book of this prophecy, God shall take away his part from the tree of life" (Rev. 22:18–19).
    b. Attitude toward the Word:
      1) "Thy word I have treasured in my heart, That I may not sin against Thee" (Ps. 119:11).
      2) "Delight in Thy statutes; I shall not forget Thy word" (Ps. 119:16).

3) "Remember also your Creator in the days of your youth" (Eccl. 12:1).
4) "He who hears My word, and believes Him who sent Me, has eternal life" (John 5:24).
5) "He who does not believe has been judged already" (John 3:18b).
6) "If you know these things, you are blessed if you do them" (John 13:17).
7) "These words are faithful and true" (Rev. 21:5b).

E. *Source Book* Keywords: Book of Life, faith, idolatry, Jeremiah, Josiah

F. Activities:
  1. Suggested Visuals: none
  2. Games, Songs, Worksheets
  3. Memory Verse: "I shall not forget Thy word." (Ps. 119:16b)
  4. Opening and Closing Prayer

LESSON ONE
THE BLESSINGS OF REMEMBERING THE WORD

If you had lived a few hundred years ago, you could not have brought a Bible to church because only the preachers and church leaders had Bibles. Since they were written by hand, there were just not enough to go around and very few people could afford to own one. Besides that, the Bible had been written in only a very few languages. How many of you thought that God gave Moses His Words to write down in our language—English? No, Moses spoke the Hebrew language, and for a long time only those who spoke Hebrew could read the Bible.

Hundreds of years after Moses wrote down God's Words, men finally began to translate them in other languages. How eager people were to read God's Word in their own language. But still there were not many copies, for it took so very long to copy all the words by hand. Then one day, more than 500 years ago, the most wonderful thing happened. In Germany a man named Johann Gutenberg invented a printing press. Now with a machine, God's Word could be copied much more quickly. But though there were more copies of God's Word, there were still none in our English language. When some men wanted to put the words of the Bible into English, James I, the King of England, brought together many Bible scholars throughout his kingdom to translate the Bible into English. Was not that a wonderful idea? Then, they were printed on the new printing press in Germany and sent back to England. Soon people were buying God's Word written in English, and oh, how they loved to read it! Many Bibles were printed, and God's Word lived on. Though many people have tried to destroy the Bible, God's Word can never be destroyed.

Why is it that some people love God's Word so much they would rather have it than all the riches in the world, and others hate it so much they want to destroy it? Is it because some people are smarter than others, or have more learning? Is it because some are rich and some are poor? No, the Bible itself tells us why. God's enemy, Satan, has made people hate God's Word. The devil has blinded their souls so that they cannot understand it (2 Cor. 4:4). It is almost as though he has bound up the Bible tight, put a big padlock on it, and hidden the key. We have already seen how Satan hates God's Word and has tried to destroy the Bible and distort its words. He has caused people to burn it; he has caused it to be forgotten and hidden. But God has kept His Word safe and will keep it safe forever (Ps. 119:89; Matt. 23:35; 1 Pet. 1:25).

Those who love the Bible have found the key which opens its pages. What do you think that key is? Faith is the key that unlocks all of its treasures. When you believe in the Lord Jesus Christ, God's Son, as your Savior, He gives you the Holy Spirit to help you understand God's Word. The Bible becomes very precious to you when you can understand it because you know it is the very Word of God. We are going to hear a story from the Word of God about a boy who learned to love God's Word.

Young King Josiah

This little boy, whose name was Josiah, had everything he could want—money, clothes, jewels, a beautiful home, his own horse, and other things that boys love. Why, I am sure he even had a chariot of his own with beautiful horses to pull it. What more could a boy want—or need? Though he had all the riches he could think of, there was still one thing he did not have—can you guess what it might have been? Yes, a Bible.

When Josiah was just eight years old, his father, who was king of Judah, died. The people in the land made Josiah, the little eight-year-old prince, the new king (2 Chron. 34:1–2). Do you think you could be the king of a whole country when you are eight years old? Well, you would have to have a lot of help, wouldn't you? King Josiah had teachers and helpers until he was old enough to rule by himself. Even though he was king and famous and had many riches, he did not become proud and selfish. Instead, the Bible says that "he did right in the sight of the LORD" (2 Kings 22:2), and that "while he was still a youth, he began to seek the God of his father David" (2 Chron. 34:3a). What is the "right" way? Many years before, King David knew the right way (1 Kings 2:3). He told his son, Solomon, that the right way was to learn God's Word and to obey it. Satan's way is to forget or disobey God's Word, and worship after idols instead.

How did Josiah learn to do what was right in the eyes of the Lord when he did not have a Bible to read? Everywhere in Josiah's country people worshiped idols of wood and stone instead of the true God. Why didn't the young king go Satan's way and make idols and worship them, too? How could he know about God? Someone, perhaps his mother or Hilkiah, the high priest, taught him what they knew about God's Word. We know Josiah listened for he wanted to know more! But no one had a copy of God's Word to teach him all that he wanted to know.

Why did they not have God's Word? Had it not yet been written? Oh, yes, part of it had been written, at least the Books of Moses. But they had been lost! Now, that may seem very strange to you that in all of Judah no one could find a copy of God's Word. But, remember there were few copies in those days. But more than that, most of the people did not care that it had been lost. Josiah's father and grandfather, the kings before him, did not care. They, too, had made idols and worshiped them. They had let the Temple, the beautiful building where God was worshiped and where His Word was kept and read, fall into ruins. No one came there anymore, and no one took care of it. Perhaps Satan thought no one would ever find God's Word again.

When Josiah was sixteen years old, he really wanted to begin to do what God wanted him to do (2 Chron. 34:3). Even though he did not have God's Word, he knew it was wrong for the people to worship idols, and he made up his mind to do something about it. At last when he was twenty years old, he could now rule the country by himself. Can you guess what was the first thing he did? He ordered that all the idols be broken, and the places where people worshiped them be torn down. Then King Josiah went everywhere to see that his word was obeyed. He did not want any false gods of wood or stone or gold or silver left in Judah that his people could bow down to and call the "true god." Was the Lord pleased that Josiah did this? Yes, He was. And the Lord had a special surprise waiting for Josiah because the young king wanted to please and obey Him.

Josiah also wanted to repair the house of the Lord, the beautiful Temple in Jerusalem where the people could come and learn about the true God and the Savior who would die for their sins. Many of the people gave money so that the Temple could be repaired. While all the workmen were busy hammering and painting, Hilkiah, the high priest, was cleaning and dusting up inside. Suddenly, he found a dusty old scroll. You remember that in those days a scroll was a book. Scrolls were scarce, and Hilkiah became very excited. Could this be the Book of the Law of the Lord which had so long been lost? Trembling, but carefully he opened the scroll. Sure enough, it was the long, lost Word of God (2 Chron. 34:14). Hilkiah quickly took the precious Book to the king's servant, Shaphan the scribe, who brought it to Josiah.

This was God's wonderful surprise for Josiah. Whenever anyone wants to know about God, He will always see that that person hears His Word (John 7:17a). Since Josiah's father and grandfather had not wanted to learn His Word, it had become buried, forgotten, and lost in the dust and rubbish of the broken-down Temple. Josiah could hardly wait for Shaphab to read the words of the Law to him. He sat down to listen to it as soon as it was brought to him. All of his important duties could wait, for nothing was as important as what God had to say.

But as Shaphan read more and more, Josiah became very sad and even afraid. He tore his clothing to show how he felt. God's Word told how God hated sin and of the punishment for sin. Josiah learned how badly he and his people had sinned because they had not kept all that was written in the Book (2 Chron. 34:21). God would destroy their whole nation if they would not listen to His Word and obey it. So eager was he for the people to hear God's Word, that he called them all together and read it to them himself (2 Chron. 34:30). Don't you think any of them were afraid when they heard what God said about those who forget Him? I am sure they were. Josiah told the people that he was going to obey God's Word and asked them to promise to obey also. They all promised to obey God's Word along with the king.

Because Josiah loved God's Word from the time he was just a little boy, he became one of Judah's greatest kings (2 Kings 23:25). And, because he made up his mind that he would always obey it, a whole nation turned to the Lord and followed Him all the days of his life (2 Chron. 34:33). If you are careful to learn and obey God's Word, other boys and girls will follow your example.

What God Wants Me to Know

Today, God's Word is not lost. Neither will God let it ever, ever be lost to those who want to know it. But there are many people who would love to get rid of it. One reason God has blessed our country and made it great is because the men who formed our country remembered God's Word and made it a part of our laws. The Bible was read and taught in the schools, and people everywhere listened to and loved it. But now, the teachers in the schools are told that they must not read the Bible because someone might not like it. They don't seem to know or care if God likes it or not. They are not afraid of the anger of God, only of the anger of men. But God will punish this nation if we forget God's Word. There are more Bibles in our country than there ever have been in all the world before. But, the Bible might as well be lost, for very few people read the Bible today. Sounds like Satan has won a victory, doesn't it? But God's Word will win out.

You must make up your mind like Josiah: "I shall not forget Thy word" (Ps. 119:16*b*). If you forget God's Word while you are young, you won't be able to find it in your mind someday when you need it. No matter what other boys and girls do, if you will hide His Word in your soul and remember it, you will be glad. Others may think they are happy reading comic books instead of God's Word, or watching television instead of going to hear God's Word taught, but only if you learn His Word and live to please Him can you be truly happy (John 13:17).

Lesson Review

Who was the boy king who loved God's Word, even though he had never read it? Josiah. Why had Josiah never read God's Word? It had been lost. How did he know about God? Someone, probably his mother or the high priest, taught him what they knew. How did God reward Josiah's desire to know more of His Word? He let the high priest find the lost Bible scroll in the ruins of the Temple. What did Josiah see in his country that he knew was wrong? Idols. What did he do about it? Had them torn down. What else did Josiah do that pleased the Lord? He repaired the Temple; he promised to do all that God said in His Word and asked that the people promise too. Why do some people hate God's Word? Satan has blinded their minds. Why do others love it? They have found the key which unlocks its treasures. What is the key? Faith.

Memory Verse
"I shall not forget Thy word." (Ps. 119:16*b*)

LESSON TWO
DIRE RESULTS OF FORSAKING THE WORD

The first thing that Josiah learned when God's Word was read to him was that he and his people were sinners. They had not kept God's Word because they did not know what it said. God's Word shows us that we have sinned, and it tells us how our sins may be forgiven. Josiah and the people believed what God's Word said about their sins, confessed them, and God forgave them. But many people only want to believe the part of the Bible they like. They do not want to believe the part that tells them they are sinners or that they need a Savior. I am going to tell you about a man like this, a wicked king, who did not want to hear about his sins.

Jehoiakim Did Not Love God's Word

Josiah had a son named Jehoiakim. He was made king of Judah when he was 25 years old, but he was not like his father at all. He did not love God's Word. He wouldn't even read it. As a result, "he did evil in the sight of the LORD his God" (2 Chron. 36:5). His father had loved God's Word, even though he did not have a copy of it when he was young. Jehoiakim had a copy of God's Word, but made up his mind to forget it. And when the king forgot God's Word, so did the people (Jer. 36:3).

God must punish sin, but He is very loving and kind to give us every opportunity to be saved. God did not want to punish King Jehoiakim or destroy his country, so He spoke to His prophet, Jeremiah, and told him to get a scroll and write words of warning to the people (Jer. 36:1–2). Jeremiah asked his helper to help him write down all the words the Lord had told him (Jer. 36:4). God's message to the king and to the people was that if they kept on worshiping idols and forgetting His Word, He would send a strong army against them to destroy their land and take them away as prisoners and even kill many of them. But, if they would believe His message and turn back to the Lord, He would forgive them and not bring all those terrible things upon them.

Then Jeremiah told his helper to go to the "house of the Lord," the Temple, and read to the people all the words which the Lord had given him. Jeremiah could not go himself, for the king had restricted him so that he could not go about and teach God's Word. His helper obeyed and read the warnings of God to all the people in the land who had come together (Jer. 36:9–10). When the princes heard the message, they were afraid (Jer. 36:16). "We must tell the king what the Lord has said," they thought. "Surely the king would listen." Quickly they ran to Jehoiakim to tell him what they had heard.

King Jehoiakim was sitting in his winter house, and since it was cold, he had a fire burning in the fireplace before him. When he heard what the princes said, he told one of his servants, Jehudi, to go and get the scroll and read it to him. Well, what do you think happened when Jehudi had read only three or four pages? The wicked king grabbed the scroll and began to cut it in pieces with his pocketknife! Then, he threw it into the fire until the whole scroll was burned up (Jer. 36:23)! He was not in the least afraid of what God would do to him, nor were any of his servants who also heard the words of the Lord. The princes begged the king not to burn up the scroll, but he paid no attention to them. He thought he could get rid of the part of God's Word he didn't like by burning it. He was certainly a foolish king.

The Bible says, "For the LORD your God is the God of gods and the Lord of lords, the great, the mighty . . . You shall fear the LORD your God" (Deut. 10:17, 20). Does this mean to be afraid of God? Yes; we should be afraid not to obey His Word because God must always punish disobedience. But to be afraid also means that we should trust the Lord because He is so great and because He loves us and will always forgive us when we turn to Him.

King Jehoiakim was not only unafraid of disobeying God's Word, but he even tried to kill Jeremiah and his helper (Jer. 36:19, 26). But, the Lord hid Jeremiah and his helper so that the king's servants could not find them. Do you think because King Jehoiakim burned the scroll and tried to kill the prophet through whom God sent His Word, that part of God's Word was gone forever? Not at all! Whenever God speaks, He sees to it that His Words are kept forever. Jesus said, "Heaven and earth will pass away, but My words shall not pass away" (Matt. 24:35). Jesus is God, and the Bible is His words to us. They will last forever (1 Pet. 1:25). The Lord told Jeremiah to write down the same thing He had told him before, and then He added more. Jehoiakim would surely be punished. Not only would a strong army come into his land and burn everything to the ground and take the people as prisoners or kill them, but Jehoiakim himself would be killed by the enemy and his body thrown over the wall. What is more, his children and grandchildren could never be kings of Judah after him.

Because he did not believe God's Word, Jehoiakim and his whole country were destroyed. How different he was from his father, Josiah, who taught his whole nation to love and obey God's Word. Everything happened just as God said it would. Jehoiakim died a terrible death, but we still have God's Word today exactly as He gave it to Jeremiah. To try and destroy God's Word is like bumping your head against a stone wall to knock it down. Which comes out the worse? Why, your head! Whenever anyone tries to get rid of God's Word, they only hurt themselves. And, do you think it is any less God's Word because people do not believe it? No matter what anyone does to God's Word or what they think about it, the Bible remains the same. It never changes—it is God's Word from beginning to end!

What God Wants Me to Know

God warns us, even as He did in the day in which the Bible was written, that we must not take anything away from His Word nor add anything to it (Deut. 13:32; Rev. 22:18–19). If you do not believe God's Word, you are taking something away from it. For you not to believe God's Word does not change it. But if you will not believe it, God will take your name out of the Book of Life.

Listen to God's warnings. "He who does not believe has been judged already [his punishment is sure], because he has not believed in the name of the only begotten Son of God" (John 3:18*b*). "He who does not obey the Son shall not see life, but the wrath [anger] of God abides [will always be] on him" (John 3:36*b*).What is the punishment for not believing in the Lord Jesus Christ? "Then He [Jesus] will also say . . . 'Depart from Me . . . into the eternal fire'" (Matt. 25:41*a*). We can hardly stand to burn just our finger; think of burning forever and ever!

God didn't want to punish King Jehoiakim, and He doesn't want anyone to go to the lake of fire. How do I know this? Because God is "not wishing for any to perish but for all to come to repentance (2 Pet. 3:9*b*). Repentance means "a change of mind." God wants us to change our minds about Jesus Christ. "God so loved the world, that He gave His only begotten Son," the Lord Jesus Christ, to take the punishment for you. He took all of our sins on Himself when he died on the cross. He changed places with us long enough to take away our sins. Now all that is left for us to do is to receive Him as our Savior. "He who believes in Him is not judged" (John 3:18*a*). "He who hears My word, and believes Him who sent Me, has eternal life" (John 5:24*a*).

Lesson Review

Listen to each sentence and tell me whether the people *did* or *did not* do what it says: Josiah did/did not love God's Word? He did. Josiah did/did not worship idols? He did not. Josiah's father did/did not love God's Word? He did not. Josiah did/did not have a Bible while he was growing up? He did not. Josiah's people did/did not promise to obey God's Word? They did. Jehoiakim did/did not love God's Word? He did not. Jehoiakim did/did not have God's Word to read He did. Jehoiakim did/did not do evil in the sight of the Lord? He did.

Memory Verse
"I shall not forget Thy word." (Ps. 119:16*b*)

Chapter Six

Hearing and Doing God's Word

OVERVIEW

A. Subject: Hearing and Doing God's Word—Matthew 13:1–23; Mark 4:1–20; Luke 8:4–15

B. Lesson Titles:
 1. Lesson One: Four Kinds of Hearers and Listeners
 2. Lesson Two: Fruit-Bearers for the Lord

C. Story Objective:
 No study of the Word of God would be complete without emphasizing the ultimate purpose of the Word in the believer's life: "to grow in the grace and in knowledge of our Lord Jesus Christ" and thereby mature and produce to the maximum for the Lord.
 The Lord warned, "Take care how you listen" (Luke 8:18). As He taught the Word, He noted several kinds of hearers: those who heard but did not understand because of negative volition; those who heard and had positive volition toward the gospel, but negative volition toward Bible doctrine; and finally those who heard the Word, understood it, grew in grace and knowledge, and produced. The latter are referred to as those who are "doers of the word, and not merely hearers."
 The Word is planted in the soul through the ear-gate. As the positive soul receives the Word, it takes root. Then, as the believer learns doctrine, he grows into a strong and spiritually healthy fruit-bearer for the Lord Jesus Christ. The Word is alive and has great power to reproduce itself, but the child must understand that what he does with the implanted Word makes the difference in his life.

D. Vocabulary and Doctrinal Concepts:
 1. Vocabulary: Egypt, hail, Israelites, missionary, Pharaoh, rod, signs and wonders, sow, sower, synagogues
 2. Doctrinal Concepts:
  a. "Foolish and senseless people . . . Who have ears, but hear not" (Jer. 5:21).
  b. "Listen to My voice, and do according to all which I command you" (Jer. 11:4).
  c. "Take care how you listen" (Luke 8:18).
  d. "Let these words sink into your ears" (Luke 9:44).
  e. "You are blessed if you do them" (John 13:17).
  f. "Being rooted and grounded" (Eph. 3:17).
  g. "Doing the will of God from the heart" (Eph. 6:6).
  h. "The things you have learned . . . and heard . . . practice" (Phil. 4:9).
  i. "Prove yourselves doers of the word, and not merely hearers" (James 1:22).
  j. "Not having become a forgetful hearer but an effectual doer" (James 1:25).
  k. "Grow in the grace and knowledge" (2 Pet. 3:18).

E. *Source Book* Keywords: hardening of the heart, Peter

F. Activities:
 1. Suggested Visuals: none
 2. Games, Songs, Worksheets
 3. Memory Verse: "Hear the word of God and do it." (Luke 8:21*b*)
 4. Opening and Closing Prayer

LESSON ONE
FOUR KINDS OF HEARERS AND LISTENERS

Do you know there is more than one way to hear? You can hear with your ears, but not really listen. Or, you can hear with your ears and listen with your soul. Your ears cannot tell you what to do. Your soul must tell you to do what you hear.

When Jesus was on the earth, He taught the people what they should do by telling them a story. The people liked to hear the stories, but some of the people did not really listen. Jesus said of them, "hearing they do not hear" (Matt. 13:13). They heard Jesus speaking, but they did not listen to what He said. Why should they listen to Jesus and to what He said? Because Jesus is God, and when God speaks it is very important. But just to hear with our ears is not enough. We must listen with our souls and obey what He says. That's what Jesus meant when He said, "He who has ears to hear, let him hear [or listen with his soul]" (Mark 4:9).

Today I want you to listen with your souls as well as hear with your ears a story that Jesus told about four kinds of hearers and listeners. How shall we hear Jesus speak? Yes, in the Bible.

The Word of God Is Planted in the Soul

A farmer went out into his field one day to plant or sow some seed. He walked up and down his land scattering good seed as he went. The farmer had made some of the soil ready for planting by plowing it up until it was soft and tender. But all of the seed which he scattered did not fall on the prepared soil. Some of it fell on the "wayside." The "wayside" were paths in the grain fields where people walked and which had become packed down and hard. Every time someone walked on the path it became harder. As the seed was thrown about, some of it fell on the hard path. Do you think seeds could get down into this kind of soil? No, they just lay on top of the ground, where the hungry birds could see them. And, sure enough, when the farmer had gone, the birds came down and ate up the good seed.

There were some places in the farmer's field where the soil looked good, but a little ways underneath it was full of rocks. Some of the seed also fell on this ground. The little seeds went into the soil and were soon covered with dirt, so that the birds did not get to them. In the soft, warm soil, the little seeds quickly split open and a little green shoot peeked out of the ground. I am sure the farmer was happy to see how quickly the plants came up in this spot. But when the sun shone hot and strong on the little plants, they withered away and died because their roots could not get down far enough through the hard rocks to get water to keep them alive. A plant must have its roots well down into the soil if it is to grow up to be a strong plant.

As the farmer went on planting the seed, some fell on another kind of ground. It, too, looked like good soil. The little seeds got safely down into the ground where they could find water and food, but there were some other seeds already in this soil. These seeds were not good seeds like the farmer's, but were sticker-weed seeds. When the good seeds began to grow, the sticker-weeds grew, too. The sticker-weeds were strong and grew very fast. Soon there were more bad weeds than good plants. They so crowded out the good plants that the good plants died before they could bear any fruit.

But some of the seeds did fall on the good, soft ground. There were no rocks in this ground, no weed seeds, for the farmer had carefully prepared it. The roots went down deep and the green plants finally came up and grew into strong, healthy plants and bore the fruit or grain which the farmer wanted. Jesus said that some of these plants had more grain than others, but that all had some fruit on them.

Did Jesus tell this story just to teach us how to plant seed? No, He told about something the people understood so that He could teach them something they did not understand. Do you understand what Jesus meant by this story? Neither did His disciples, so He told them what it meant. "The good seed," Jesus explained, "is the Word of God" (1 Pet. 1:23). The Word of God, you remember, is the Bible. When someone teaches you the Word of God, it is planted in your heart (Matt. 13:19). The Bible uses the word "heart" to describe our souls by which we can think and understand. Just as the little seed has life in it and grows, so the Word of God is alive and has power to give life to those who believe it (1 Pet. 1:23–25).

Who was the farmer or "sower" in the story? Perhaps, Jesus was first of all thinking of Himself who came down to earth to plant the Word of God in the souls of men and women and boys and girls. But you and I are sowers, too. We are to plant God's Word to others so that they can hear and believe and have eternal life and grow in the Lord.

As I told you the story, did you notice that quite a bit of the seed which the farmer scattered was lost? Why was that? Was some of the seed not as good as some of the other? No, the seed was all alike. It was all good. Some of it was lost because of the ground on which it fell. Can you guess what the ground or soil represents? Yes, our hearts or souls. Jesus was saying that our souls are like the soil in a garden, but not all souls are alike, just as not all soil is the same. Some souls are hard and some are tender; some are full of worries and some are ready for planting. When Jesus taught His Word to the people of His day, there were four different kinds of people who heard it. Let's see what kind of 'soil' is in your soul. Of course, your soul does not really have soil in it, but we will pretend it has so that we can see how God sees us.

The Wayside (Hard) Soil, Luke 8:5, 12

The first kind of ground was very hard. The seeds could not get down into that soil, and the birds, who just love seeds, came and ate them all up. This is like the boy or girl who hears God's Word over and over again, but does not believe it. He hears his teacher in Bible class tell him that the Lord Jesus Christ died for his sins, but he will not listen. He may think, "I'm not so bad, or I don't need anyone to save me. God is too good to punish anyone in the lake of fire, so I'll get to heaven anyway."

Every time that boy or girl hears the way to be saved and does not believe it, his heart or soul becomes hardened. Most boys and girls have very soft and tender hearts that love to learn God's Word. But when they do not, Satan, like the big bird, comes along and snatches away the Word so that they will not believe and be saved. How the old devil hates God's Word! How he hates for anyone to be saved and become a child of God!

The Rocky Soil, Luke 8:6, 13

Of course, not everyone hardens his heart when he hears God's Word. Some boys and girls hear God's Word, and right away they believe it and are saved. They are very happy at first, but pretty soon someone comes along and laughs at them because they love God's Word and they become ashamed and pretend they are not children of God. They quit learning God's Word for fear someone will make fun of them. What kind of soil does this boy or girl have in his heart? Jesus called it "rocky soil." It had a little good dirt on top and the plants sprang up quickly. But there were rocks underneath which kept the roots from going down deep, and when the sun shone very hot upon the tender plants, they withered and died.

The Thorny Soil, Luke 8:7, 14

The third kind of soil God sees in our souls is filled with sticker-weeds. When someone planted God's Word in this soul, the soil looked good, and the seed went down in the soil. This boy or girl heard God's Word, and he believed in Jesus as his Savior and was saved. He started to grow in the Lord. He began to learn the Word of God, but soon something else came up in his life. Jesus called it sticker-weeds or thorns. If you have ever planted a garden, you know that there are always weeds which come up right along with the good plants. What happens if you do not pull them out? Why, they soon choke out the good plants. Weeds are tough and strong and will take over any garden if allowed to grow.

Jesus told us what some of these weeds are which can choke out the Word of God in our lives. He called them "worries and riches and pleasures of *this* life." What are the worries of this life? To live in this world we must work. We must have homes, food, and clothes. There are also many other things we would like to have. All these things take a lot of our time and sometimes we begin to worry about them. We worry that we might not have enough, or we worry that we might lose them. To worry about these everyday things is to let 'sticker-weeds' grow up in your life. Jesus told us that we are not to worry about what we shall eat or drink or wear. Why? Because He will take care of us. He said that every day we must first take time to hear God's Word. Then we must do what the Word says and trust Him, and He will help us to take care of our needs (Matt. 6:25–34).

What are the riches and pleasures of this life? Some boys and girls think that having a lot of money so that you can have many things and go many places will make you happy. But Jesus said that you will be happy only if you will learn God's Word and obey it (John 13:17). It is not wrong to have money or to have fun, but we must not let these things crowd out the Word of God. Sometimes boys or girls stay home from Bible class because they don't want to miss a television program, or maybe they want to go on a picnic instead. This is a sticker-weed that Jesus told us to watch out for.

The Good Soil, Luke 8:8, 15

Not all of the seed fell on bad soil. You will remember that some of it fell on the good, soft earth which the farmer had made ready for planting. What did the seed do in this kind of soil? It grew. The roots went down deep and became strong. The hot sun did not wither it, and all of its stalks had beautiful grain or fruit on them.

The good soil is like a soul also. This soul is like your memory verse: It heard the Word of God and obeyed it. It brought forth much fruit and pleased God. In our next lesson we will find out what this fruit is, and we will learn about four people in the Bible who had these four different kinds of heart-soil.

What God Wants Me to Know

God wants us to learn and know His Word. His words are true and pure. It is not good enough for our ears just to hear His Word; we must listen with our souls and obey His Word. Jesus said, "He who has ears to hear, let him hear" (Mark 4:9).

Lesson Review

The 'good seed' is the Word of God, and it gets planted in your soul. What kind of soil is in your soul? The soul with wayside or hard soil hears the Word of God over and over again, but does not believe it. The soul with the rocky soil hears the Word and believes it, but the rocks keep the Word from taking root and soon the hard soul quits learning. The soul with the thorny soil is filled with sticker-weeds. This soul began to learn the Word of God, but soon other things came up in his life so that the sticker-weeds choked out the Word of God. The soul with good soil heard the Word of God and obeyed it.

> **Memory Verse**
> "Hear the word of God and do it." (Luke 8:21*b*)

LESSON TWO
FRUIT-BEARERS FOR THE LORD

The people we read about in the Bible were real people, just like you and me, even though they lived many, many years ago. God has told us about them so that we would understand about ourselves. I want to tell you today about four of them whose souls were like the four soils we have been learning about.

Pharaoh—The Hard Heart, Exodus 5

Pharaoh was a man who heard God's Word many, many times. Each time he heard the Word of God he would not obey it so that his heart became harder and harder. Pharaoh was the ruler of Egypt when God's people, the Israelites, were living there. Pharaoh was afraid that God's people would become stronger than his own nation, so he made them his slaves. He made them work very hard, and had them beaten with whips to make them work even harder. At last God told His servant, Moses, to go to Pharaoh and tell him that God said to let the Israelites leave his country.

God had promised Moses, "I will help you to do many wonderful things so that Pharaoh will believe my word." Moses went to the Pharaoh and spoke God's words to him. "God has said to let His people go." Did Pharaoh do what God said? No, he didn't. He said, "Who is the LORD that I should obey His voice to let Israel go? I do not know the LORD, and besides, I will not let Israel go" (Ex. 5:2). Then Moses showed Pharaoh God's great power. He and Aaron threw down Aaron's rod and it became an ugly, wiggling, poisonous snake. When they picked up the snake by the tail, it became a rod again.

But, Pharaoh hardened his heart and would not obey God's Word. Moses showed Pharaoh many signs and wonders of God's great power so that Pharaoh would listen to God. He turned the river into blood. He made frogs come up all over the land—frogs hopped into everything—into the beds, into the soup, into the drinking water. But still Pharaoh hardened his heart. Moses brought forth little insects, called lice, that bit and stung. He made millions of flies come; he caused all the cattle to die and brought a terrible disease of sores on the people. He called down hail and fire that ruined the farmer's crops and many other things, but Pharaoh would still not listen to or obey God's Word.

Moses was really a sower or farmer, planting the good seed of God's Word in Pharaoh's heart or soul, wasn't he? But Pharaoh's heart was hard. Satan took the seed away since Pharaoh would not believe and be saved. It does not pay to harden your heart against God's Word. If you do, it is harder and harder to be saved, and what a terrible thing it is to die without being saved!

Peter—The Rocky Heart-Soil
Matthew 26:69–75

When Peter was first saved, he was very much like the rocky soil. He was a big, rough, tough fisherman. One day Peter's brother, Andrew, brought him to see Jesus. Andrew had believed in Jesus, and now he was sowing the seed of the Word so Peter would believe, too. When Peter saw and talked to Jesus (John 1:40–42), he gladly believed in Him. He became one of Jesus' disciples.

But, only three years later when Jesus was taken away to be crucified on the cross, Peter became afraid that he, too, would be arrested and ran away. He hung around outside the palace where Jesus had been taken to find out what would happen to Him. While out there, a girl noticed him and said, "You were with Jesus, weren't you?" This was a hard test for Peter because he was afraid he might be killed along with Jesus if he said he was a friend of Jesus. Peter had not grown much in the Lord, for he was not yet rooted and grounded in the knowledge of God's Word. He pretended that he did not know Jesus.

Pretty soon another girl recognized Peter as one who had been with Jesus. Again, Peter just wilted instead of courageously answering as he had once before: "Jesus is the Christ, the Son of the living God." Then, a third time Peter was accused of being one of Jesus' followers, and a third time Peter said, "No, I am not!" You see, Peter's soul had not been well-prepared. The good seed of God's Word had not gotten down very deep because the 'rocks' of fear and worry had not been 'dug out' of his soul. So when the 'hot sun' trouble came, he just shriveled up.

But Peter confessed his sin and Jesus forgave him. After that Peter began to learn God's Word. He prepared his soul carefully by learning and doing God's Word, and he became a strong believer. Years later, Peter wrote two books in the Bible. He told us to "grow in the grace and knowledge of our Lord and Savior Jesus Christ" (2 Pet. 3:18), so that we too will have roots which will make us strong enough not to turn away from the Lord when the hot sun of testing or trouble comes along.

Demas—The Sticker-Weed Heart-Soil
2 Timothy 4:10

The great missionary, Paul, had a helper named Demas. When Demas heard in God's Word that Jesus died for his sins, he right away believed in Jesus as his Savior. At first he wanted very much to do what God's Word said. He listened to Paul teach. He began to grow in grace and in knowledge. Demas wanted to help Paul tell people about Jesus too. So Paul made Demas his helper. He went everywhere with Paul.

It was hard work helping Paul, for Paul traveled in rough places. Often he did not have enough food to eat, and many times the people he preached to were cruel to him. Satan did not want Paul to tell people how to be saved and go to heaven, so he stirred up hatred in the people wherever Paul went and tried to snatch away the good seed whenever he could. But Paul was faithful to the Lord, and many people were saved in spite of Satan.

Pretty soon, Demas got tired of going hungry. He got tired of walking and walking over mountains and deserts and in the cold and in the hot sun. He began to wish he had more food and a nice place to live. He wished he might have more fun. He wanted some new clothes. He quit listening to the great teacher, Paul. He thought more of the things he wanted than he did of God's Word. He didn't care anymore if people did not hear how to be saved. Finally, he quit helping Paul and left for the big city where he could have what he wanted.

Demas had a soul full of sticker-weeds, didn't he? They crowded out God's Word so that the good plant that had started to grow from the seed which the sower, Paul, had planted in his soul did not bear much fruit.

Timothy—The Good Heart-Soil
Acts 16:1–5; 2 Timothy 1:5; 3:15

Now, I want to tell you about a boy who did prepare his soul carefully—how he grew up to be a strong believer in Jesus Christ and bore fruit which pleased the Lord. When Timothy was just a little boy, Paul came to his town of Lystra preaching about Jesus. Sometimes, Paul preached in the Jewish churches called synagogues, and sometimes he preached in the streets. It might be that Timothy, like other Jewish boys, went to school in the synagogue, and there he heard the great missionary. Or, perhaps he was playing in the street when he stopped to listen as Paul preached. But, wherever it was that he heard Paul preach and teach God's Word, Timothy believed it. His mother and grandmother, Eunice and Lois, also believed in the Lord Jesus and were saved.

All three of them loved God's Word. They wanted to know more and more. Lois and Eunice studied it every day. They taught what they learned to little Timothy. Timothy took time to listen. He came in from his play each day to hear his mother and grandmother tell him about God's Word. When he grew older, he began to study it for himself. Nothing was so important to Timothy as learning God's Word. He learned what pleased God and what didn't. He wanted to make the Lord happy with the things he did. He wanted to obey God and do what God's Word said. Timothy became "rooted and grounded" (Eph. 3:17) in God's Word. It went way down deep into his soul. No matter if his friends made fun of him for studying God's Word and pleasing Him, Timothy did not turn away from it. In God's sight he became a beautiful, strong plant. Don't you imagine that Timothy told other boys and girls about Jesus, too? This is what Jesus meant by "sowing, or planting, the seed." When you learn God's Word and want to do what it says, you can do many things for the Lord. God had a big job for Timothy to do, and he would bear much fruit for the Lord.

Paul came back through Timothy's town after Timothy had grown up. Many of the believers in the town told Paul what a fine young man Timothy was. They told how he had studied the Word ever since he had accepted Christ as Savior. Maybe even some of them had been saved themselves because Timothy told them about Jesus. Paul wanted Timothy to go with him and be his helper. Wasn't Timothy excited! There was nothing he would rather do. He got his things together in a hurry and was ready to go. His mother and grandmother were glad, too. They knew from God's Word that serving the Lord was the best thing he could do. Because the Word of God had taken deep root in Timothy's soul, he did not get tired and want to quit when things got hard like Demas. He stayed with Paul and was a faithful helper. Timothy became a great preacher himself. Many people came to know the Lord because Timothy listened to God's Word and obeyed it. This was some of the "fruit" Timothy brought to the Lord (John 4:36). Two books in our

Bible are named after Timothy. They are letters in which Paul wrote Timothy what God wanted him to do.

What God Wants Me to Know

As you heard about the four different kinds of souls, did you think which one might be like your own? Perhaps you have heard many, many times that Jesus died for your sins. You have heard that in order to have everlasting life and go to heaven you must believe that Jesus died for you. But every time you heard it, you went away and did not do anything about it. You have never told God the Father, "I believe that Jesus died for me. I am taking Him as my Savior." Each time you hear the Word and do not do what it says, your heart becomes a little harder.

The good seed of the Word of God has been planted in your heart today. Will you let Satan snatch it away so that you will never be saved? Are you going to let Satan tempt you to pay no attention again today, to think of other things instead of what God is saying to you through His Word? "Believe in the Lord Jesus, and you shall be saved" (Acts 16:31).

Jesus was also talking to those who have already believed in Him. He said, "Take care [watch out] how you listen" (Luke 8:18). If you pay no attention to what you hear, you will soon sin and you will stay out of God's fellowship circle. You will not do anything to please the Lord. I am sure you would rather have a soul like the last one we talked about—"an honest and good heart, and hold it fast, and bear fruit with perseverance [keep doing it]" (Luke 8:15).

What will an "honest and good heart" do to please the Lord and bring forth fruit? You will love God's Word and want to hear about it every day, like Timothy. The Bible should be your favorite Book. When your mother wants to read you a story, you will ask her to read from God's Word. You will remember to confess your sins, to tell God what you have done wrong. That way you can get back in His fellowship circle, because sin does not please God at all (1 John 1:9). You will talk to God in prayer every day, and you will want to come to Bible class to hear God's Word more than you want to play or sleep. When you come to Bible class, you will listen with your soul. Maybe some boy or girl you know does not believe in Jesus as his Savior. You will want to tell him a Bible verse which would show him how he might go to heaven. Then you will become a sower or planter of the good seed of the Word of God.

When we do what God's Word says and please the Lord, it is like growing good fruit for Him. God will gather up all the things you do to please Him, just as a farmer gathers his grain, and one day you will hear Him say to you up in heaven, "Well done, thou good and faithful servant" (Matt. 25:21, KJV).

Memory Verse

"Hear the word of God and do it." (Luke 8:21*b*)

Teaching the Essence of God

In order that we might learn about Him, God has designed in the Scriptures themselves a remarkable and simple approach to the complex truths about Himself. Taking into account our inherent limitations and basic ignorance, the Bible often resorts to language of accommodation to describe God's infinite character and functions. God is ascribed human anatomy, human emotions, human passions, human thoughts, even human sins, none of which He actually possesses, to communicate to us His thoughts, policies, decisions, and actions. Designated theologically as anthropomorphisms and anthropopathisms, these human characteristics are used by God as teaching aids to communicate aspects of His perfect Person and plan.

Anthropomorphisms ascribe to God some physical characteristic of man. God is said to have hands, arms, eyes, a face (Ex. 15:5; Deut. 5:15; John 10:28–29; 1 Pet. 3:12), yet God possesses none of these physical characteristics. They are used to describe the true functions of His righteousness and justice in blessing and disciplining; to depict divine guidance; to explain His protection and provision.

Anthropopathisms ascribe to God such human attitudes as hate, wrath, anger, repentance, as well as many others. The Bible declares that God "dost hate all who do iniquity" (Ps. 5:5), that He executes "judgments against you in anger, wrath, and raging rebukes" (Ezek. 5:15*b*). However, God does not hate, and is never angry, full of rage, or wrath. Hatred and anger are sins. God is not a sinner; God is perfect righteousness or goodness. His immutable, eternal goodness cannot be diminished by any failure of man. Hatred, anger, and wrath are human characteristics for which we have a frame of reference. God uses them to express the function of His righteousness and justice in His condemnation of the unbeliever who rejects salvation and His discipline of the believer who is disobedient to His will. The Bible also says that "the LORD was sorry that He had made man on the earth," (Gen. 6:6*a*). Repent means "to change one's mind." God is immutable; He cannot change His mind (Ps. 102:25–27; Isa. 46:10; Heb. 4:13). Furthermore, He is omniscient; He knows eternally and perfectly all that is knowable. There is no circumstance that ever comes as a surprise to Him or that would cause Him to change His mind. Thus, when Scripture says God "repented," it is simply explaining in terms of human frame of reference God's divine policy of judgment as called for by differences and changes in man and in history.

The terms "anthropopathism" and "anthropomorphism" are not used in these lessons. However, the concepts should be understood by the parent and teacher so as *not* to leave the child with the idea that God hates or is angry or changes His mind. Rather the child must know that as the Supreme Ruler over all, God has absolute righteous and just standards; He is absolutely fair. He knows all and is all powerful. He is absolute truth and never changes. The child must learn that God loves him with an infinite love and whenever the child fails, God has graciously provided the way for the child to recover fellowship with Him. These divine truths instill in the child a confident hope that God provides maximum blessing and reward in life and for all eternity to those who seek to know Him and are obedient to His will.

Chapter Seven

The Sovereignty of God

OVERVIEW

A. Subject: The Sovereignty of God—Daniel 4; Book of Acts

B. Lesson Titles:
   1. Lesson One: Nebuchadnezzar's Dream
   2. Lesson Two: The Mightiest King of All

C. Story Objective:
   God is sovereign. Sovereignty is that expression of the character of God which denotes that He is the Supreme Being, the Sovereign of the universe. There is none greater than He (Heb. 6:13). From God's sovereignty stems His absolute will. From His will comes a twofold plan for the entire human race: first, salvation and second, post-salvation conduct and provision or the Christian way of life.
   Though our Sovereign is not willing that any should perish, He cannot and will not coerce the volition which He gave man. The sovereignty of God and the free will of man coexist in human history by divine decree. The decree is the sovereign choice of divine will by which all things are brought into being and controlled, made subject to His pleasure, and produce His glorification (Isa. 46:10; Rom. 11:36; Eph. 1:9; Rev. 4:11). However, nothing is directly determined or caused by the decree; the decree merely establishes what will occur. God does not interfere with man's free will.

D. Vocabulary and Doctrinal Concepts:
   1. Vocabulary: Babylon, clever, dew of heaven, drenched, essence, just, king, kingdom, palace, pride, sovereign, stump, throne
   2. Doctrinal Concepts: The sovereignty of God (1 Sam. 2:6–8; 1 Chron. 29:11*b*–12; Ps. 8:1, 24; 115:3; 135:6; Isa. 40:12–15; 66:1; Heb. 6:13; 8:1; Rev. 4)

E. *Source Book* Keywords: Christ (birth, wise men), Daniel, essence of God (sovereignty), plan of God

F. Activities:
   1. Suggested Visuals: Daniel, young; Nebuchadnezzar; Nebuchadnezzar mad; sovereignty symbol; Trinity
   2. Games, Songs, Worksheets
   3. Memory Verse: "The earth is the LORD'S, and all it contains, The world, and those who dwell in it." (Ps. 24:1)
   4. Opening and Closing Prayer

Lesson One
Nebuchadnezzar's Dream

Have you ever wondered what God is like? As I look at you this morning, I can tell what most of you are like. You are a boy about 7 years old; your hair is brown and your eyes are blue. You pay attention in Sunday school; you are polite. I can tell all these things because I know you, and because I stand here where I can see you. I know what God is like too, but does that mean that I can see God? No. I cannot see God and neither can you. The Bible tells us that no man has ever seen God (John 1:18*a*). But someday, all who have believed in the Lord Jesus as their Savior will see Him. Yet even though we cannot see God now, we can still know Him. Do you know how? We can know God through His Word.

We have learned much about the Word of God and now, we will learn from God's Word what God is like. Where shall we begin? I know! We will let the Bible show us word pictures of God's essence. Let's make a box and call it God's essence. In this box, we will put all the word pictures about God as we learn them. Do you remember what essence means? Yes, what God is like. Let's look at the first word picture in Psalm 24:1. "The earth is the LORD'S, and all it contains, The world, and those who dwell in it." This verse and many others like it tell us that God is SOVEREIGN.

That's a big word, is it not? Can you say it with me? Sov-er-eign. God is sovereign means that God is King. Not just a plain king, like a king over a country, but King of the whole world! He is the highest, heavenly King. The sun, moon and stars, the oceans and mountains, the animals and birds, and all the people in the world belong to God. He made them and He owns them. He is King over all. Because God is the highest king, there is none greater than He (Heb. 6:13). Let's learn the words of Psalm 24:1, for they tell us that God is the mightiest King over all heaven and earth. Then you can tell others what you have learned today.

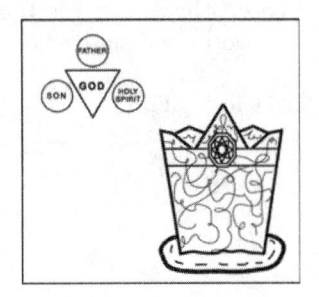

Kings sit on thrones, and God's throne is set far above the sky we see, higher than the stars, all the way up to the highest heaven. If you were in a very high place and looked down, the people below would seem like tiny specks to you. You might say they remind you of teeny little ants busily running around an anthill. Yet when the heavenly King looks down on each one of us, we are very, very important to Him. He has created us and placed us right here on this earth. He has a perfect plan for us. He owns everything and can do with it as He desires and thinks best for us (Job 1:21).

Often people do not realize that God alone is King of heaven and earth. Yet, God wants everyone to know of His sovereignty. Sometimes He must even take away what He has already given before people will learn what He is like. Listen, and I will tell you the true story of someone who found out the hard way that God is sovereign.

A Mighty King

Almost twenty-five hundred years ago in faraway Babylon, there lived a mighty king named Nebuchadnezzar. Say it with me, Ne-bu-chad-nez-zar. Nebuchadnezzar was king when Daniel was taken to Babylon to live there. Daniel was one of the men whom God had chosen to write a part of our Bible. Now King Nebuchadnezzar was very rich and powerful, and he had a great kingdom. He had everything he wanted. He even thought that he had everything he needed, but that was not so. Nebuchadnezzar did not have God's salvation. He did not believe in the Lord Jesus Christ as his Savior. And, if we do not believe in the Lord, we really have nothing at all.

Do you know who had given Nebuchadnezzar all that he owned? Do you know who had made him a great king? Yes, God did. But King Nebuchadnezzar did not know this, nor did he know that the Lord wanted to save him or that he needed to be saved at all. Remember, he thought he needed nothing else. He was so puffed up with pride that all he could think of was himself. No, King Nebuchadnezzar made no room in his life for the Lord God of heaven and earth.

The King's Dream

One night, as the king lay asleep in his bed, he had a strange dream. He saw a great big tree full of fruit and leaves. Animals rested in its shade, and birds nested in its branches. Oh, what a lovely tree that was. But suddenly, an angel came and spoke! He said that the tree must be cut down and only the stump left in the ground. The animals fled. The birds quickly flew off. Now, only the stump was left with an iron fence all around it. What a strange and frightening dream that was! Long after the king awoke, he kept thinking about the dream. What did it all mean? Nebuchadnezzar shook his head. He was frightened and could not understand the dream at all (Dan. 4:4–5, 10–15).

Do you remember why the men who were with Daniel at the river did not see the Lord nor understand the angel's words? See if you can think back to the story we had about Daniel. Only Daniel could understand God's words and God's plan. The others could not because they did not believe in the Lord Jesus Christ (Dan. 10:7; cf., 1 Cor. 2:14). King Nebuchadnezzar was also an unbeliever. That was why he was so frightened and puzzled. He called for all the wise men in his kingdom. Perhaps they might tell him what the dream meant (Dan. 4:6).

The wise men stood by the king's throne and listened to him tell of his dream. They shrugged their shoulders and shook their heads sadly. No, they did not have any idea what the dream was all about. They could not even make a guess (Dan. 4:7). At last, Daniel came into the king's throne room (Dan. 4:8).

"Daniel," said the king, "you are a clever man and God has shown you many secrets. I will tell you a dream I have dreamed. Then, you must tell me what it means."

"I dreamed," began the king, "that I saw a tree in the middle of the earth. It was a huge tree and kept growing taller and taller until it almost reached up into heaven. People all over the world could see that tree. It was full of leaves and had enough fruit on it to feed the whole world. Animals rested in the shade of the leaves, and birds made their nests in its branches. It was a lovely sight to be seen."

"But suddenly an angel appeared and shouted, 'Cut down the tree; cut off the branches; shake off the leaves, and scatter the fruit. Chase away the animals and the birds. But do not tear out the tree stump. Let the stump stay in the ground. Let it get wet with the dew of heaven. Let it live among the animals in the grass of the field. Give him the mind of an animal in exchange for his own mind until seven years are over.' Then as the angel finished speaking, he announced the purpose of the dream, 'This must be done to show that God is sovereign, the highest King of all. He alone rules over the earth. He puts kings on earth to rule over countries, but God Himself rules over the whole world'" (Dan. 4:8–17).

After the king told his dream to Daniel, he waited to hear what Daniel might say. But Daniel was perplexed and remained silent for quite awhile. Had God not shown Daniel the meaning of this strange dream? Yes, God had shown Daniel. But Daniel was alarmed and was thinking how he might best tell the king, for the dream had a disturbing and sad meaning. It was possible that the king would be very angry when he found out what the dream meant (Dan. 4:19a).

Nebuchadnezzar's Dream Interpreted

"Speak up, don't be afraid," said the king. Then, Daniel told him, "This is what the mighty King of heaven wants you to know: You are that tree. It is healthy and increasing in size and riches of fruit like your kingdom. You, O king, are high and mighty because God made you so. But you are proud, too proud to accept God's plan for you. So God will take everything away from you, and all that you have seen in the dream will come true. God has given you your kingdom; He can also take it away. He has given you great power, and He can take away your power. For seven years you will live out in the fields with the wild animals. You will even think that you are an animal yourself. You will eat grass like cattle and be drenched with the dew from heaven until you believe that God is sovereign King over your life. God surely wants you to know, King Nebuchadnezzar, that He alone is the great Sovereign of heaven and earth and that He alone gives kingdoms to whomever He wishes. He will give you back your kingdom after you have learned that God is the greatest King of all."

Then, Daniel warned Nebuchadnezzar: "Please listen to what I will say now, O King. If you will believe on the Lord as your Savior and accept God's plan for your life, perhaps God will keep your dream from coming true" (Dan. 4:19–27).

What God Wants Me to Know

The king was listening to every word Daniel had spoken, but I wonder what he thought about God's warning to him? Do you think he recognized the sovereignty of God?

You, too, have heard that God is sovereign. What does that mean? You don't need Daniel to tell you, do you? No, you already know that sovereign means king. Nebuchadnezzar was sovereign over a country. God is the Sovereign of heaven and earth. If you have believed in the Lord Jesus as your Savior, then God is sovereign of your life. That means you should obey all that He says to you in His Word. Do you even try? Do you know that all you have, your home, your parents, your health, your food and clothing—everything—was given to you by God (James 1:17)? Have you ever thanked Him for giving you and planning for you what is best?

The one thing God wants to give you more than anything else is the gift of salvation. Salvation is God's perfect plan for every boy and girl, man and woman. God's plan of salvation is written down in God's Word. It says, "But these have been written that you may believe that Jesus is the Christ, the Son of God; and that believing you may have life in His name" (John 20:31). When you take Jesus as your Savior, God's plan for you comes true and you become a child of the heavenly King.

Lesson Review

We have learned that God is King. Who can tell me the big new word that means "God is King"? Yes, God is sovereign. Where is God's throne? Who is the mightiest King of all? Yes, God.

King Nebuchadnezzar was a mighty king. All that he had was given to him by God, but Nebuchadnezzar did not know this. Neither did he think he needed God's plan of salvation, God's perfect plan for his life. But God showed him that he was wrong. What kind of a dream did God send Nebuchadnezzar? Who told the king what the dream meant? What was going to happen to the king? What did Daniel advise the king to do?

Memory Verse
"The earth is the LORD'S, and all it contains, The world, and those who dwell in it." (Ps. 24:1)

LESSON TWO
THE MIGHTIEST KING OF ALL

Today, we want to find out what the king decided to do about God's warning dream to him. But first, we want to be sure you can say the verse we learned about God's sovereignty. "The earth is the Lord's and all it contains, The world, and those who dwell in it" (Ps. 24:1).

The Dream Comes True

One whole year had passed, for God was giving Nebuchadnezzar plenty of time to think about the dream and its meaning. What did Nebuchadnezzar do? When he saw nothing happening day after day, week after week, month after month, he forgot all about God's warning and Daniel's words.

Then, one fine day King Nebuchadnezzar walked in his gardens. He looked about him and proudly said, "Look at my great kingdom. I made it great. My own power has built it and made it famous. I have made it for myself and all by myself" (Dan. 4:29–30).

While he was still bragging, a strong and mighty voice called from heaven: "O king, your kingdom has been taken away from you." Who took it away? The same One who gave it to Nebuchadnezzar—God, the heavenly Sovereign. Why did God take his kingdom away from Nebuchadnezzar? To teach him that God, not Nebuchadnezzar, is the greatest King of all.

Now, the king could no longer live in his fine palace. Day in and day out, he lived outside in the fields with the animals. He ate grass like the cattle and sheep. He slept in the fields, not in his royal bed, and he woke up wet with the dew of heaven. His hair grew as long as eagle's feathers, and soon, his nails were like a bird's claws. His mind was sick. He no longer looked or felt like the proud king he had once been. And so he continued for seven long years, just as in his dream (Dan. 4:31–33).

Nebuchadnezzar Realizes God Is Sovereign

Do you know how long seven years are? Would it not be awful if you had to live out in a field all that time with never a meal, never a bath, and never having your hair or your nails cut? Just imagine how Nebuchadnezzar must have felt!

After seven years, Nebuchadnezzar finally looked up to heaven and understood what God was like. At last he knew that God's plan was much better than his own. Nebuchadnezzar's kingdom was not nearly as important as he thought it was; it would belong to him only as long as he lived. Now, he knew that God's kingdom would last forever and no one could take God's kingdom away from God. No one was more powerful than God. He alone is the

Sovereign of the world. Yes, Nebuchadnezzar had finally found out what we already know, that God sits on His throne in heaven and that He is the mightiest King of all. He owns the earth and everything in it.

Long ago, God planned and made the world, the animals, the birds, and the people who live in it. He knew exactly how to make them and where to put them. God's plan for His creatures is perfect, but He has a very special plan for mankind.

God's plan for mankind was to send His Son, the Lord Jesus Christ, into the world to die for the sins of the whole world. Whoever will believe in Him will become a child of the heavenly King and will live forever with Him in heaven. Many people do not want to understand that God's plan is best for them, they want to have their own way. Then, they learn that their way was not the right way at all. That's what happened to King Nebuchadnezzar, is it not?

Nebuchadnezzar Believes in the Lord

From now on things were going to be different, for what happened to Nebuchadnezzar is the very best thing which can happen to any of us. He believed on the Lord Jesus Christ, God's promised Savior. That very moment God made Nebuchadnezzar's mind well again. He remembered that he was a man and not an animal. He remembered he was a king and had a palace in which to live. He had a great country, a throne, and power. Would God give it back to him again? Oh, how foolish he had been not to want God's better plan for his life.

Nebuchadnezzar's Restoration

What do you think God did? Did He give back the great kingdom to Nebuchadnezzar now? Yes, you are right; He did. Soon the king's friends and wise men came from the palace. They asked Nebuchadnezzar to be their king once again. Once Nebuchadnezzar learned that God is sovereign, he became a better and wiser king trying to please God. God rewarded Nebuchadnezzar by making him even greater than he had once been (Dan. 4:36*b*).

Nebuchadnezzar's Declaration

Let me tell you what King Nebuchadnezzar did after he got back to his palace. He sent some very important news to all people in his great country. This is what he said: "I, King Nebuchadnezzar, am writing you to tell you about the greatness of God. He alone is most high and has done many wonderful things. His kingdom is an everlasting kingdom, and He rules forever and ever. All the things which have happened to me taught me to praise and honor sovereign God whose works are truth and whose ways are just" (Dan. 4:1–3, 37). The story about King Nebuchadnezzar and how he learned the hard way is written down in God's Word for all to read, as is his letter. Now you, too, have heard it.

Only you have learned the easy way that God is what? Yes, sovereign.

What God Wants Me to Know

Some day, when all the children of the heavenly King are with the Lord in heaven, we will have a wonderful time together. We will meet King Nebuchadnezzar and Daniel. We will see Moses and all those who have received God's gift of salvation. Everyone who accepted God's perfect plan for their lives will be there.

Now while we live on this earth, we know that the whole earth belongs to the highest King, our Father in heaven. Think how rich our heavenly Father is. The stars, the mountains with all the gold in them, and the seas with all the precious pearls belong to Him. You belong to Him, and you are far more precious to Him than all the stars, all the gold in the mountains, or all the pearls of the sea. You are more important than all the children of the kings on earth because you are a child of the heavenly King.

Can you still remember the name of the proud king who thought he did not need the Lord Jesus as his Savior? Yes, it was Nebuchadnezzar. God sent an angel to warn him and show him what would happen if he did not believe. God gave this king one whole year to change his mind and believe on the Lord Jesus as his Savior. But Nebuchadnezzar did not want God's plan of salvation. So, God had to punish him for his pride. Seven years were wasted before the king would believe in the Lord Jesus Christ.

Does God still speak to us in dreams? No. Does He still send angels to tell us His plan? No, today God speaks to us through His Word, the Bible.

In the Bible, His perfect plan of salvation is given to us clearly. The Bible says that Jesus died for our sins. Have you sinned? Have I? We are all sinners (Rom. 5:12). We all need to be saved, whether we think we do or not. We can be saved and go to heaven only one way, by believing on the Lord Jesus Christ (Acts 16:31). How long will God wait for you to make up your mind? A day? A year? Ten years? No, as long as you live. But we do not know how long any of us will live, do we? That is why God's Word says, "Behold, now is 'the acceptable time,' behold, now is 'the day of salvation'" (2 Cor. 6:2). Will you decide right now to become a child of the heavenly King? Only you can do it; no one can do it for you. How? Believe on the Lord Jesus Christ.

Lesson Review

Let's all say Psalm 24:1 together: "The earth is the Lord's, and all it contains, The world, and those who dwell in it." Can anyone tell me why the earth and all it contains belongs to the Lord? Yes, He created them and owns them. God has a perfect will for all of His creatures. His will is best, for He is the Sovereign of heaven and earth. Not everyone knows that God is the highest King.

Nebuchadnezzar certainly did not know until God showed him. Do you remember the true story about the two kings, King Nebuchadnezzar and God, the heavenly King? I wonder how well you remember it. I will tell you the story just one more time. But listen carefully, and tell me if what I say is true or false.

Many years ago in the land of Babylon lived a proud king. His name was Nebuchadnezzar. True or false? True. One afternoon he had a dream. True or false? False—one night. He dreamed he saw a tiny little tree. True or false? False—a big tree. This tree could be seen throughout all the earth. The animals found shelter in its shade, and the birds nested in its branches. Suddenly three angels came down from heaven. True or false? False—one angel. The angel said, "Cut down the tree and leave only the stump in the ground. Let it stay out in the field for one year." True or false? False—seven years. The king told his dream to Daniel. True of false? True. When Daniel heard the dream he said nothing for awhile. Then he warned the king, saying, "You, O king, are that tree. Unless you accept the Lord as your Savior, your kingdom will be taken from you." True or false? True.

At the end of another year, King Nebuchadnezzar walked alongside a river. True or false? False—in his garden. He was as proud as ever and bragged of his power. Just then, a voice called from heaven: "Your kingdom is taken from you." True or false? True, that same hour his dream came true! The king now lived out in the field with the animals and ate grass for seven years. He grew wings. True or false? False—his hair grew as long as eagle's feathers. He had long nails like a bird's claws. True or false? True. When he finally believed in the Lord, his mind cleared and he knew how foolish his pride had been. Nebuchadnezzar had learned that God is the most high King, the Sovereign of heaven and earth, who rules forever and ever. True or false? True.

Memory Verse
"The earth is the LORD'S, and all it contains, The world, and those who dwell in it." (Ps. 24:1)

Chapter Eight

Sovereignty and Serving the Heavenly King

OVERVIEW

A. Subject: Sovereignty and Serving the Heavenly King—Acts 9:1–25; 23; 27—28

B. Lesson Titles:
 1. Lesson One: Saul Meets the Heavenly King
 2. Lesson Two: Paul Serves His Sovereign

C. Story Objective:
 The sovereignty of God coexists with the free will or volition of man. God, who planned and created the world and all that dwells therein, upholds the whole universe in His sovereign hands (Ps. 24:1; Col. 1:16–17). From His throne, our heavenly Sovereign watches the very steps of His creatures and through His Word directs their paths (Ps. 33:13–14). His sovereign will supersedes man's plans (Ps. 135:6). Yet, He never coerces the volition of man. He uses our free will to work out all for the purpose of His good pleasure (Phil. 2:13). "The LORD nullifies the counsel of the nations; He frustrates the plans of the peoples" (Ps. 33:10). But blessings come to those whom He has chosen for His own (Ps. 33:12).
 Every believer in the Lord Jesus Christ has the right and privilege to choose to be of service and allegiance to the King of glory (Ps. 24:10). He may confidently look to the Lord, knowing that the divine plan of salvation does not overlook man's temporal needs (Phil. 4:1), whatever they may be.

D. Vocabulary and Doctrinal Concepts:
 1. Vocabulary: cargo, cause, Christians, courage, Damascus, faithfully, Festus, former, God's will, island, Italy, Jerusalem, natives, nephew, persecute, Rome, servant, serve, shipwrecked, solemnly, sovereign, synagogue, witness, witnessed
 2. Doctrinal Concepts:
  a. God enthroned (Ps. 45:6; 47; 93).
  b. God plans and provides for every need of man.
   1) Temporal (Ps. 8:3–9)
   2) Eternal (John 3:16, 36)

E. *Source Book* Keywords: Paul, volition, witnessing

F. Activities:
 1. Suggested Visuals: bright light, Saul blinded
 2. Games, Songs, Worksheets
 3. Memory Verse: "For God is the King of all the earth." (Ps. 47:7*a*)
 4. Opening and Closing Prayer

Lesson One
Saul Meets the Heavenly King

Now, let's see how perfect God's will and God's plan really are.

Just as your mother plans what you will have for dinner, prepares it, and calls for you to come and get it, so God planned everything for the first man and woman long before He put them on this earth. He knew exactly what they would need. Who showed God, and who taught Him what to do? No one did. God is sovereign and He did as He pleased in heaven and on earth (Ps. 135:6). He made plants for man to eat (Gen. 1:11). He made the sun to shine by day and provided nighttime to rest. He placed the moon and stars in the sky as lights in the darkness (Gen. 1:14). He filled the oceans and rivers with fish (Gen. 1:20). He made the plants, the cattle, the birds, and the food for all to eat (Gen. 1:24). When everything was ready, God created the first man and his wife and said that the earth and everything in it was his and he was to rule over all of it (Gen. 1:28). Everything was perfect because perfect, sovereign God had planned it so.

Since then, sin has changed many things (Rom. 5:12). Yet, you and I still rule over the plants. Have you ever bent down to pick a flower? Did you ever hear the flower say, "Don't you dare pick me"? No! The flowers still obey God's plan for them, don't they? You may rule over the flowers, but who rules over you? Over your parents? Over presidents and kings? God does! The heavenly King is sovereign over all.

Because we all have sinned, God made the plan of salvation. This means that He made a way for us to have our sins taken away so that we could go to heaven. Now, suppose you have already accepted God's salvation plan by believing in the Lord Jesus Christ. Is God's plan for you now finished? Did He take you to heaven the moment you believed in Him? No, He left you here on earth. His plan for you has just begun. Our heavenly King wants you and me to serve Him of our own volition, just like He wanted a man named Saul, who lived long, long ago, to serve Him. Let's hear how this man's life was changed because of God's perfect plan, shall we?

Saul, the Enemy of Christ and Christians

Everyone knew that Saul of Tarsus hated all Christians. Who are Christians? Those who have believed in the Lord Jesus Christ. Saul had put many Christians in jail and even had some of them killed for their belief in the Lord Jesus Christ! You see, Saul did not believe that Jesus was God's Son who had died for the sins of all mankind. Now, he threatened to go all the way to Damascus to find more Christians and bring them back to Jerusalem in chains. In his pocket, Saul had a letter from the high priest which said that he could do with these Christians as he pleased (Acts 9:1–2).

Surely God did not plan to save a man like Saul? Or did He? Yes, He did, for the Lord Jesus died on the cross for every person in the world, even Saul (Rom. 5:6, 8).

Saul Meets the Risen Lord

Now, Saul and his helpers were on their way to Damascus. As they walked down the long road, a bright light from heaven flashed around Saul and Saul fell to the ground. He heard a voice say to him, "Saul, Saul, why are you persecuting me?" Had Saul tried to hurt the bright light from heaven? Whose voice was that? Do you remember what the Lord's face was like when He spoke to Daniel by the river? Yes, like a bright light. I am sure you know who spoke to Saul now. Who was it? Yes, it was the Lord Jesus Christ, but Saul did not know this yet. "Who are You, Lord?" he asked. The Lord answered, "I am Jesus whom you are persecuting" (Acts 9:3–5, NKJV).

Saul's Conversion

You see, every time Saul had persecuted or hurt a Christian, he was also persecuting the Lord Jesus (Zech. 2:8b; Eph. 5:30). Now, Saul was trembling with fear. Jesus was God after all, and he had not believed it! "What do you want me to do, Lord?" he asked. "Rise, and enter the city, and it shall be told you what you must do," said the Lord (Acts 9:6). Then, the Lord Jesus was gone as suddenly as He had appeared.

The men who came with Saul heard the voice, but had not seen anyone. "What was happening to Saul?" they wondered. But Saul knew, for he had seen the Lord. Now, he understood God's plan of salvation. Now, he wanted God's plan for his life. He changed his mind about the

Lord Jesus and believed in Jesus as his Savior. When Saul stood up he could see nothing, for he had been blinded by the Bright Light from heaven. Have you ever looked into a camera flash when your picture was taken? Afterwards, you see dark spots before your eyes, don't you? God is much brighter than a camera flash, or even the sun, for "God is light" (1 John 1:5b). Just looking at the Lord Jesus made Saul blind for three days and nights. Now helpless, Saul's men had to guide him by the hand into the city. There, Saul waited for God to show him what to do. For three days and nights he did not eat or drink anything, but prayed to the Lord (Acts 9:7–9).

Saul Receives His Sight Back

In Damascus lived a man whose name was Ananias. He was a Christian who loved the Lord and had learned much about God and His Word. One day, the Lord spoke to him. "Ananias, go to Straight Street and find a man named Saul of Tarsus. He is blind and is waiting and praying. Touch him with your hand to make him see once more" (Acts 9:10–12). Ananias did not trust his ears for he knew that Saul had persecuted many Christians and why should God give Saul his eyesight back? "Lord," he said, "I have heard some awful things about Saul. He kills your people, and now, he has come to our city to put us in chains and make us suffer" (Acts 9:13–14). Ananias was not at all sure that he should go to such a wicked man as Saul.

God's Plans for Saul's Life

The Lord answered Ananias: "Go to him. I have special plans for Saul. I have saved him, and chosen him to tell the plan of salvation and to teach My Word to the people of the world and to their kings" (Acts 9:15). Then, Ananias obeyed His heavenly King and went to Saul.

Remember, everyone knew Saul hated Christians. Can you imagine how frightened the believers in Damascus must have been when they heard that he was coming to their city? But now, they heard that Saul had begun to tell about the Lord Jesus Christ, His own Savior, and how wonderful He was. How surprised they were to hear these words from Saul's lips! Why, Saul was one of them now! He loved the Lord Jesus as much as they did, and He was teaching that Jesus is God (Acts 9:17–22).

Saul's Enemies and New Friends

What did Saul's former friends and helpers from Jerusalem think? They became so angry with Saul that they planned to kill him. They hid near the city gate, watching day and night for Saul to leave Damascus. They planned to murder him, for he was of no use to them now. He was on the side of the Christians (Acts 9:23–24). Sooner or later, Saul was sure to leave the city, and when he came out of the gate, they would get rid of him once for all.

But God helped Saul to find out what these bad men were trying to do. One night, Saul's new Christian friends in Damascus lowered Saul over the top of the city wall in a basket so that he got away safely (Acts 9:24–25). God had much work for His new servant Saul.

What God Wants Me to Know

God had a special plan for Saul, just as He has a plan for you. Do you remember what Saul asked the Lord? "Lord, what do you want me to do?" How can we find out what our heavenly King wants us to do for Him? God speaks to us in the words of the Bible. He says, "Children, obey your parents" (Eph. 6:1). Obedience to your parents is obeying God. How else can you serve the heavenly King? By telling others about God's perfect plan and how He sent His Son to die on the cross for the sins of the whole world.

Saul's sins were forgiven as soon as he believed in the Lord Jesus Christ. No one is too bad to be saved; no one is too good to be saved. If, while you are here on earth, you do not accept God's perfect plan to serve the mightiest King and live with Him forever in heaven, then some day, you will stand before the King's throne in judgment and hear God say, "Why did you not believe in the Lord Jesus Christ?"

As sovereign, the heavenly Father has the power to force you to accept His plan for your life, but He does not force anyone to obey. God does not say, "You must." He has provided salvation as a gift for you. To receive His gift, all you have to do is believe in the Lord Jesus Christ. God wants everyone to choose by their own volition to obey Him. Why don't you tell Him right now, quietly in prayer, that you want His plan, that you are believing in the Lord Jesus Christ. Right now, you can become a child of the heavenly King and have His perfect plan for your life from now on.

Lesson Review

We talked about God's plan always being perfect and better than man's plans. Do you recall what Saul planned to do in Damascus? But God planned for Saul to be saved. Whose plan came true? What did Saul's former friends plan to do when they found out Saul had believed in the Lord Jesus Christ? What was God's plan for Saul from now on? That's right, to tell others about God's Son and God's Word. Whose plan came true? How did Saul get away without going through the city gate? His new friends lowered him over the city wall in a basket. God protected Saul like He protects all who believe in Him.

Memory Verse
"For God is the King of all the earth." (Ps. 47:7a)

Lesson Two
Paul Serves His Sovereign

Have you ever made special plans for your vacation or a holiday, only to have everything go wrong? Maybe you had planned to go on a picnic, or swimming, or on a hike, and when you woke up it was storming and raining so hard you had to stay indoors.

We often make plans, but we have no way of making sure they will turn out all right. That is why people will say, "If everything is all right, we will do such and such." But we need not be disappointed when we cannot have our way, if we will only remember that God's way is always better than our own.

Once a man made careful plans to visit his family whom he had not seen for a long time. He had bought his plane ticket and had written his wife and children when and where to meet him. They could hardly wait for that special day. Then all went wrong. The man missed his plane, and he was terribly upset. "Why did this have to happen to me?" he grumbled. Later, he found out that the plane had crashed. God's better plan had saved his life.

From His throne in heaven, God watches all the people on earth (Ps. 33:13–19). He sees what they are doing and knows what they are planning. He sees us and knows all about us and about our plans. Will you trust Him to know what is best for you?

God Protects Paul

Saul of Tarsus, whom we met in our last lesson, is none other than the great Apostle Paul. God used him to write many of the books in the New Testament. In our story today, we will find that his name was changed to Paul and we will hear how he served his heavenly King.

The Roman soldier slammed the heavy iron door shut, and Paul was alone in his prison cell in the tower of the fortress of Antonia (Acts 23:10*b*). How quiet it now was. Only a few minutes ago, there was a lot of shouting as the leaders of the synagogue quarreled about something Paul had said (Acts 23:7–10*a*). What do you think that might have been? Yes, Paul told them that the Lord Jesus was not dead any longer, that He had come back to life, and that all who believed in Him would also live forever with Him (Acts 9:15; cf., 23:6). Some of the leaders were so angry with Paul they wanted to kill him. Others tried to help Paul. Oh, what a lot of noise they made! They shouted and pulled Paul this way and that. They would have surely pulled him in pieces if the Roman soldiers passing by had not heard their angry voices. The soldiers came in to see what was the matter. Then, they took Paul away with them and put him in prison until they could find out what had happened that day (Acts 23:10*b*).

God's Plan Made Known to Paul

Now, night had come and all was quiet. I am sure Paul thanked the heavenly King for saving his life. Suddenly, Paul looked up. What was that? He was no longer alone in his cell; the Lord Jesus stood beside him. The Lord said, "Take courage; for as you have solemnly witnessed to My cause at Jerusalem, so you must witness at Rome also" (Acts 23:11). Then, the Lord was gone, and Paul was glad to know the Lord still had work for him to do.

Do you remember what Paul asked the Lord on the road to Damascus? "Who are You, Lord?" he asked (Acts 9:6, NKJV). Jesus told Paul who He was and what to do, did He not? He did. He told Paul when He was on the road to Damascus, and He was telling Paul now in prison. Paul must go to Rome to witness, to tell about God's plan of salvation. He must obey the heavenly Sovereign. Do you think Paul wondered how he could go to Rome when he was still in prison? Rome was a long, long way from Jerusalem. But Paul soon would find out.

Paul's former friends in Jerusalem were now his enemies. They had tried to kill Paul once before, but his new Christian friends had helped him escape over the city wall. Now his enemies were going to try to kill him again. This time, they watched and waited near the great Antonia tower where Paul was kept. They numbered forty men, and they planned to snatch Paul away from his Roman guard when Paul was to be taken for questioning the next day (Acts 23:12–15). But God had another plan for Paul's life; He did not want Paul killed. And God's plan is always greater than any plan man can make.

God Works Out His Plan

God is sovereign, and God worked out His better plan this way. When Paul's enemies talked and made their wicked plans, God made Paul's young nephew pass by, just close enough to hear what they were saying. Quickly, the boy ran to the prison to tell his Uncle Paul what these bad men were planning to do (Acts 23:16).

Paul listened carefully to his nephew, and then he called the captain of the guards. "Take this young man to the chief captain of the guards, for he has something very important to tell him," he said (Acts 23:17–18). Yes, God the heavenly Sovereign can even use children to do His will. This boy was ready to do what God wanted. Are you? So Paul's life was spared again, for the chief captain sent two hundred of his soldiers, seventy riders, and two hundred men with spears to bring Paul safely to another city (Acts 23:19–23). God certainly takes care of His own does He not? He uses people to carry out His will and plans (Ps. 33:13–19).

Paul Serves the Heavenly King

Two years passed, and Paul had told many people, even kings and queens and other rulers like Festus about our Savior, Jesus Christ. But Paul's adventures had only just begun. Where must he go next to take God's message? Yes, to Rome. This king and queen and Festus would see to it that Paul was sent there.

A Dangerous Journey

Before long, a ship was on its way sailing to Italy. Rome is in Italy, and who do you think is sailing on that ship? You are right, Paul. But will the ship ever get to Italy? The wind blew and blew, but it was blowing from the wrong direction. Sailing was becoming more dangerous every day (Acts 27:6–8). The ship kept close to the shore, hoping to find shelter from the storm. Paul had warned the captain and the Roman officer not to sail, but neither one would listen, as they hoped the weather would soon be better (Acts 27:10–11). Instead, the storm only grew worse. The ship tossed helplessly in the raging sea, threatening to drown every one on board (Acts 27:13–18*a*). The next day, they threw the cargo they carried overboard to lighten the load. Only the captain and his sailors, and the Roman officer, his soldiers, and their prisoners were left aboard (Acts 27:1, 18*b*, 32). But it was no use. All seemed lost (Acts 27:20).

Now, Paul spoke up: "You did not listen to me when I warned you not to sail, but believe me now. The ship will sink, but not a man shall be lost" (Acts 27:21–22). The men looked at each other in disbelief. How did Paul know? "I know," said Paul, "because last night the heavenly King, whom I serve, sent an angel to tell me this. And I also know that what God plans, He will surely bring to pass. Soon, we will be shipwrecked on an island" (Acts 27:23–26).

All happened as the angel had told Paul. The ship ran aground and broke into many small pieces (Acts 27:41). When the soldiers saw that their prisoners were now free to escape, they wanted to kill them (Acts 27:42). But God's plan was to keep Paul alive. So the heavenly Sovereign helped the Roman officer know what to do. He quickly shouted an order to his soldiers: "No, do not kill anyone! Let them swim to the nearby island or keep afloat by holding on to the wooden planks of the broken ship" (Acts 27:42–44). The shipwrecked men reached the island safely.

They were wet and cold. They shivered. But, the people who lived on the island welcomed them kindly and lit fires to warm and dry their visitors. Paul helped gather the wood. As he bent down to place some sticks on the fire, a poisonous snake crawled out and bit his hand. Everyone watched. Would Paul die? Paul shook off the snake. No harm came to him (Acts 28:1–6). God, the heavenly King, looked after His servant.

To Rome, At Last

Every day, the men looked out over the ocean. Was there no ship near that could take them away from the island and bring them to Rome? One month passed, two months, three. At last a ship! How the men must have waved and called, for the sailors heard them. They picked up the stranded men and sailed to Italy (Acts 28:10–15). At last, Paul arrived in Rome.

What was Paul to do in Rome? To speak about God's perfect plan for every man, woman, and child. And did he? Let's see what the Bible says. Paul lived in Rome for two years. Many people had heard about Paul and now, they came to see him. Paul told them about God's plan and God's Son. He spoke from morning until evening, and some believed the things he told them (Acts 28:16, 23–24), but others did not.

What God Wants Me to Know

Wasn't God's plan for Paul perfect? His plan is just as perfect for you, too. Even boys and girls your age can serve their heavenly King. All they need to do is to obey His Word and His will. Did you know that serving God is the most wonderful adventure in the world? Some day, if you have served God well and faithfully, you will hear Him say to you as you stand before His throne in heaven, "Well done, good and faithful servant" (Matt. 25:23*a*). Who knows, He may even have a crown for you (Rev. 2:10*b*)!

Some of the people who listened to Paul did not believe what he said was true. But, it is true that Jesus died on the cross for your sins and mine. He alone can save you and give you eternal life (Acts 4:12). Right now, God is waiting to save you, too. He loves you and wants you to believe on the Lord Jesus Christ. He wants you to serve Him. Will you believe on the Lord Jesus Christ right now?

Lesson Review

God has a perfect plan for every man, woman, boy, and girl. God is the King of heaven and earth, which means that He is what? That's right, sovereign. Once there was a man named Saul who hated the Lord Jesus and all Christians. Who did Saul meet on his way to Damascus? From that day on he believed on the Lord Jesus and served who? Yes, sovereign God. But now, Saul's former friends had become his enemies. They tried to kill him. But God had other plans for his servant, whom we also know as Paul. One time, Paul got away from his enemies in a what which was lowered over the city wall? Yes, a basket. Another time, God sent Roman soldiers to take Paul away from angry people and put him into a what? That's right, a prison. During the night the Lord visited Paul and said, "Be courageous."

God wanted Paul to go all the way to Rome to tell of His wonderful plan of salvation. Paul must go by ship to Rome. What a lot of adventures he had after he got on the ship. The winds and waves were so terrible that those aboard ship almost drowned. God sent word to Paul that no one would be lost; only the what would break up? That's right, the ship. But all the men swam to the nearest island where the people welcomed their visitors and lit a what? Yes, fire. Paul helped gather wood for the fire. As he bent down to place the sticks on the fire, a what crawled out and bit his hand? Yes, a poisonous snake. But Paul did not die.

After some time a ship came to take the men and Paul to Rome. For two years Paul told everyone he met about God's perfect plan of salvation. He served his heavenly King well for as long as he lived. Surely some day God will say to him, "Well done, good and faithful" what? Yes, "Well done, good and faithful servant."

Memory Verse
"For God is the King of all the earth." (Ps. 47:7a)

Chapter Nine

The Righteousness of God

OVERVIEW

A. Subject: The Righteousness of God—Genesis 1—3; Luke 18:9–14

B. Lesson Titles:
1. Lesson One: God's Righteousness and Man's
2. Lesson Two: The Pharisee and the Publican
3. Lesson Three: The Test in the Garden

C. Story Objective:

God is righteous (Deut. 32:4). He is perfect goodness, free from sin or wrong in His Person (Ps. 11:7; 116:5; John 17:25a). God's concept of righteousness, by means of His own perfection, is one of absoluteness. In contrast, man's concept of righteousness, by means of his sinful nature, is one of relativity, not perfection. Righteous God cannot have a relationship with that which is sinful or wrong, but demands the same righteousness in His creatures.

Since "all have sinned and fall short of the glory of God" (Rom. 3:23), we cannot measure up to the divine standard of righteousness. Neither can we achieve God's righteousness through self-effort (Titus 3:5). Yet, God does not desire to be separated from us (2 Pet. 3:9) but has provided the means to be reconciled to Him: "Even *the* righteousness of God through faith in Jesus Christ," is available for "all who believe" (Rom. 3:22).

God's righteousness is seen in all His attitudes and actions (Ps. 145:17; Rev. 19:2a); He never acts apart from His righteousness and justice (Ps. 145:17; Dan. 9:14b). God has absolute right and authority over His creatures by virtue of creation (Col. 1:16–17; Rev. 4:11). However, God does not coerce any creature's volition. He can sovereignly dispose of His works as it may please Him (Ps. 135:6; Dan. 4:35).

God gave man righteous laws (Gen. 2:16–17; Rom. 7:12; 8:2). He never condones sin. He demands that disobedience to His laws and Word be punished without partiality (2 Chron. 25:4; Rom. 2:11–12).

D. Vocabulary and Doctrinal Concepts:
1. Vocabulary: adulterers, altar, goodness, holy, innocent, jealous, Pharisee, praise God, publican, reconciled, relationship, righteousness, swindlers, Temple, white linen cloth, worship
2. Doctrinal Concepts:
   a. The righteousness of God (1 Sam. 2:2; Ps. 7:9; 22:3; 47:8; 97:6; 111:3; Rom. 1:17; 10:3; 1 John 1:5)
   b. The holiness of God (Lev. 19:2b; Ps. 22:3; 111:9)
   c. Man's righteousness (Isa. 64:6; Rom. 3:10–12; 2 Cor. 10:12)

E. *Source Book* Keywords: Adam and Eve; Adam's original sin; angels; essence of God (righteousness); fall of man; Garden of Eden; heavens, three; human spirit; integrity of God; righteousness (+R); righteousness (−R); Satan; sin; soul; tabernacle

F. Activities:
1. Suggested Visuals: Christ on earth, righteousness symbol, Trinity
2. Games, Songs, Worksheets
3. Memory Verse: "And the heavens declare His righteousness." (Ps. 50:6a)
4. Opening and Closing Prayer

Lesson One
God's Righteousness and Man's

Let's look at our Essence Box again to see what we have learned about God so far. God is sovereign. That means God is King, the highest King of heaven and earth. Now let's see another word picture the Bible shows of God. "And the heavens declare His righteousness" (Ps. 50:6a). Let's be sure we understand what this verse tells us so that we can all learn it.

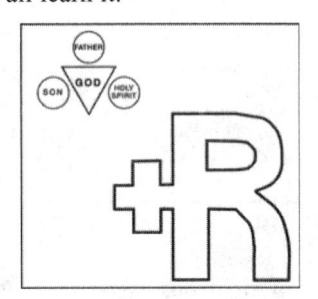

We all know what the heavens are. We look up into the sky and can only think how great heaven must really be, for the sky we can see with our eyes is only the first heaven. There are two more heavens beyond that, the second and the third heavens (2 Cor. 12:2b). The third heaven is God's home. Now, how do the heavens declare God's righteousness? And what does the word "righteousness" mean? First of all, to declare means "to tell" or "to show." In school you have a time called "Show and Tell," don't you? Well, the heavens both show and tell that God is RIGHTEOUS. "Righteousness" means perfect goodness. "God is righteous" means that God is perfectly good—not just sometimes, but always and forever.

But how do the heavens show and tell us that God is perfect goodness, or righteousness? Think about the countless stars, suns, and moons of heaven. Do they ever crash or bump into each other as do our cars? No, God put each in its own place and keeps them there (Col. 1:16–17). Everything God does is perfect and good because God is perfect goodness. He can do no wrong.

What about men and women? Are they perfectly good? Some are a little better than others, some are worse than others, but none is altogether good as God is good. How good is God's goodness? And how good is man's goodness? Well, that's what we will find out.

The Righteousness of Man as Seen by God

God looks down from His heavenly throne, and this is what He sees: "filthy rags" (Isa. 64:6a, KJV). Now, you say, "But I don't look like that. I am nice and clean and good, at least right now. I don't tell lies—very often that is. Just yesterday I helped my mother clean the house, or helped my dad mow the lawn. I go to church and to Sunday School. I even saved some of my allowance and put it in the offering plate. Surely, when God looks at me, He could not see filthy rags on me." So, you don't believe it? See if you can find Isaiah 64:6a in your Bible and follow along as I read what it says. "But we are all [not just some—ALL—you and I and everyone] like an unclean *thing*, and all our righteousnesses *are* like filthy rags" (Isa. 64:6a, KJV). Listen to another verse I will read. This one is Romans 3:10: "THERE IS NONE RIGHTEOUS, NOT EVEN ONE." What makes us all like unclean and filthy rags? What makes us all unrighteous? Yes, sin. Man's righteousness is *un*righteousness.

Have you sinned? Have I sinned? The Bible says, "All have sinned and fall short of the glory of God" (Rom. 3:23). That means we are not as good as God is good. Now that we have seen what we are like, it certainly does not make a pretty picture, does it? But it is true just the same.

The Righteousness of Man as Seen by Man

Many people do not like to see themselves as God sees them. They hope that somehow all the good things they have done will make them good enough to go to heaven some day. They hope that God will notice how good they have been. But being good will never get us to heaven, and being bad will never get us to the lake of fire. Sure, God knows all the good and bad things we have ever done and will ever do, but they make no difference. What matters is that we have believed on the Lord Jesus Christ!

Not Good Enough

Just for fun, let's pretend we can watch God adding up all the good things boys and girls your age can do, and see how you come out. (1) Helped mother make the beds. (2) Picked up my clothes and toys. (3) Cleared the table every day this week. (4) Helped do the dishes. (5) Took out the garbage. (6) Brought in the papers. (7) Said my prayers. (8) Washed my hands without being told. (9) Went to church. (10) Gave money. These are all good things, and you should certainly do them. God draws a big line underneath your good works and begins to add them up. What will the total be? Let me give you a clue. "But we are all like an unclean *thing* and all our righteousnesses *are* like filthy rags" (Isa. 64:6a, KJV). In other words, no matter how hard we try, we are just not good enough to be acceptable to God.

The Righteousness of God

Now, we are ready to look at God's righteousness, that is, God's perfect goodness. God's goodness is like a spotless, white linen cloth. He is perfect, good, pure, and white. The Bible says that "God is light and in Him is no darkness at all" (1 John 1:5b). Because God is perfect goodness He cannot have anything to do with sin or unrighteousness. He cannot and will not let filthy rags come near Him. We must first have God's goodness, then we can be children and friends of God (1 Pet. 1:16). Listen, and I will tell you how you may have God's righteousness for your very own.

Christ Was Punished for Our Sins

Do you remember when we learned *how* God gave the Law to Moses. The Law is part of God's Word. In it He tells His people what they must and must not do. But do you know *why* God had to give them a Law at all? He gave them a Law to show them that they were *all* sinners (Rom. 3:20). Remember, "All have sinned and fall short of the glory of God" (Rom. 3:23). If we were perfectly good, we would not need to be told not to do bad things, would we? If you never told a lie, your mother would not have to say to you, "Don't lie to me." If you always obeyed your parents, God would not have written down in His Word, "Children, obey your parents" (Eph. 6:1a). God knew that we could never, ever keep all His commandments, for we are all born with a sin nature and we all sin. Every time we disobey God, we show that we are sinners (James 2:10). Since righteous God can have nothing to do with sin, He had to find a way to bring mankind into a relationship with Him. God the Father would send His own Son, the Lord Jesus Christ, to "show and tell" and share God's righteousness with all who want it (John 1:18; Heb. 1:3).

The Lord Jesus is absolute righteousness, for Jesus is God. Remember, the Lord Jesus left His heavenly home and was born into the world to save sinners. He came to *show* us that God loves us (John 3:16) and wants to forgive our sins (1 John 1:9). Never once did the Lord Jesus do a wrong or bad thing; never once did He disobey God's Word (1 Pet. 2:22). One day, He let Himself be nailed to a cross. While He hung on that cross, He took everyone's sins, yours and mine also, and let Himself be punished in our place (2 Cor. 5:21a; 1 Pet. 2:24). God the Father loved the world so much that He let the Lord Jesus take the punishment for our sins, our filthy rags (1 John 1:7). "For He [God the Father] made Him [God the Son] who knew no sin *to be* sin on our behalf" (2 Cor. 5:21a). The righteousness of God the Father was satisfied with our Lord being our substitute, taking our place because He was without sin.

Made Righteous in Christ

And now, the Lord Jesus wants to share His righteousness, the very same righteousness which God has, with us (2 Cor. 5:21). When we believe in the Lord Jesus Christ, He gives us His own righteousness (Rom. 4:9). Now that we have God's goodness or righteousness, we are the children of God.

What God Wants Me to Know

Some of you already have God's righteousness. How did you get it? By being especially good? No, you received God's righteousness by believing in the Lord Jesus Christ. Now, you have God's perfect goodness. But you still sin don't you? In fact, you will still do bad and wrong things as long as you live. Yet, when the Father in heaven looks at you, He can see His own righteousness in you.

True, you will still go to heaven even though you sin, but sin breaks your fellowship with God. Sin puts that ugly splotch of uncleanness between God and you. Is there any way to remove it? There certainly is: "If we confess our sins, He is faithful and righteous to forgive us our sins and to cleanse us from all unrighteousness" (1 John 1:9). Just be sure to tell God right away whenever you have done or thought something wrong, and He will restore you to fellowship with Him.

And talking about uncleanness, if you came home with your clothes and shoes all dirty and muddy, would your mother let you track the dirt into her nice, clean house? No, she would make you take off your dirty things before you came in and send you to wash up.

God has a wonderful home in heaven. He loves us all and wants us all to come there. Because He cannot let sin come into heaven, He sent the Lord Jesus Christ to die as a substitute for us. Only by believing in Him do we receive His righteousness so that we can live with God forever in heaven. The Lord Jesus Christ did not stay dead, did He? No, He came back to life and went back up to heaven. Now, He is just waiting to share His righteousness with anyone who will believe in Him.

You cannot make yourself good enough for God. You cannot do enough good works to be acceptable to the righteousness of God. Only accepting the salvation work of the Lord can do it. Will you receive God's righteousness this minute? How? By believing in God's perfect Son as your Savior.

Lesson Review

What is God like? God is sovereign, and God is righteous. What do those two words mean? Yes, God is King and God is perfect goodness. Can you say the memory verse we have learned about God's righteousness? "And the heavens declare His righteousness" (Ps. 50:6a).

What is God's righteousness like? It is spotless, pure, white, and without sin or wrong. Is man's righteousness like that also? No, the Bible says that all of our righteousnesses are like what? Filthy rags. God's perfect righteousness cannot have a relationship with those who do not have God's perfect righteousness.

Is there any way whereby we can become good enough to be friends with God and go to heaven? Can anyone change his own unrighteousness into the righteousness of God? Of course not, but we can receive the righteousness of God by believing in the Lord Jesus Christ so that we will live with God forever. Because we possess God's righteousness, He can restore us to fellowship with Him when we are cleansed through confession of all known sins.

Memory Verse
"And the heavens declare His righteousness." (Ps. 50:6a)

Lesson Two
The Pharisee and the Publican

Do you ever think you are better than the girl or boy down the street? You have nicer things than they, and you would never, never do some of the bad things they do. They steal and tell lies, they tattle on others, they are very naughty. When you compare yourself to them you seem to be so much better. People will often do this. They measure themselves against other people (2 Cor. 10:12) and come up pretty good in their own sight. But we are not to do that. We are to measure ourselves against God's perfect goodness. When we do, we will find that we are not good at all.

I want to tell you a story which the Lord Jesus told when He was on earth. But before I do, I want to ask you a question. Why did the Lord Jesus come to earth? So He could pay the penalty for our sin—that's right. We may be different in our ways, our looks, in the things we do or say or think, but there is one way in which we are all the same. We are all sinners (Rom. 3:23) and not nearly as good as God is good.

To show the people that the Lord Jesus would die as a substitute for them some day, God taught them to bring animal offerings to the Temple. The animals must be killed and burned on the altar. Now, when God's people saw that the little lambs died in their place, they understood the perfect righteousness of God and His promise to send the Lord Jesus to save them from their sins.

The Pharisee and the Publican

Many years had passed, but at last God's perfect and good Son, the Lord Jesus Christ, had come into the world. He had come to seek and to save lost sinners (Luke 19:10). The only trouble was that most people thought they were so good they did not need a Savior. Whatever made them think that? Yes, they had been comparing themselves to others, but not to God. Soon they began to look down their noses at those they thought were bad. What they did not know was that when God looked at them, He did not see one better or worse than another; He saw them all alike—sinners every one (Rom. 3:10, 23). That was why the Lord Jesus told them the story which I will tell you now.

Once, two men went up into the Temple to pray. One of them was a Pharisee, the other a publican (Luke 18:10). Just what is a Pharisee and what is a publican? A Pharisee belonged to a group of Jewish people who tried hard to keep every part of the Law God had given to Moses, and many, many more laws besides. They hoped to please God by the things they did. But remember, no one can keep the Law perfectly. If they broke even one little part of it, they were just as guilty as if they had already broken the whole Law. But the Pharisees did not believe this. They thought God would surely see their good works and let them come to heaven. Can you tell me what our righteousnesses, our own good works, are like in God's sight? Right, "filthy rags" (Isa. 64:6a, KJV). It is not by the good things we try to do, but by the good thing the Lord Jesus did for us that we may be saved and given the righteousness of God (Titus 3:5). The Pharisees went to the Temple twice a day and made a big show of giving money. They usually prayed loud and long to make sure everyone heard and saw them. One of the two men who had come to the Temple was this kind of a person, a Pharisee.

The other man was much different. He was a publican. Now what is a publican? A publican is a tax-collector.

Matthew, who wrote the first book of the New Testament, was a publican. Often the publicans collected more tax money than the Jewish people owed the Roman government and put it in their own pockets.

The Pharisees knew that. They hated the publicans and called them "sinners." Sure, it is wrong to steal, but never forget that the inner sins, the bad things we think—prideful, hateful, or jealous thoughts—are every bit as wrong and sinful as the bad things we do.

This time the proud Pharisee had come to pray silently. The Lord Jesus tells us what he said. Listen to this man's prayer and count to see how many times he said "I." "The Pharisee stood and was praying thus to himself, 'God, I thank Thee that I am not like other people: swindlers, unjust, adulterers, or even like this tax-gatherer. I fast twice a week; I pay tithes of all that I get'" (Luke 18:11–12). Five times he said, "I, I, I, I, I." He had just told God, "God, look at me. I am a good man. Twice every week I pray at a time when others eat. I give you a tenth of all that I own (that means if he has ten dollars, he gives God one dollar), and I thank you that I am different from all these other bad people, especially people like this publican here." What kind of a prayer was that? Had the man really come to worship and praise God? No, he had come to praise himself before God.

Far off, in the back of the Temple, stood the publican. He bowed his head and did not dare look up to heaven. He, too, prayed silently: "God, be merciful to me, the sinner!" (Luke 18:13b). His prayer went something like this: "God, show your love to someone who does not deserve it. I know I am a sinner, and I should die for my sins. But I saw the little lambs die outside the Temple for my sins. I understand and I believe that some day the Savior will come to take my place and pay the penalty for my sin. Only through believing on Him will I receive your righteousness and be acceptable to You."

God looked down at the two men in the Temple. He saw one man who trusted in his own righteousness, and another who trusted in the righteousness of God. Did God think one was better than the other? No, God saw that they were both sinners. Neither was good enough to go to heaven; neither had the righteousness of God. Remember, "All have sinned and fall short of the glory of God" (Rom. 3:23). Both men were unrighteous or –R (minus righteousness) while God is perfect righteousness or +R (plus righteousness). Both men needed salvation, but only one believed in the Lord Jesus Christ. Which one was given the righteousness of God? Yes, the publican. The Lord Jesus had finished His story, but we are not quite through with it yet.

What God Wants Me to Know

The people who had listened to the Lord knew that He was speaking straight to them. He was asking them what kind of people they were. Did they trust in themselves and in their own righteousness? Were they like the proud Pharisee who thought he could work his way to heaven? Or were they like the publican who realized that he was a sinner and needed the Lord to save him? And, now I am asking you the same question. What are you like?

I know about some saved boys and girls. Once they trusted the Lord Jesus, but now, they have started trusting in themselves. They think they are smarter than others and better than others. Pretty soon they become all puffed up with pride. They have forgotten that all they have, and all they are is theirs because God gave it to them (1 Cor. 4:7; 15:10). Should they not be thankful instead? Should they not think how great and good God is instead of how they are? Boys and girls who trust in themselves sooner or later will get into trouble. Never forget the perfect goodness of God!

But, what about boys and girls who still have a –R before their names because they have not yet trusted the Lord Jesus to save them? Many of them, too, are like the Pharisee. They think only of themselves. With them it is "I" all the way. They strut about saying, "Hey, look at me! See how good I am!"

And, then there are those boys and girls who are shy and timid and want to hide behind their mother's and dad's back. Does that mean they are any better? Who do you think God loves more? Well, I have a big surprise for you. God loves all of you the same. He loves you so much that He gave the Lord Jesus to die for your sins and to rise again to give you the righteousness of God in Him.

Now I wonder if you will walk away with +R. Will you? You can, if you will believe on the Lord Jesus Christ. Right now, you may bow your head and tell God the Father, "Father in heaven, I know that I, too, am a sinner. I need the Lord Jesus to save me and give me His righteousness so that I may go to heaven. I believe in Him and thank you that you will share your perfect righteousness even with me."

Lesson Review

I am curious to know how much you have learned since we started to find out what God is like. Can you quote Psalm 24:1? "The earth is the LORD'S, and all it contains, The world, and those who dwell in it" (Ps. 24:1). Yes, God is sovereign.

Do you know Psalm 50:6a? "And the heavens declare His righteousness." Yes, God is also righteous. Well, I see you have learned a lot, but really we have only just begun. And we must be sure to tell others what we have learned about God.

Memory Verse
"And the heavens declare His righteousness." (Ps. 50:6a)

Lesson Three
The Test in the Garden

Did you remember to tell anyone about God? The heavens did. The sun rises and sets, and the twinkling stars come out with the moon every night to show and tell what God is like. But, there are others who also praise our wonderful God. They are the angels in heaven. They stand about God's throne and call out, "Holy, Holy, Holy, is the LORD of hosts, The whole earth is full of His glory" (Isa. 6:3*b*).

Can you tell me what "holy" means? No? Well, then, let me tell you. "Holy" means absolutely pure and perfect and set apart from all others. God's holiness is made up of God's righteousness and God's justice. We are still learning about God's righteousness, but soon we will learn about His justice. Did you know that we are not the only ones who are learning what God is like? The angels watch and listen all the time to find out more about God (Eph. 3:10; 1 Tim. 3:16; 1 Pet. 1:12). Can you be like them? Then watch and listen as I tell you what the angels found out long, long ago.

The Creation

The angels sang together and shouted for joy (Job 38:7). Why were they so happy? They had just watched God make the earth out of nothing and hang it in space (Gen. 1:1; Job 26:7; 38:4–6; Isa. 45:18*a*). What a lovely sight that first earth must have been! But, it did not stay perfect and lovely for very long. One of God's angels, Satan, had sinned and with the help of other bad angels ruined the beautiful earth (Gen. 1:2; Isa. 14; Ezek. 28). God had to repair the earth and make it ready once again, for He had special plans for it. He wanted people to live on the earth (Isa. 45:18*b*). So, God decided to make the first man. You know how God did that, don't you? He took some chemicals found in the soil and formed them into the shape of a man. Then God breathed into this man, Adam, and made him come alive (Gen. 1:26; 2:7). And so that man would not be lonesome, God made a wife, Eve, for him (Gen. 2:18, 21–22).

Adam and Eve were perfectly made. They were innocent, that is, free from sin, and had a body, a soul, and a human spirit. We all know what a body is, don't we? It is that part of a person which we can see and touch. Adam and Eve saw each other. They knew they were very much alive. They could not see their souls and spirits, and neither can we, but their souls helped them to understand each other and to know how beautiful everything around them was. Their spirits helped them to understand and love God.

But there was something else God had given them—volition of their own. God let Adam and Eve choose what they wanted; they could say, "I will" or "I won't."

Adam and Eve in Eden

Adam and Eve were happy in the Garden where God had placed them. It was a perfect place to live. The weather was lovely. They had all the food they could eat, with fishes, animals, and birds for their playmates. Yes, God had given them all they needed, and there was no hard work for them to do. There were rivers in that garden, and gold and precious stones, and every kind of tree (Gen. 2:9). Some trees were pretty to look at; others were good to eat; but the very best thing about living in the Garden of Eden was that Adam and Eve could walk and talk with God.

The Test Declared

God spoke to Adam and said, "Of every tree of the garden you may freely eat; but of the tree of the knowledge of good and evil you shall not eat, for in the day that you eat of it you shall surely die" (Gen. 2:16–17). There were many trees in the Garden, including the tree of life. But God only forbid eating from one tree—the tree of the knowledge of good and evil. Was God mean to forbid Adam and Eve to eat of that one tree in the Garden? Not at all. God is perfect goodness. What was that big word we learned which tells us that God cannot do anything mean or wrong? That's right, righteousness. God was going to test Adam and Eve, to see if they would obey Him or not. While you and I can sin in many, many ways, there was only one way in which Adam and Eve could sin against God. What was it? Disobedience.

The Temptation

Some time had passed since God had told Adam about the tree in the middle of the Garden. Then one day, when Eve was all by herself, Satan, the devil, entered into the serpent and called to Eve: "Say, Eve, did God say that you should not eat of every tree in the Garden?" Why, Satan was trying to trick Eve and make her think that God was keeping something good from them. Eve answered, "No; God said we may eat of all the trees in the Garden, but not of the tree of the knowledge of good and evil." Then Eve added, "God said we must not even touch that tree or we will die" (Gen. 3:1–3).

Had God said they would die if they *touched* the tree? Of course not. Eve made that part up, didn't she? But it was true that they would die if they *ate* of the tree of the knowledge of good and evil.

Satan did not give up easily. Again he spoke through the serpent. "You will not die. God just does not want you to know good and evil as He does." Why, that was a lie, wasn't it? Oh, how the angels watching must have wanted to shout, "Don't listen to the serpent with the devil's voice. Remember what God said to you!" But the angels could not do that. That would not have been fair. God had given Adam and Eve free will, their volition. They must make up their minds by themselves to see if they would pass the test. The angels watched, trembling to see what Eve would do. Oh no!

The Fall of Man

It was only too true. Eve reached up, took the forbidden fruit, and bit into it. Satan had not forced her to do it; the devil had only tricked her (1 Tim. 2:14). Eve listened to Satan, and not to God. Later, Eve gave some of the fruit to Adam and he ate of it also (Gen. 3:4–6). What had they done? They had decided to disobey God. The first man and woman had become sinners. What would God do now, the angels wondered? They knew that God is righteous and can have nothing to do with sin. Sin is bad, but God is perfect and good.

All happened just as God had warned. From the moment they sinned, Adam and Eve lost their innocence. They also lost their human spirit and acquired a sin nature. They were incapable of having a relationship or fellowship with God. They could no longer understand or love God for they were now spiritually dead. Many years later, their bodies would also die, and return to the dust from which God had made them. But now, for as long as they lived, there was no place found for them in God's beautiful Garden. God had to send them away so they could not eat of the tree of life and live forever in the state of spiritual death (Gen. 3:22–24*a*).

What God Wants Me to Know

What had spoiled God's perfect fellowship with Adam and Eve? Yes, sin. And just so it is with God and us. When God's children have disobeyed God, they cannot talk to Him in prayer (Ps. 66:18; Gal. 3:26). But we need not disobey God and His Word. God gave us all volition. We may decide for ourselves if we will obey Him or not. God does not merely want us to hear His Word, but also to do it (James 1:22). Still, if we have decided to disobey, there is a way back to fellowship with God. "If we confess our sins, He [God] is faithful and just to forgive us our sins and to cleanse us from all unrighteousness" (1 John 1:9). You who have trusted the Lord Jesus should never forget this verse. It is God's guarantee of fellowship for as long as you live on this earth.

Now, maybe you think, "Now, if I had been Adam or Eve, I would not have eaten of that tree. I would not have disobeyed God." Are you sure you would not have? Do you obey Him now? Let's see if you do.

God provided another tree. It was not pretty to look at, nor good to eat. It was made of wood in the shape of a cross. Jesus died on that tree for you and for me, for all of us (Rom. 3:23). Now God invites you to come to His tree and accept a gift from Him. That gift is God's righteousness, and you may have it by believing on the Lord Jesus Christ (2 Cor. 5:21). Which way will you decide, for God or against Him?

Lesson Review

When God created the first man and woman, He made them perfect and free from sin. What four things did God give them? Let me give you a hint: Only one of these four things could be seen. Yes, God gave them a body, a soul, a spirit, and volition. Let's remember what the soul inside of man can do. The soul can love and understand people and things. What about the human spirit? The spirit can love and understand God and His Word. As long as Adam and Eve had a human spirit they could walk and talk with God.

Where did Adam and Eve live? They lived in the Garden of Eden. What special tree stood in the middle of the Garden? Yes, the tree of the knowledge of good and evil. What rule did God make about that tree? Adam and Eve were not to eat of it. What was the punishment if Adam and Eve disobeyed? Spiritual death. What happened to Eve in the Garden one day? She disobeyed God and ate from the tree of the knowledge of good and evil.

Could Adam and Eve have decided to obey God instead of disobeying Him? Of course they could have. Volition can say "no" just as easily as "yes" to doing bad things. Certainly Adam and Eve had not been hungry, for God had given them all the food they could eat, and more. Nor had Satan forced them to take and eat the fruit. No, Adam and Eve decided by themselves to disobey God, and no one was to blame except the two of them.

Memory Verse
"And the heavens declare His righteousness." (Ps. 50:6*a*)

Chapter Ten

The Justice of God

OVERVIEW

A. Subject: The Justice of God—Genesis 1—3; Rom 8:1; 14:10*b*; Rev. 20:11–15

B. Lesson Titles:
 1. Lesson One: The Fall and Judgment of Man
 2. Lesson Two: The Great White Throne Judgment

C. Story Objective:
  God is infinitely holy (Isa. 6:3; Rev. 15:4). His holiness or integrity is composed of His righteousness and justice. While righteousness is the divine standard, justice is the function. God's justice is absolutely fair in all its actions (Lev. 19:2; Deut. 32:4; Ps. 19:9*b*; Isa. 2:2; Rom. 3:26; Heb. 11:30–31; Rev. 3:7). Divine justice can best be seen in the plan of redemption and its execution.
  Through His vicarious, efficacious death on the cross, the Lord Jesus Christ transferred the guilt of the sinner upon Himself and thus satisfied the perfect righteousness and justice of God. Because the penalty was exacted in full, God is now free to pardon and justify the sinner who accepts His saving grace (Rom. 3:26; 8:1). At the same time God is equally free to justly condemn all who reject the divine provision of salvation (Deut. 18:18–19; John 3:18, 36; 5:28–30; Rev. 20:11–15). The basis of their indictment is *works*, never sins, and the judgment is committed to Him who was judged as a substitute for us, our just God and Savior (Isa. 45:21; John 5:22; Heb. 9:27–28).
  This study is not an attempt to teach, or even cover in part, the various judgments recognized in Scripture, but it is merely intended to bring out the assurance of "no condemnation" for the believer in the Lord Jesus Christ and the contrast of "condemnation" for the unbeliever.

D. Vocabulary and Doctrinal Concepts:
 1. Vocabulary: blame, condemnation, evaluated, evaluation, fellowship, great white throne, guilty, judge (noun), judgment seat of Christ, lake of fire, production, thrown
 2. Doctrinal Concepts:
   a. The holiness of God (Lev. 19:2*b*; 1 Sam. 2:2; Ps. 22:3)
   b. His righteousness and justice (Deut. 32:4; Job 37:23; Ps. 50:6*b*; 58:11; 89:14; Isa. 45:21; Rom. 3:26; Heb. 12:23; Rev. 15:3)
   c. The judgment of believers (Rom. 14:10; 2 Cor. 5:10)
   d. The judgment of unbelievers (Ezek. 20:33–38; Matt. 25:30; Rev. 20:11–15)
   e. The Book of Life (Ps. 69:28; Rev. 3:5; 21:27)

E. *Source Book* Keywords: Adam and Eve, blood of Christ, Book of Life, essence of God (justice, righteousness), the great white throne, judgment seat of Christ, justice of God, lake of fire, Last Judgment, origin of sin

F. Activities:
 1. Suggested Visuals: justice symbol, sin circle, Trinity, volition
 2. Games, Songs, Worksheets
 3. Memory Verse: "For God Himself is judge." (Ps. 50:6*b*)
 4. Opening and Closing Prayer

Lesson One
The Fall and Judgment of Man

Let's pretend we can tiptoe into the Garden of Eden and see Adam and Eve before and after they sinned. But before we do, let's learn a new verse which will show us another word picture of what God is like. That verse is found in Psalm 50:6*b*. You have already learned the first part of the verse. Can you say it with me? "And the heavens declare His righteousness" (Ps. 50:6*a*). Now we will see what the last part of the verse says: "For God Himself is judge" (Ps. 50:6*b*). That's easy and short, is it not? But what does it mean?

Do you know what a judge is and what he does? A judge is someone who decides what punishment is best for a guilty person who has broken the law. He must be absolutely fair and just. Would it be right for the judge to feel sorry for a person who had killed another and to let him go free? No, that would not do. That would be very unfair to those who did not break the law. To be fair, a judge must declare the right punishment to be carried out.

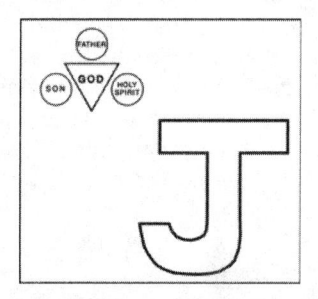

Sometimes judges on this earth are not fair and just as they should be, but God is always fair and just. And, He is the highest Judge of all. So, now we will add a new word picture of God, justice, into our Essence Box with those we already know. God is perfect JUSTICE. Now let's say our verse: "For God Himself is judge," over and over as we tiptoe softly into the Garden of Eden.

Adam and Eve before the Fall

Remember, we are pretending to be with Adam and Eve in the Garden. Just imagine them coming down the path between the trees. There is a happy look on their faces. And who is that walking with them? Why, it is the Lord Jesus Christ, God Himself, and they are talking with one another. And look! Do you see that dazzling light about the Lord?

Do you remember learning about the bright light from heaven which Saul saw along the road to Damascus (Acts 9:3)? God's clothing is a bright and flashing light. The Bible tells all believers that, "But if we walk in the light as He [God] Himself is in the light, we have fellowship with one another" (1 John 1:7*a*). To "walk in the light" is just another way of saying that we should make sure all our sins are confessed so that our fellowship with God will not be broken.

The Wages of Sin

God had told Adam and Eve exactly what would happen if they disobeyed His rule. He had said they would die on the very same day that they ate of the forbidden tree (Gen. 2:17*b*). But the serpent with the devil's voice said that it would not be so; that they would not die, that God was only being mean and unfair and did not want them to know as much as He knew (Gen. 3:4–5). Who would be right, God or Satan? God is always right. And, He is never mean or unfair; He is always righteousness and *justice*. Adam and Eve certainly did die the same day they sinned. What part of Adam and Eve died first? Right, their human spirits.

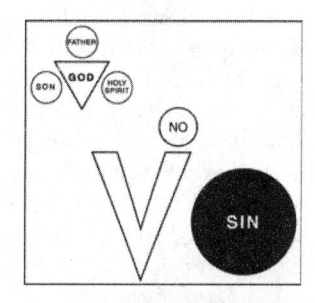

Was God fair and just to let them die spiritually—in their spirits? Yes, indeed. Remember God never forces anyone to obey or disobey. Everyone has volition to make a choice for or against God. He had clearly warned them and told them this would happen. A fair Judge must make the guilty person pay the penalty. Adam and Eve disobeyed God and were guilty and must be punished.

Operation Coverup

As soon as Adam and Eve knew they were sinners, for they had eaten of the tree of the knowledge of good and evil, they knew they had done a terrible thing. They had disobeyed God. They felt ashamed and afraid. Sin always makes us feel ashamed and afraid to be found out. The Bible tells us that they now realized that they were "naked" (Gen. 3:7) and, for the first time in their lives, they were afraid. They thought, "What will God do when He sees that we have disobeyed Him?" They hoped that if they made for themselves coverings of fig leaves, their sins would be hidden from God (Gen. 3:7).

Sin Discovered

By now it was late in the afternoon and lovely and cool. Adam and Eve heard the voice of the Lord as He walked in the Garden. Then Adam and Eve, who had so loved to walk and talk with the Lord, hid themselves among the trees. If they had only known it, they did not need to hide from God, for even if they had tried to come near Him they could not have done so. Sin, like a big wall, had come between them and God.

Then, the Lord called to Adam: "Where are you?" (Gen. 13:9). God knew well where Adam was and he knew why he had hidden among the trees. But God wanted Adam to admit what he had done. Adam answered, "I heard Your voice in the garden, and I was afraid because I was naked; and I hid myself" (Gen. 3:10, NKJV). Now, God wanted to know, "Who told you that you *were* naked? Have you eaten from the tree of which I commanded you that you should not eat?" (Gen. 3:11, NKJV).

Oh, oh! What will Adam say now? Will he admit what he has done? That's not what my Bible says. Instead, we read that Adam pointed to Eve and said, "The woman whom You gave *to be* with me, she gave me of the tree, and I ate" (Gen. 3:12, NKJV). Adam blamed Eve and God and he made it sound as if it were all their fault. Now, God turned to Eve and asked her, "What *is* this you have done?" Eve began to make excuses and blamed the serpent for having tricked her to disobey (Gen. 3:13, NKJV).

Sounds familiar, does it not? Have you ever blamed someone else for what you have done? Sure you have; we all have. But it is wrong just the same. We must all take the blame and the punishment if we have it coming to us.

God Judges

How did God judge Adam and Eve and the serpent? In a fair and just way. First, God judged the serpent for letting Satan use him. Once the serpent had been the loveliest and cleverest of all the animals in the Garden; now it became an ugly snake. Since that day all snakes must crawl and slither along on their bellies. Next, He judged the earth on which sinners now walked; it would bring forth thorns and thistles. And last of all, God judged the man and the woman. How did He judge them? Well, they had already died in their spirits, but now God told them that they must work hard for as long as they lived. Sin had brought sorrow and pain, sickness and death to them and to the children they would have someday. In the end their bodies would die and return to the dust of the ground from which God had taken them (Gen. 3:14, 16–19; Rom. 5:12).

How sadly the day had ended! But wait, God is not through yet. He had something wonderful to say to Adam and Eve. He had judged Adam and Eve in a fair and right way; now He wanted to help them. He told them how they may be made alive in their spirits to be friends with God once more. He promised them a Savior (Gen. 3:15). He promised to send His Son, the Lord Jesus, to die as a substitute for them and pay the penalty for their sins. Would Adam and Eve believe God this time? This was God's second test for Adam and Eve and this time they turned their volition the right way. They decided to believe what God had told them (Gen. 3:15, 20). True, they had to leave the Garden, and God made sure they would not come back and eat of the tree of life. He placed angels and a flaming sword to guard the Garden and the tree of life (Gen. 3:23–24). But Adam and Eve did not leave the Garden naked, or covered with fig leaves. God gave them a new covering; He made them coats of animal skins (Gen. 3:21). Their new covering was a picture of what God did for them when they trusted in the Lord Jesus, providing them with His own righteousness. The new covering was also a reminder of God's promised Son. Because they believed in the Lord Jesus, they now possessed God's perfect righteousness and were acceptable to God once more. Now, they could walk and talk with God.

What God Wants Me to Know

There is only one way to get the skins off an animal. You must kill the animal first. Their blood must be shed. The animals had to die before Adam and Eve could be clothed. Just so, the Lord Jesus had to die as our substitute before we could be made acceptable to God (Heb. 9:22). And because He paid the penalty for all our sins, the ones we have already done and the ones we will still do, we need only confess them to our heavenly Father. God is free to forgive us and just to cleanse us from all our unrighteousness (1 John 1:9).

It is very important that we never be like Adam and Eve and not own up to what we have done. As we have seen, God knows anyway. We must name our sins to God so that we can be restored to fellowship. But, if we know what is good for us, we will listen to His Word and decide to obey Him.

I wonder what kind of animals gave their lives for Adam and Eve? I think they were lambs. When the Lord Jesus Christ walked on the earth in His perfect goodness and fairness, John the Baptist saw Him and said, "Behold, the Lamb of God who takes away the sin of the world!" (John 1:29*b*). Just think, the skins of the animals that made a covering for Adam and Eve only pictured the righteousness that is provided by the substitutionary death of the Lord Jesus. But the death of the Lord Jesus Christ actually paid the penalty for all of our sins and only by believing on Him can we receive His perfect righteousness (Gal. 3:6). Adam and Eve passed God's second test. They made the right decision to believe on Him (John 11:25).

God gives you a test. Will you take the covering of God's own righteousness by believing on the Lord Jesus

Christ (Isa. 61:10)? Will you let Him be your Friend? Listen to what will happen if you do. You will become God's child (1 John 3:2) and be made alive in your spirit (1 Pet. 3:18). You will live with God not in the Garden of Eden, but in His heavenly home forever.

And, now listen to what God says will happen if you decide against God. You will fail the test and have to meet God as your Judge. You will not go to heaven, but to the lake of fire (Rev. 20:15). That's a terrible thought, is it not? But you need not go there; no one needs to go there. God made this lake of fire for the devil and his bad angels (Matt. 25:41), but He wants you in heaven. He loves you; that's why He sent His Son to die for you (John 3:16). Will you pass the test right now?

Lesson Review

Listen carefully, and tell me if what I say is true or false. Adam and Eve were created good and free from sin. True or false? True. God gave them a body, a soul, and volition, but not a human spirit. False. God also gave them a human spirit. With their souls, Adam and Eve understood and loved people and things. True or false? True. With their human spirits, they understood and loved God. True or false? True. God did not tell Adam and Eve what would happen if they disobeyed. True or false? False. The serpent broke off the fruit and gave it to Eve. True or false? False. Eve gave some fruit to Adam and he ate of it. True or false? True. When Adam and Eve sinned they dropped dead. True or false? False. Only their human spirits died. God is sovereign, righteous, and just. True or false? True. God judged Adam and Eve unfairly. True or false? False. Angels died to let God make a new covering for Adam and Eve. True or false? False. Animals. God promised Adam and Eve to send a Savior to take away their sins. True or false? True. Adam and Eve believed God and were saved. True or false? True.

Memory Verse
"For God Himself is judge." (Ps. 50:6*b*)

LESSON TWO
THE GREAT WHITE THRONE JUDGMENT

Do you know what opposites are? True and false are opposites; then and now are opposites. Adam and Eve lived on earth "long ago"; "now" is when you and I live. Now, I will just say one word and you must tell me another which means the opposite of my word. Suppose I say "black," what would you say? White, very good. "Hot"—cold. "Light"—dark. "Long"—short. "Quiet"—loud. "Good"—bad. "Fair"—unfair. "Just"—unjust. "Believer"—unbeliever. "Heaven"—hell. Our lesson is about some of these words. They are very different from each other because they are opposites, and they tell us about two opposite kinds of people who live on earth.

Two Teams

When God looks down from His throne in heaven, He sees a big difference in the people who live in the world. He sees them divided into two teams. One team is for God; the other against God. Who may decide which team they might belong to? Does God? No, each one of us does. God has given every one of us free will, or volition. So, God cannot say, "You *must* join My team." That would be unfair. Suppose I asked you, "Which do you want, the apple or the orange?" and you said, "I want the orange." Then I told you, "No, you must take the apple." "Well," you would say, "that's not fair." And you would be right. If I wanted to decide for you, I should not have asked you in the first place. God is *just*. He cannot be unfair. He has given you volition and He wants you to use it. You must certainly decide for yourself when it comes to believing in the Lord Jesus Christ.

Two Places

At the moment, the members of the two teams live side-by-side on the earth (Matt. 13:30). But the day will come when God must separate the two teams. We call this separation "the judgment" (Heb. 9:27). God is a just and fair Judge. He has prepared two places, as different from each other as were our words. Can you think what the names of these places might be? The one place is heaven; the other is hell. Who will go to heaven? All the tall people? No, that would not only be unfair, but silly. Do all the "good" people go to heaven and all the "bad" people go to hell? No, not that either. Let's find out how God separates the two teams.

The Qualifying Rule

There are rules for belonging to any team, and God, too, has made a law or a rule for those who want to get on His team. "And this is His commandment [rule]: that we should believe on the name of His Son Jesus Christ" (1 John 3:23a). Those who qualify by believing are called "believers." They are for God and on His team forever. Those who do not obey the rule and do not believe are called "unbelievers." They are against God and not on His team. But until a person dies, he has the opportunity to be on God's team by choosing to believe that Jesus Christ died for his sins.

The Teams Separated and Judged

God knows who belongs to His team and who does not (2 Tim. 2:19b). He knows exactly on what team you are. All teams have a score, don't they? Calling the score is something like judging. The Bible tells us that we must all stand before God and be judged. "All" means all the believers (Rom. 14:10b; 2 Cor. 5:10) and all the unbelievers (Ezek. 20:33–38; Matt. 25:30; Rev. 20:11–15). All believers will stand before the judgment seat of Christ and be evaluated for their production in time, and all unbelievers will stand before the great white throne and be judged. Not one will be forgotten (Eccl. 12:14).

The Book of Life

God has all the names of everyone who has ever lived, who lives now, or who will ever live. We know the names of the first two people who ever lived—Adam and Eve, but we do not know what the name of the last person will be. When you were born, God wrote your name into His Book of Life (Rev. 21:27b). If you are on God's team by having believed that Jesus died for you and rose again, your name will stay in the Book of Life forever.

Your name in the Book of Life is like a ticket or pass to heaven. You need never fear standing before the heavenly Judge. He has promised you that there will be "no condemnation," judgment or punishment, for any believer (Rom. 8:1). You are no longer guilty because Jesus took your guilt on Himself. He has already been judged for you (Heb. 9:27–28a). You are free to live with God forever. You will rule with the heavenly Sovereign for a thousand years (Rev. 20:4). You will be with God when He judges the unbelievers (Mal. 3:18). Won't that be exciting?

What about the unbelievers? Are their names also in the Book of Life? Yes, as long as they live, for Christ died for everyone in the world. But when someone dies without believing in Christ, his name is blotted or wiped out of the Book of Life (Ps. 69:28; Rev. 3:5). As long as anyone lives, he still has a choice. He may decide which team he wishes to join, but he can only come to God in God's way.

Suppose the believer says, "I am going to be real good. I am going to do so many nice things that God will say to me, 'You are a good man, Joe. You may come to heaven because of all the good works you have done.'" Will Joe make it? Will he get to heaven this way? Not any more than the proud Pharisee who boasted of his own righteousness. Remember, our own goodness or –R is just not good enough (Titus 3:5). No, I am afraid Joe is in for a big disappointment on the day of judgment. What will that day be like?

The Last Judgment

God in His sovereignty, righteousness, and justice is seated upon the great white throne. This is the day of the Last Judgment (Rev. 20:11–14) and "God Himself is judge" (Ps. 50:6b). Joe is there and so are many, many others. Who are they? They are all the unbelieving dead, small and great, rich and poor, good and bad. There are boys and girls, men and women. Where did they all come from? They came out of their graves and from the bottom of the oceans. Why are they there? Because they did not believe in the Lord Jesus Christ as their Savior. Some just did not care. Some did not accept His work on the cross on their behalf. They thought they were good enough to go to heaven by their own good works. Joe was one of them, and now Joe's turn has come. He is standing before the righteous Judge.

God had written down all the good works Joe did as long as he lived in the Books of Works. What a long list of nice things are said about Joe, and Joe gets prouder by the minute. Perhaps God even says, "You certainly have done many good works." And now, Joe waits eagerly to hear the righteous Judge, the Lord Jesus Christ (John 5:22) say, "All right, Joe, you may go in to heaven." But instead, the Lord Jesus says that he did "not believe in Me" (John 16:9).

God closes the Books of Works from which Joe's good deeds have been read and opens another book, the Book of Life. Joe looks and sees a big blot where once his name had been written. Oh, how Joe wishes he had believed that Jesus was the only way to get to heaven. But it's too late to change his mind now. Finally, Joe understands that all his good works did not measure up to the perfect righteousness of God. Joe's good works are not good enough. He sees that Jesus Christ did all the work that was necessary to get him into heaven. Jesus Christ had died for all of Joe's sins. Joe need not have done anything at all, except believe in the Lord Jesus Christ (Acts 4:12).

The Deciding Factor

We know what will happen to Joe and to those others who have decided not to be on God's team. "And anyone not found written in the Book of Life, was cast into the lake of fire" (Rev. 20:15). Joe and the other unbelievers will have company, for Satan and his bad angels will all be there with them (Matt. 25:41). Is there a way out for Joe? For the others? No, they must stay in hell forever and ever.

People do not go to the lake of fire or hell because they have sinned; they go because they have not believed that Jesus died for their sins. They have refused to come to God according to God's rule. When Joe decided against God's way of salvation, he lost his ticket to heaven. God in His justice must decide a fair punishment for Joe's unbelief. That punishment is written down in God's Word: "He who believes in Him is not condemned [judged]; but he who does not believe is condemned [judged] already, because he has not believed in the name of the only begotten Son of God" (John 3:18).

What God Wants Me to Know

But, happily there are others who will spend eternity in heaven. Who are they? All who are on God's team. The Bible says, "Whoever believes in Him should not perish, but have eternal life" (John 3:16*b*). Put your name in the place of "whoever." Mary, John, Mike shall have eternal life because they believed in the Lord Jesus Christ. Their names shall never be blotted out of God's Book of Life. God is a fair and just Judge. Because His Son took all your punishment, you need not fear, but have confidence in the day of judgment (1 John 4:17). God meant it when He said, "There is therefore now no condemnation for those who are in Christ Jesus" (Rom. 8:1). No matter what happens, you can be sure of that!

God is fair and just. He can do no wrong. He does not want you to go to hell, nor even to have to stand before His great white throne. He is "not wishing for any to perish but for all to come to repentance" (2 Pet. 3:9*b*), that is to change their minds about Jesus and accept Him as their Savior. That's why He sent His Son into the world, to save us, not to condemn us (John 3:17). He lets you decide for yourself. But you cannot afford to wait. "Now," not "later," is the time for you to make your decision to obey God and believe on His Son. Are you ready to join God's team today? "Believe in the Lord Jesus, and you shall be saved" (Acts 16:31*a*).

Lesson Review

What two teams live side by side on this earth? Believers and unbelievers. Who decides to which team he wants to belong? The person himself. How many sets of books are there in heaven? Two. What are the names of these books? Book of Life, Books of Works. Into which of these books are our names written when we are born? Book of Life. Whose names stay in the Book of Life forever? Believers. What happens to the names of those who die without believing on the Lord Jesus Christ? Blotted out. Who will sit on the great white throne? The Lord Jesus Christ. Who will be with Him on the day of the Last Judgment? Angels and believers. Who will stand before the throne to be judged? All unbelievers of all time. What will God see in the Books of Works? All of the unbelievers' good works. How good are these works? Not good enough. Do good people go to heaven and bad people to hell? No. Who goes to hell, or the lake of fire? Unbelievers. What three words tell us that God is King, God is perfect goodness, and God is fair and just? Sovereignty, righteousness, justice. What will God ask people, like Joe, who think their own good works will get them into heaven? "Why have you not believed on the Lord Jesus Christ?" Who else will be in the lake of fire? Satan and his bad angels. What did God give each one of us so we can decide for ourselves? Volition.

Can you say our memory verses? "The earth is the LORD'S, and all it contains, The world, and those who dwell in it" (Ps. 24:1). "And the heavens declare His righteousness" (Ps. 50:6*a*). "For God Himself is judge" (Ps. 50:6*b*). Now, listen to this verse: "For God so loved the world, that He gave His only begotten Son" (John 3:16*a*). Why did God give His Son? Because He loved the world so much.

Memory Verse
"For God Himself is judge." (Ps. 50:6*b*)

Chapter Eleven

The Love of God

OVERVIEW

A. Subject: The Love of God—1 Samuel 17:34; John 10:1–6

B. Lesson Titles:
 1. Lesson One: The Grace of God
 2. Lesson Two: The Good Shepherd

C. Story Objective:
God is eternal and unchangeable love (Jer. 31:3). His love is infinite, pure, and strong. God's love compels Him to give Himself for the well-being of the ones He loved (John 10:17; 15:13; Gal. 2:20; Eph. 2:4).

Though man in his fallen state had doomed himself to eternal separation from God, God's infinite love reached out to save the sinner (Isa. 63:9b; Luke 19:10; Rom. 5:8–11). God's righteousness abhors sin. His justice demands that the penalty for sin be paid in full. His righteousness must be satisfied. In setting forth His saving grace (Eph. 2:8), God removed the obstacle, sin, through the outpouring of His divine love (John 3:16; 1 John 4:9a—the Father's love; 1 John 3:16a—the Son's love; John 16:8–11; 1 Cor. 2:9–11—the Spirit's love).

Those who appropriate the grace of God in salvation are accepted in the Beloved (Eph. 1:6) and come under the principle of God's "much more" grace (Rom. 5:9–10, 15, 17; 8:32). They can never be separated from the love of God (Rom. 8:38–39). The very love of God is produced in the life of the Spirit-filled believer (Rom. 5:5; Gal. 5:22) and overflows into the lives of others (1 John 4:7–21).

D. Vocabulary and Doctrinal Concepts:
 1. Vocabulary: anointed, barrier, branded, deserve, echo, flock, forsook, goodness, grace, lovingkindness, obstacle, pasture, righteousness, satisfied, sheep-fold, sheltered, shepherd, staff
 2. Doctrinal Concepts:
  a. The love of God (John 10:1–18; 15:9–13; Rom. 5:8, 10; Eph. 5:25; 1 John 3:1; 4:10, 16; Rev. 1:5)
  b. The obstacle (Gen. 2:17; cf., Rom. 6:23a)
  c. The obstacle removed (Ps. 22:1–3; Rom. 6:23b)
  d. Disciplined by love (Heb. 12:6)
  e. Response to God's love (1 John 4:18–19)
  f. Love reflected (2 Cor. 5:14; 1 John 3:16–17)

E. *Source Book* Keywords: the barrier, Christ (good shepherd), essence of God (love), grace, grace pipeline, love

F. Activities:
 1. Suggested Visuals: Christ on the cross, cross with open door, heaven symbol, love symbol, Trinity
 2. Games, Songs, Worksheets
 3. Memory Verse: "We love Him, because He first loved us." (1 John 4:19, NKJV)
 4. Opening and Closing Prayer

Lesson One
The Grace of God

Today we want to add our next word into the Essence Box. We have already seen that God is sovereign. He rules the heavens and the earth; His Word is law and must be obeyed. Disobeying God is called "sin." God is also righteous; He cannot stand sin. From His justice, God must punish sin. Who took the punishment for us and was judged for all our sins? Jesus Christ. None of us deserved this. We are saved only by God's *grace* (Eph. 2:8–9). Grace is God doing something for us which we cannot earn, do not deserve, and can never work for. God's grace comes to us because of God's love, righteousness, and justice. That is our new picture word of what God is like. God is LOVE (1 John 4:16).

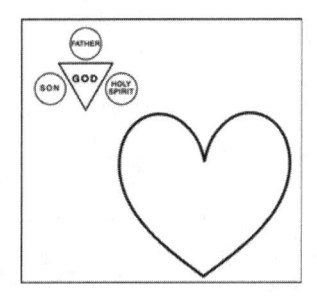

God loved us long before we were even born. The Bible tells us that this is the reason why "We love Him, because He first loved us" (1 John 4:19, NKJV). Let's see if you can find 1 John 4:19 in your Bible. Let's read it together. "We love Him, because He first loved us." Who loves God? We do. Who are "we"? Believers. Why do we love Him? Because He first loved us. Today we want to hear the story of God's great love for us. Are you ready to listen?

God's Love and the Sin Barrier

Long before there ever was a man upon the earth, God, the heavenly Sovereign, made a decision. Even though He knew that man would become a sinner, He decided to treat mankind, that means all people, in *grace*. He would love us and be kind to us, though we certainly do not deserve it (Luke 6:35). Remember, after Adam and Eve had disobeyed God and became sinners God still wanted to have a family relationship with them. He wants to have a relationship with us also. He wants to send free gifts of His great love all the way from heaven to us for as long as we live (James 1:17).

But God, who is perfect goodness, or righteousness, cannot have a relationship with spiritually dead, sinful mankind. Sin stands like a big wall or barrier between God and man.

God knew that sinful man deserved to be punished. He had said, "The wages [punishment] of sin is," what? "Death" (Gen. 2:17; Rom. 6:23). To be just, God must punish the sinner, which means the sinner must die. When Adam and Eve sinned, they died spiritually. That means they died to God. They could not have a relationship with Him any longer. Since then, all the children of Adam have been born with the sin of Adam (Rom. 5:12). When you were born, you were born with eyes or hair like your father's; you look or act like him in many ways. So, as your father's looks were passed down to you, so Adam's sin was passed down to all of us. We cannot help being born sinners and we could never have a relationship with God unless God would make a way possible. And He did! God is *love* (1 John 4:16). His love is so great, no one can measure it.

God hates sin, yet He loved the sinner so much that He wanted to bring him back into relationship, not only now, but forever and ever. God wanted to pour out His love to man, but His righteousness and justice stood in the way.

What should God do? Should He just pretend that man had not really sinned? That would not be just, would it? There was only one thing God could do. God the Father decided that if someone could be found who was absolutely perfect and without sin, who was willing to take man's place and be judged for man, then God's righteousness and justice would be satisfied and God would be free to give His love once more. Our own Lord Jesus Christ, God the Son, said, "I will go." What? God's only begotten Son, whom He loved the most? Would God want to send His beloved Son to be a substitute for sinners?

John 3:16

God did want to send His Son. "For God so loved the world, that He gave His only begotten Son" (John 3:16*a*). This was God's greatest way to show how much He loved all the world. He sent His only beloved, perfect Son to die on the cross in our place, to remove the barrier of sin. Now, God's wonderful love can be poured out on all mankind.

Could not someone else have died for the sins of the world? No one else could have done it. Why not? Before Adam had disobeyed God, he had been sinless. Since then, all people except Jesus Christ have been born with Adam's sin nature, and all have sinned. Someone who was without the sin nature and sin would have to obey God. Jesus Christ is the only One who was born without a sin nature, and lived His whole life without one sin. Therefore, Jesus Christ was the only One who could die as a substitute for sinful man. Jesus proved His love for us when He gave His life for us (1 John 3:16*a*).

Oh, how our Lord Jesus suffered when He hung on the cross, for He carried a great burden. What do you think that great and heavy burden was? God the Father had laid on God the Son the sins of the whole world (Isa. 53:5–6). That was when "He made Him who knew no sin *to be* sin on our behalf" (2 Cor. 5:21*a*) and He punished Jesus for our sins. God was well-pleased with His obedient Son (Phil. 2:8–9). The only trouble was that now that Jesus was bearing our sins in His own body, God could not have a relationship with His beloved Son. And so it was that God the Father forsook or turned His back on the Lord Jesus Christ as He hung there on the cross.

Why was that, you wonder? Well, the Lord Jesus had to become sin for us. God had to judge Him for our sins. Jesus had to die spiritually as a substitute for us; sin separated Him from God the Father. For three hours on the cross, Jesus Christ paid the punishment for the sins of the whole world. A short time later His body also died. By then, God had forgiven us because of what Jesus did for us. Jesus Christ had made a new way whereby we can come to God by Him because sin no longer blocks the way.

What God Wants Me to Know

The Lord Jesus once said, "Greater love has no one than this, that one lay down his life for his friends" (John 15:13). God, the Lord Jesus, did more than that. He died for His enemies, for those who hate Him and laugh about Him; for those who beat Him and nailed Him to the cross, and He died for those who were His friends and loved Him. That is why we can say, "We love Him, because He first loved us" (1 John 4:19, NKJV).

If God loved us that much and did the most for us when we were His enemies, how much more will He do for us now that we are His friends (Rom. 5:8–11)? Should we not love God more than anyone or anything? Yes, we should. We must love Him because of what He has done for us. When we know what He is like we will love Him. He is sovereignty, righteousness, justice, and love. In His grace, He gives us what we don't deserve. That is "greater grace" (James 4:6*a*). When He disciplines us, He does it in grace to teach us to please Him. Your parents still love you even though they must sometimes correct you, don't they? Of course. So it is with the Lord: "For those whom the Lord loves He disciplines [corrects]" (Heb. 12:6*a*).

Remember, God's love is for everyone, not just for you. It is meant even for the meanest or most unlovely boy and girl. When we believe in Jesus Christ, God puts His love into our hearts, our souls, so that we might show it to others. "Hope does not disappoint, because the love of God has been poured out within our hearts through the Holy Spirit" (Rom. 5:5*a*). Others need God's love, too. We must love them and pray for them. We must ask the Heavenly Father to help us tell of His great love.

God the Holy Spirit helps people understand God's plan of salvation and His love which opens up a way for everyone who wants to come to God. Jesus says to all who want to know the way to heaven, "I am the way, and the truth, and the life; no one comes to the Father, but through Me" (John 14:6). It is so easy. You can come right now. God loved you long before you were even born. He wants to have a relationship with you. He is waiting to give you His greater grace, but it cannot come until you tell God "Father, I believe in the Lord Jesus Christ, who loved me and died for me." His love provided the way for you to come to the Father. Will you accept His love?

Lesson Review

What was the last thing we learned about God? That He is love. The greatest way He could show His love for us was by sending Someone to do something for us that we could not do for ourselves. Whom did God the Father send, and why? The Lord Jesus Christ, His Son, to die for our sins and to save us. Why could God's love not be poured out on us? The sin barrier. God's righteousness and justice had to be satisfied. What removed the barrier? Christ's death on the cross. Can God pour His love out on us now? Yes.

Who remembers what "grace" means? Grace is something we cannot buy, earn or deserve; grace is what God does for us. God's love toward us is grace, isn't it? Why does God love the world so much? What did you ever do that God would love you enough to send the One whom He loved best to take your place and be punished for your sins? Could it be that you are such a nice girl or boy that God just had to do this for you? Or perhaps He did it because you are always good and obedient to your parents and teachers? Or because you never fight with your playmates and never tell a lie? No, no one ever deserves God's love. He loves us because He is love. Can you say our memory verse? "We love Him, because He first loved us" (1 John 4:19, NKJV).

Memory Verse

"We love Him, because He first loved us." (1 John 4:19, NKJV)

Lesson Two
The Good Shepherd

Did you ever lose something you loved very much, maybe a puppy or a kitten or a bird? Would you try to go out and find it? Or would you say, "Oh well, never mind, I'll just forget I ever had a pet." Of course not, you would go out and call it by name; you would ask all your neighbors and friends whether they had seen your pet. And would you not be unhappy and cry if you never found your pet again?

God loves us far, far more than you ever loved a pet; more than you love your parents, and even more than they can love you. When man became a sinner, he got lost from God. But God loves man, and He did not want him to be lost in sin forever. So, God went out to call for man and try to find him and bring man back to Himself (Luke 19:10). Remember, God called Adam's name in the Garden, and came looking for him (Gen. 3:9). The Lord Jesus came into the world to seek and save us from sin.

The Bible tells us that people are very much like sheep (Isa. 53:6), we easily wander away. And just like sheep, we need a shepherd who will love us and take care of us. The Lord Jesus is the Good Shepherd who loves His sheep. Our story today is about His loving care of His own.

Watching the Sheep and Shepherds
John 10:1–6

In the evening, the shepherds came back from their pastures. They always brought their sheep into the sheepfold this time of night. The little woollies would enter in through the one and only gate. They would be sheltered, safe, and snug until the next morning. Then, the shepherds would come by again to take them out to feed. There were many sheep. They were not branded, nor marked in any way. They all looked the same. But the sheep knew their own shepherd. They knew his voice and came when he called. No shepherd ever went off with sheep that did not belong to him, because the sheep would run away from a stranger.

The Good Shepherd, John 10:7–19

THE DOOR TO HEAVEN

The Lord Jesus Christ stood by close enough to watch the shepherds and their sheep. Now, He turned to the crowd that usually followed Him. Many of them were unbelievers. He said, "I am the door of the sheep" (John 10:7b). They wondered just what He might be talking about. How could He be a door? You see, what they did not know and could not believe was that right here before them stood God. He had left heaven to come and save them.

But how could God be like a door? How do you come into your classroom? Through a door. There is only one door into the room. Just the same there is only one Savior, one door which leads into heaven (John 10:8; cf., Acts 4:12). Remember Jesus says, "I am the way, and the truth, and the life; no one comes to the Father, but through Me" (John 14:6). Just like the sheep go in and come out through that door and find pastures and places to feed, so Jesus said, "If anyone enters through Me, he shall be saved, and shall go in and out, and find pasture" (John 10:9). When sheep find good, green grass they grow healthy and strong. How do you think the Lord Jesus, our own Good Shepherd, feeds us? He feeds us through His Word. When we read and learn His Word we grow up to please Him (1 Pet. 2:2; 2 Pet. 3:18). Do you believe that He is the only door into heaven? Anyone who tries to go to heaven any other way is just like a thief or a robber breaking into a house; he won't get in (John 10:8).

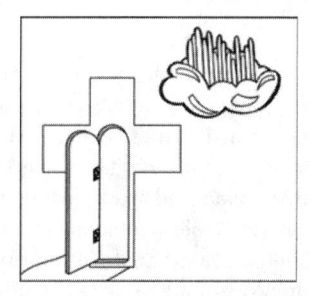

No one deserves to go to heaven and no one deserves God's loving care, but God is love. To prove His love for us, God the Father was willing to send His Son (John 3:16). To prove His love, God the Son had come down from heaven to be the gracious Shepherd, full of love, to look tenderly after His sheep and protect them (John 10:10–13).

HIS LIFE FOR THE SHEEP
JOHN 10:14–15

Then the Lord Jesus said, "I know my sheep, and they know me. I have come to give my life for the sheep." No one made Him do it. Jesus Christ gave Himself as a free gift to us. He died to save His sheep as He had promised, but He came back from the dead when He rose three days later. After fifty more days He returned to His heavenly home to prepare a place where His "sheep" may be with Him forever (John 10:18).

HIS LOVE AND CARE OF THE SHEEP
JOHN 10:12–13

Jesus, our Shepherd, loves His sheep. He cannot help loving them, because He is love. His sheep belong to Him (John 10:12–13). You belong to your parents. They cannot help but love you and they want to care for you because you are theirs. They show their great love for you every day in many different ways.

What can a shepherd do to show how much he loves his sheep? He leads his flock to the best meadows and hills where they might feed. He watches over them tenderly. If one of his sheep wanders off, the shepherd looks for it and often carries it on his shoulders to bring it back safely. The shepherd carries a long staff with a crook on the upper end. He uses this staff or rod to guide the sheep or to rescue them in case they slip. With it the shepherd beats off attacks by thieves or wild animals, and with it he also corrects the sheep if they should wander off or do not mind him.

The Lord watches over us every day and every night. He alone keeps us safe so that no harm can come to us. He even shows us that He loves us by correcting us when we have disobeyed His Word (Heb. 12:6). He is truly our great Shepherd, and we can safely trust Him moment-by-moment. We need never be afraid.

THE SHEPHERD PSALM

In the Bible in Psalm 23 is a beautiful song. We sometimes call it "The Song of the Shepherd." David wrote it long ago. David knew all about sheep, for he was a shepherd boy long before he became king (1 Sam. 17:34). Listen to what happened to David one day as he kept his father's sheep. First a lion came and made off with a little lamb. Soon after that a bear stole another lamb out of the flock. What do you suppose David did? Did he run away? Did he just shrug his shoulders and say, "Oh well, that's too bad, but we still have a lot of sheep left"? No. The Bible tells us that David was a good shepherd. He ran after the lion and the bear and killed them to rescue his little lambs. You see, David loved his sheep, every one of them; he did not fear for his own life. His only thought was to save the lambs. And because he was such a good and faithful shepherd, God made him a king over God's own people.

David never forgot that he had once been a shepherd. He often thought how God had taken care of him, much like he had taken care of his own sheep, so he wrote this song. "The LORD [Jesus Christ] is my shepherd, I shall not want. He makes me lie down in green pastures; He leads me beside quiet waters. He restores my soul; He guides me in the paths of righteousness For His name's sake. Even though I walk through the valley of the shadow of death, I fear no evil; for Thou art with me; Thy rod and Thy staff, they comfort me. Thou dost prepare a table before me in the presence of my enemies; Thou hast anointed my head with oil; My cup overflows. Surely goodness and lovingkindness will follow me all the days of my life, And I will dwell in the house of the LORD forever" (Ps. 23).

Would you say that David knew his Shepherd? Indeed, he did. Would you say that the Lord Jesus knew David as one of His sheep? He most certainly did. Jesus had said, "I am the good shepherd; and I know My own, and My own know Me" (John 10:14). "When he puts forth all his own, he goes before them, and the sheep follow him because they know his voice" (John 10:4*b*). "I am the good shepherd; the good shepherd lays down His life for the sheep" (John 10:11).

What God Wants Me to Know

Is the Lord your Shepherd too? If you believe that He loved you and died for your sins, then you are His own. Just think of it, billions and billions of years ago, God loved you. And billions and billions of years from now, He will still love you every bit as much. Do you know His voice? Where do we hear God's voice today? He speaks to us in the words of the Bible. He wants us not only to hear what He has to say, but also to be doers of His Word (James 1:22). He wants us to be an echo of His love. An echo is a sound carried by sound waves which hits a surface in the distance and bounce back to you. In His great love, God gave us all He has to give. Once we have received His love, we must let it bounce back to others. Have you ever told anyone that God loves him? You can show your love for God and for others by telling them of Jesus Christ, our Good Shepherd, our only door to heaven.

God says that we must love other believers (1 John 4:21), even that mean child next door. God loves him as much as He loves you. However, God also knows we cannot always love others in our own power, but with the power of God's Holy Spirit which is inside of us we can love other believers (Rom. 5:5). Will you ask the heavenly Father to help you be an echo of His love?

The greatest way that anyone could ever show his love would be to die to save the life of his friend (John 15:13). God's love is even much, much greater. He died to save not only those who would love Him in return, but He died even for His enemies (Rom. 5:8). If you have never believed on the Lord Jesus Christ, you are still God's enemy. But He died to save you. He loves you and has prayed for you long ago. What did He pray for you? That you might believe what you hear about God and His wonderful love for you (John 17:21*b*, 23*b*). God knew that David was one of His own sheep. But He said, "I have other sheep, which are not of this fold; I must bring them also, and they shall hear My voice; and they shall become one flock *with* one shepherd" (John 10:16). Was He talking about you?

Jesus prayed for you long before you were born. He said, "I do not ask in behalf of these alone, but for those also who believe in Me through their word" (John 17:20). You have heard of God's love for you. You can believe on Him right now, for He opened wide the only door to heaven. Just decide to trust Him this very moment. Then you, too, can love the Good Shepherd because He first loved you (1 John 4:19).

> ### *Memory Verse*
> "We love Him, because He first loved us." (1 John 4:19, NKJV)

Chapter Twelve

Eternal Life, the Great I AM

OVERVIEW

A. Subject: Eternal Life, the Great I AM—Exodus 3; John 8:20, 50–59

B. Lesson Titles:
1. Lesson One: Moses Learns That God Is Eternal Life
2. Lesson Two: The Great I AM

C. Story Objective:
God is eternal life. He has neither beginning nor end, but is "from everlasting to everlasting" (Ps. 90:2). The Lord of absolute existence declares, "I AM WHO I AM" (Ex. 3:14*a*); "I live forever" (Deut. 32:40*b*).

Jehovah, "the existing One" who reveals himself, promises all who will accept Jesus Christ as their Lord and Savior, "I give them eternal life" (John 10:27–28*a*). He warns the unbelievers (John 8:24) that they "will go away into eternal punishment" (Matt. 25:46*a*).

Believers thus have the assurance of everlasting life in the presence of the Eternal One (John 8:51) and can rest in the knowledge that in this life "the eternal God is thy refuge" (Deut. 33:27*a*, KJV).

D. Vocabulary and Doctrinal Concepts:
1. Vocabulary: afraid, death, eternal
2. Doctrinal Concepts:
   a. The eternal life of God (Gen. 1:1*a*; John 1:1, 4; 8:58; Heb. 9:14).
   b. "He is before all things" (Col. 1:17).
   c. Immortal (1 Tim. 1:17*a*).
   d. God is in eternity future (Ps. 135:13; Rev. 4:8–9).
   e. Believers are given eternal life in Christ (John 3:16; 1 John 5:11).

E. *Source Book* Keywords: essence of God (eternal life), John, Moses

F. Activities:
1. Suggested Visuals: Christ on the cross, eternal life symbol, Trinity
2. Games, Songs, Worksheets
3. Memory Verse: "Even from everlasting to everlasting, Thou art God." (Ps. 90:2*b*)
4. Opening and Closing Prayer

LESSON ONE
MOSES LEARNS THAT GOD IS ETERNAL LIFE

The better we know God, the better we can love Him. So, the next thing we need to do is to find out more about Him and what He is like. We have already learned that God is sovereignty, righteousness, justice, and love. Today we will learn that God is ETERNAL LIFE.

What kind of life is eternal life? It is forever life, a life which has no beginning and no ending. Do you have that kind of life? Do I? No, our life has a beginning and an end—at least our life on this earth. But if you will listen carefully you will hear that God wants to share His forever life with you.

I have in my hands a piece of string and a ring. Which one of these objects has a beginning and an end to it? Which one does not? That was easy, wasn't it? Of course, the string has a beginning and an end to it. That's what our lives are like. When do our lives begin? Yes, when we are born. And when do they end? When we die. But are our lives really over then? There is a much better kind of life waiting for all who will believe in the Lord Jesus Christ—God's kind of life, eternal life.

Now, look at this ring; it has neither beginning nor end. That's what God's life is like. We show His eternal life as a ring or circle in our Essence Box. God is eternal life. As Psalm 90:2*b* tells us, "Even from everlasting to everlasting, Thou art God" (Ps. 90:2*b*).

I want to tell you two stories about God's eternal life. Our first story is from the Old Testament; the next story is from the New Testament. Let's call our first story "Moses Learns That God Is Eternal Life."

A Question You May Have Asked

Moses wrote the first five books of the Bible: Genesis, Exodus, Leviticus, Numbers, and Deuteronomy. Did he just 'make up' these books and write what he wanted? Of course not. You already know from your lessons that "All Scripture is inspired by God [that is God-breathed]" (2 Tim. 3:16). That's how Moses knew to start the Bible with these words: "In the beginning God" (Gen. 1:1).

Did Moses ever wonder, "Where did God come from? Does He have a beginning?" Perhaps he looked up into the starry sky and thought about God, wanting to know more about God. For you see, Moses did not have a Bible to tell him what God is like. Perhaps you, too, have asked those questions. Well, Moses found out, and today so will you.

How God Counts Time

Moses had been a shepherd for forty years. He had done a good job looking after his father-in-law's, Jethro's, sheep. God knew that Moses was now ready for greater things. He would now let Moses lead people instead of sheep. Maybe those forty years with sheep seemed long to Moses, but they were not long to God—just long enough for Moses to be made ready for the job God wanted him to do.

How do we tell time? By the sun and moon, by our clocks: we count the seconds, minutes, hours, days, months, and years. But God does not count time as we do. There are no clocks in heaven to tick off the hours of the day. When a thousand years have gone by, they seem just as short to God as yesterday seems to you right now (Ps. 90:4). Who said so? Moses did, and God told him to tell us. We also read in the New Testament that "One day is with the Lord as a thousand years, and a thousand years as one day" (2 Pet. 3:8*b*, KJV). God's life is timeless, without beginning or end. God is eternal life.

Moses Sees a Strange Sight

On the day when God told Moses about His eternal life, Moses had taken the sheep to graze or feed by Mount Horeb. The people called Mount Horeb "the mountain of God" (Ex. 3:1). Moses was watching over the animals, when suddenly he looked up, for he had seen a strange sight. He saw a bush on fire! But what was so strange about that burning bush was that it did not burn up into ashes. It was just a plain old thornbush, but it didn't burn up (Ex. 3:2–3). "Why, that is strange," thought Moses; "I must go and see this great fire." Although the bush was just a plain old thornbush, the fire was not just a plain old fire.

No, the Lord Jesus was in that bush, in that fire, and now, He was showing Himself to Moses.

God Speaks to Moses out of the Burning Bush

As Moses came closer and closer to the burning bush he heard a voice, calling his name, "Moses." And there it was again: "Moses!" Whose voice could that be? It was the voice of God—God the Son, the Lord Jesus. But where was it coming from? Why, right out of the middle of the burning bush (Ex. 3:4). Moses stopped and answered, "Here am I." Then God said, "Do not come near here; remove your sandals from your feet, for the place on which you are standing is holy ground" (Ex. 3:5). Holy ground is ground set apart by God's presence.

Moses did as he was told. He listened carefully as God spoke to him. Now, if you listen just as carefully, you, too, will hear how Moses learned that God is eternal life. God said, "I am the God of your father, the God of Abraham, the God of Isaac, and the God of Jacob" (Ex. 3:6*a*).

The Great I AM

Had Moses heard right? Had God said "I AM"? Abraham, Isaac, and Jacob had long since died. What could God possibly mean? God meant just what He said. True, Abraham, Isaac, and Jacob's bodies had died, but their souls and spirits were still living (Luke 16:22–23). They had God's kind of life—eternal life. God is still their God, just as He was when they lived upon the earth (Matt. 22:32). God *was*, *is*, and always *will be*! He is the great I AM.

Now, God was saying, "Moses, I will come and set my people free. I will send you to bring them out of the land of Egypt, where they are slaves." At first Moses was not so sure that he wanted to do what God wished. Only forty years ago he had run away from Egypt, and now he was to return to lead God's people out? He did not think he could do that (Ex. 3:7–11).

Whatever was the matter with Moses? Did he not trust God to know best what Moses could and could not do? Besides, God had promised that He would set His people free. Moses would only be God's helper with the people. It seems that Moses, too, had to learn that he must not only be a hearer of the Word, but a doer also (Luke 8:21*b*).

Just now though, Moses was still asking a lot of questions (Ex. 3:13–14). "When I go to the Israelites and tell them, 'The God of your fathers has sent me to you,' and they ask me 'What is his name?', what shall I say?" Then God told Moses, "I AM WHO I AM' . . . Thus you shall say to the sons of Israel, 'I AM has sent me to you.'"

You did not know that God's name is "I AM," did you? Well, Moses had not known this either. But now, both you and Moses know it. Do you think this is a strange name for God? It isn't. I AM WHO I AM simply says that there never was a time when God was not. There once was a time when you and I were not. When was that? Before we were born. There once was a time when Moses was not—before he was born. But God always *was*, *is*, and *will be*. Why? Because He is eternal life.

Moses Tells Us of the Great I AM

At last Moses understood. He became the leader of God's people, in fact, he was one of the greatest leaders God's people ever had. How Moses led the Israelites out of Egypt and how God made a way for them right through the middle of the sea we will soon learn.

Did God want Moses to keep His eternal life a secret? If you have listened carefully to our lesson, you will know that He did not. God said, "Tell them who I AM." And did Moses tell us? Indeed he did, in many places of our Bible. Listen to one of them which I will read now, and when you think I get to a part you know, say it with me. Ready? "Lord, Thou hast been our dwelling place in all generations. Before the mountains were born, Or Thou didst give birth to the earth and the world, Even from everlasting to everlasting, Thou art God" (Ps. 90:1–2).

What God Wants Me to Know

Right from the very beginning, God wanted to share His eternal life with us, for in ourselves we do not have eternal life. Eternal life is God's forever life, without beginning and without end. Our lives have a beginning, but they need not have an end. How can God give us His eternal life? He has told us in the Bible in the words of John 20:31: "But these have been written that you may believe that Jesus is the Christ, the Son of God; and that believing you may have life in His name." You already know that verse, don't you? But do you believe what it tells you? You may have eternal life this minute. It does not take any longer than, "Believe in the Lord Jesus, and you shall be saved" (Acts 16:31*a*).

Perhaps you have already believed in the Lord Jesus Christ. Does that mean you have eternal life? Yes, that's exactly what that means! You don't have to wait for it; you already have eternal life. The Bible says, "And the witness is this, that God has given us [all who have believed in Christ] eternal life, and this life is in His Son" (1 John 5:11). God has already shared His eternal life with you so that you can live with Him in heaven forever. Now you never need be afraid of death any more, for you know that when time on earth stops for you, eternity, the forever, happy time in heaven, begins. And for now, as along as you are alive on the earth, you are safe. You have the Son, His eternal life is your life, and "the eternal God is a dwelling place, And underneath are the everlasting arms" (Deut. 33:27a). He will take care of you.

Lesson Review

Do you know how long eternal life is? It is life without beginning and without end. Who has that kind of life? God. This same life is in God the Father, God the Son, and God the Holy Spirit. God *was*, *is*, and always *will be*. We learned about God's eternal life in our lesson. Who else learned it in our lesson? Yes, Moses.

When did Moses learn that God is eternal life? When God spoke to him out of the burning bush. What did God tell Moses about himself? His name. What is God's name? "I AM." What does that name mean? "I AM" means there was never a time when God was not. With whom will God share His life? With all who believe in the Lord Jesus Christ.

Memory Verse

"Even from everlasting to everlasting, Thou art God." (Ps. 90:2b)

LESSON TWO
THE GREAT I AM

Since God is eternal life, He is both the First and the Last. No one, or nothing was before God. Now, I promised to tell you a story from the New Testament about God's eternal life, and I will. But first, I want to ask you a question: How long have you lived on this earth? Seven years? Eight years? Where were you, say, ten years before then? You were not anywhere? That's right. Your life only began seven or eight years ago.

Our story today is about Someone whose life on earth had a beginning just like yours, but whose life in heaven *had* no beginning and *has* no ending. Can you guess whom I am thinking about? You are right. I am thinking about our wonderful Lord Jesus. Let's call our story "The Great I AM."

The Eternal Word

Like the Book of Genesis in the Old Testament, the Book of John in the New Testament starts out, "In the beginning" (John 1:1). Before all time began, God the Father, God the Son, and God the Holy Spirit lived together in God's heavenly home. Listen to me read you this most wonderful of all stories. "In the beginning was the Word, and the Word was with God, and the Word was God. He was in the beginning with God. All things came into being by Him, and apart from Him nothing came into being that has come into being. In Him was life" (John 1:1–4a).

The Lord Jesus Christ is God's *eternal* Word. He made all things in the heavens and on earth (Col. 1:16). We call the Lord Jesus Christ "the Word" because God spoke to men through Him, just like God speaks to us in the pages of His written Word, the Bible. He was always in heaven; but to share His life with us, He must leave heaven and come down to earth to die for the sins of the world.

God Cannot Die

Can God die? Never! God is, what? Eternal life! How then can God's Son come to die for us? Well, as God He cannot die; but as man He can die. So it was decided in heaven that God the Father and God the Holy Spirit would prepare a special human body for God the Son which could die. God the Son took on a human body and was born as the baby in the manger. The Baby Jesus had a beginning, just like you had. But *eternal* God the Son who was inside that special baby had no beginning. He was the same great "I AM" whom Moses met at the burning bush.

The Baby Jesus grew up and had birthdays just like you. He was a real person, and yet He was also *eternal* God. How would people know this? Jesus Christ was going to tell them just as He once told Moses. Do you think they would listen to Him and believe His words? Let's make believe that you and I can go back in time almost two thousand years, back to the days when Jesus walked on the earth.

Come with me to the great temple in Jerusalem, for there the Lord Jesus, the great I AM, is teaching about Himself. Look at all those people! Do you think they will make room for us? Can you see the Lord Jesus? Ah, yes, there He is! I can see Him now. Hush, be ever so quiet, so we can hear what He will say.

"Unless you believe that I am *He* [that I am always God], you shall die in your sins," He says (John 8:24*b*). But the people wonder, "Is He trying to tell us that He is God?" Why, they would never, never believe that. Would you believe His words? Then hear what He promises: "Truly, truly, [He is telling us a very important doctrine, so listen carefully] I say to you, if anyone [a man, a woman, a girl, or a boy] keeps [hears and does] My Word, he shall never see death" (John 8:51). What a wonderful promise that is! Surely all the people will believe Him now. Or will they?

Oh my! Suddenly there is a lot of shouting (John 8:52–53). Do you see the angry faces? Do you know what they are shouting at the Lord Jesus? "You say that those who believe you won't die? What about Abraham? He believed God, and he died. And what about all those others who lived long ago and trusted God? They, too, are dead. So who do you think you are, telling us you can give us eternal life?" The Jews continued to shout at Him: "Now we know that You have a demon. Abraham died, and the prophets also; and You say, 'If anyone keeps My word, he shall never taste of death.' Surely You are not greater than our father Abraham, who died? The prophets died too; who do You make Yourself out to be?"

Who is the Lord Jesus Christ? Do you know? Would you need to ask Him? Jesus is God! And think of it, the people asked the Lord Jesus such stupid questions that day (John 8:53). They said, "Are you greater than Abraham?" Who is greater, Abraham or the Lord Jesus Christ? The Lord, of course! We know it, for we believe His Word; but most of the people in the Temple that day would not believe Him. Isn't that sad? But Abraham knew it. He believed that the Son of God would come into the world some day (Gen. 15:6).

Before Abraham Was Born, I AM

That's why the Lord Jesus said to the people, "Your father Abraham rejoiced to see My day, and he saw *it* and was glad" (John 8:56). Abraham was happy when he found out that the Lord Jesus would come. Do you know what the people did then? They just laughed at the Lord Jesus. They pointed their fingers at Him and made fun of God's Son. "The Jews therefore said to Him, 'You are not yet fifty years old, and have You seen Abraham?'" (John 8:57). Why, Abraham had been dead hundreds and hundreds of years. How could Jesus have seen him? Do you know?

Let's hear what the Lord Jesus answered them: "Truly, truly, I say to you, before Abraham was born, I am" (John 8:58). Where did we hear God say those words "I am" before? Yes, to Moses at the burning bush. Jesus is God, and God is the great I AM. He is eternal life. Remember, Jesus had a beginning only as man; as God, He always *was*, *is*, and *will be*. That's why the Lord Jesus could say, "Before Abraham was born, I am."

Had the Lord Jesus ever seen Abraham? Oh, yes, many, many times. The Lord Jesus of the New Testament is the same "Lord" we find in the Old Testament. God had always known Abraham, even long before Abraham was born. He had called Abraham and had told him to leave home and go to a land which God would show him (Gen. 12). He had promised Abraham a son (Gen. 15:4). He had asked Abraham to prove how much he loved God by offering up his son Isaac (Gen. 22). Yes indeed, the Lord Jesus knew Abraham well, but He said nothing about these things to the people. They would not have believed Him anyway.

Yes, Abraham "was," but God *is*. Abraham's body had died and had been buried. But God had kept His promise to Abraham. Abraham *is* still alive in the presence of God, and some day God will let him live on the earth once more in the very land He had promised.

Rejection of the Son of God

Do you know that when the Lord was on earth His words fell on "hard ground"? Oh, how terribly hard-hearted those people were! They did not want to believe in the Lord Jesus. They wanted to kill Him so they picked up rocks to throw at Him. Were there any rocks in the Temple, I wonder? We don't know, but we do know that the Lord Jesus calmly walked past them, and not one stone, not one rock was thrown (John 8:59). The Lord Jesus' time to die had not come yet. But when the time did come, He would not die under a heap of rocks. How would the Lord Jesus die? Yes, on the cross.

What God Wants Me to Know

As I told you before, the life of the Lord Jesus on this earth had a beginning and an end. He died on the cross for our sins. His body was buried in a tomb. But did He stay dead? No! A dead Savior cannot help anyone. We have a living Savior! Because He is also God, He has eternal life. The grave could not hold Him. He rose from the dead on the third day. Now He lives in heaven, ever ready to help us (Heb. 7:25*b*). Right now, the Lord is preparing a place for you in heaven (John 14:3). Why? Because He loves you and wants to have you with Him.

The Lord Jesus kept His promise to Abraham and gave him eternal life. He shared this same life with you the moment you believed in Him. Just wait and see; some day, maybe real soon, the eternal God the Son is coming back to take us up to heaven with Him. What a glad day that will be! We just cannot thank Him enough for sharing His life with us!

What the Lord Jesus said to those people in the Temple, He says to you right now in the words of the Bible: "If anyone keeps My word he shall never see death" (John 8:51*b*). Would you like to live forever? "Christ Jesus came into the world to save sinners" (1 Tim. 1:15*b*). We are all sinners but we can all be saved!

Can the Lord Jesus give you eternal life? Is it His to give away? Why, yes it is. He is God, and therefore He is eternal life. He is sovereign. So He may do as He pleases. But He cannot give you life unless you are willing to believe in Him. Will you believe in Him right now?

Lesson Review

Well, I see that you have learned your lessons well. I am sure God is pleased that you are getting to know Him better. You see, we cannot love someone we do not know; and the better we get to know God, the more we will love Him.

We learned that God is eternal life. Can you remember what the Lord Jesus taught about Himself in the Temple that made the people so angry they wanted to kill Him with rocks? That's right. "I AM."

Memory Verse
"Even from everlasting to everlasting, Thou art God." (Ps. 90:2*b*)

Chapter Thirteen

Omniscience: How God Looks at Man

OVERVIEW

A. Subject: Omniscience: How God Looks at Man—1 Samuel 16; Psalm 139

B. Lesson Titles:
   1. Lesson One: The Story of David
   2. Lesson Two: God Reveals a Secret

C. Story Objective:
   God is omniscient, absolute and "perfect in knowledge" (Job 37:16). "His understanding is infinite" (Ps. 147:5b). He knows and understands us better than anyone. Our very thoughts and actions (Ps. 139:2, 4), our yet unspoken words—"are open and laid bare to the eyes of Him with whom we have to do" (Heb. 4:13b).
   Darkness hides nothing from God (Ps. 139:12). He knows the end from the beginning (Isa. 46:10). And because He is omniscient, He knows what is best for those who trust Him. "The LORD is good, A stronghold in the day of trouble, And He knows those who take refuge in Him" (Nah. 1:7).

D. Vocabulary and Doctrinal Concepts:
   1. Vocabulary: anoint, know, knowledge, secret
   2. Doctrinal Concepts:
      a. The omniscience of God (1 Sam. 16:7).
      b. God knows the ways of men (Prov. 5:21; 34:21; Jer. 16:17; Ezek. 11:5).
      c. God examines our motivations (Ps. 26:2; Prov. 17:3b).
      d. The Lord Jesus knew all things and all men (John 2:24; 21:17b; 1 John 3:20).
      e. The Holy Spirit "searches all things" (1 Cor. 2:10–11).

E. *Source Book* Keywords: David, essence of God (omniscience), volition

F. Activities:
   1. Suggested Visuals: omniscience symbol, Samuel anointing David, Trinity
   2. Games, Songs, Worksheets
   3. Memory Verse: "O LORD, You have searched me and known *me*." (Ps. 139:1, NKJV)
   4. Opening and Closing Prayer

Lesson One
The Story of David

Since God is eternal life, no one or nothing was before God. That's why the Bible begins with the words, "In the beginning God" (Gen. 1:1*a*). We learned that last time, didn't we? Does anyone know what God did in the beginning? Yes, He "created [He made out of nothing, for there was nothing but God] the heavens and the earth" (Gen. 1:1*b*).

Who showed God how to take nothing and make something out of it? Who taught Him to form a man out of the dust or chemicals of the ground? Have you ever wondered about those things? Could it be that God went to school to learn all He knows? Of course not; God needs no one to teach Him. He is all knowledge! We have a big new word for God's "all knowledge." It is OMNISCIENCE. Can you say this big new word with me? Om-nis-cience, omniscience!

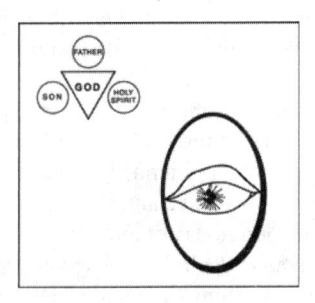

Now let's take this big word and divide it in two: "omni" and "science." "Omni" means "all." Soon, you will learn two other new words that tell us what else God is like. Both of them also begin with the same four letters: o-m-n-i. And what did I tell you those letters mean? Right, all! "Science" means "knowledge." There are many kinds of knowledge. We get our knowledge by learning. That's why you must go to school, but God did not have to go to school to learn. He knows all things, for He is what? Yes, omniscience. Let's add the "O" to our Essence Box; that will stand for God's omniscience.

All our knowledge about God comes from the Bible. Let's open the Bible and see what it says about God's omniscience. I am turning to the Old Testament, to 1 Samuel 16. First Samuel is the ninth book in your Bible; see if you can find it: Genesis, Exodus, Leviticus, Numbers, Deuteronomy, Joshua, Judges, Ruth, and 1 Samuel. There it is. Now turn to chapter 16, where our story begins.

God Knows Israel's Next King

Billions upon billions of years before David was ever born, God knew all about him. He knew that some day David would be a great king. How did God know this? Did anyone tell Him? No! God is omniscient; He need not be told what will happen. He has always known all about David, all about you, and all about me!

God Knew a Prophet

God knew that some day the Prophet Samuel would serve Him in Israel, in a town called Ramah. A prophet is a servant of God who brings a special message of God to the people. God had often talked to Samuel—in fact, from the time Samuel came to live at the Temple, when he was still a very small boy. Now, Samuel was an old man and the right time had come for him to do a special job for God.

God Sends Samuel to Anoint David

So, one day God called Samuel and said, "Fill your horn with oil, and go; I will send you to Jesse the Bethlehemite, for I have selected a king for Myself among his sons" (1 Sam. 16:1). Samuel did as he was told. He filled a ram's horn with olive oil and set out on the road to Bethlehem.

I wonder what Samuel was thinking about? Perhaps he wondered how many sons Jesse had. He did not know Jesse, and he did not know his sons. But what Samuel did know was that God is omniscient. God knew, and that was all that mattered. When the right son of Jesse would stand before him, Samuel would know it for God would tell him (1 Sam. 16:3).

How God Looks at Man

Maybe Samuel stopped some people and asked, "Do you know a man named Jesse who lives here? He has some sons." Maybe the people nodded, "Sure we know Jesse and his eight sons." Then Samuel ordered, "Bring them here."

Don't you think Jesse was pleased when he heard that the prophet Samuel wanted to meet him and his sons? How surprised he would be when he finds out why Samuel had come! "This is my oldest son," Jesse said. "His name is Eliab." Samuel looked hard at Eliab. What a tall, fine looking young man he was, and an officer in King Saul's army, too. "He would make a splendid king," thought Samuel to himself; "Surely this one must be the Lord's anointed [or chosen]" (1 Sam. 16:6). Just then Samuel heard the Lord's voice, though no one else did: "Do not look at his appearance or at the height of his stature, because I [God] have rejected him [do not want him]; for God *sees* not as man sees, for man looks at the outward appearance [how a man looks from the outside], but the LORD looks at the heart [the soul or mind]" (1 Sam. 16:7).

You see, the Lord is not impressed with us because we wear nice clothes, or because we look pretty and neat, though I am sure He wants us to be neat and clean. He is not impressed with our good manners, though He would want us to be polite. God can see beyond the outside. He looks straight into our minds and reads our thoughts.

Are you sometimes like Samuel was that day? Do you think that just because some girl or boy "looks bad" that they really are, or that because they "look good and nice" that they are good and nice? Only God can tell what a person is really like. Never forget that!

God knew that Eliab was not His man. Eliab would never make a good king. Then Jesse called his second son, Abinadab. But Samuel shook his head and said, "No, the Lord had not chosen Abinadab either." What about Shammah, the third son? No, not that one either. "These are my four next sons," said Jesse. And still Samuel kept shaking his head, for the Lord had said "No" to him each time (1 Sam. 16:8–10).

Let's count and see how many of Jesse's sons Samuel has met up to now: Eliab—one, Abinadab—two, Shammah—three, and the next four sons. Three and four adds up to? Seven! And how many sons does Jesse have? Eight.

"Are these all of your children?" asked Samuel. He was sure that God had said one of Jesse's sons *would* be the new king! "Well, no," answered Jesse. "I still have another son, my youngest, but he is out keeping the sheep." Jesse would have never thought that young David might be God's chosen king. Why, David was only a shepherd boy! Jesse had almost forgotten about David in all the excitement.

But God had not forgotten! He knew what David was like, for He had looked right inside of David. And what did God see there? Just as plain as you can see a show on your television screen, so God saw that David would love God and obey God's Word (Acts 13:22). David was the very one God had sent Samuel to "anoint."

Do you know what anoint means? In those long ago days, when a man was to serve God as prophet, priest, or king, oil was poured on his head to show that God had indeed chosen him and that He would help this man. That's what Samuel had come to do. He still stood there holding the horn with oil in it. Then Samuel ordered, "Send and bring him [David]; for we will not sit down until he comes here" (1 Sam. 16:11*b*).

What God Wants Me to Know

In His omniscience God looks right into our souls as well. I wonder what He sees in your soul? Did He see that you listened to every word I said? Or did He know that you paid no attention? I'll never really know; but God knows, and that is all that matters.

God has always known you. He knows all your secrets (Ps. 44:21). And do you know what else He knows about you? He knows how many hairs each of you has on your head (Matt. 10:30). He knows when you have sinned, even if you were all by yourself and thought no one had seen you (Heb. 4:13). He knows when you are frightened and alone, and He wants you to trust Him.

He knows where your favorite toy is when you think you have lost it. Have you ever thought of asking the Father to help you remember what you did with it? He knows what will happen to you tomorrow, in ten years, in twenty years, in eternity! He knows what you are going to do or think or say long before you do. And because He knows you best, you can safely trust and love Him.

God also knows who does not believe in the Lord Jesus Christ. Once a boy named John wanted very much to go to heaven. He had heard that God is holy, that is, righteous and just. He had also heard that God hates sin. John, too, thought that sin was a bad and dirty thing.

Because of all the bad things he did and all the dirty words he said, John decided he must do something to be better. Maybe God would let him come to heaven then. He would begin by taking a bath every day, keeping his clothes real clean, and being as good and obedient as he possibly could. Yet as fine as this idea sounded to him, things just did not work out the way he planned. The truth was that John wasn't always good. Too often he disobeyed and said ugly things.

What was John's problem? The same problem we all have—a sinful nature on the inside! Then, one day John went to Sunday School with a friend. He heard the teacher say, "You children all look so nice and clean this morning, at least to me you do. But God does not look on the outside; He looks right into your souls. Psalm 139:1 (NKJV) says, "O LORD, You have searched me and known *me*." He knows that we all have sinful natures inside us. The sin nature is bad all the way and it wants its own way, not God's way (Jer. 17:9).

John was nodding his head; and wasn't he glad to hear the teacher say next, "But class, God did something for us we could never do for ourselves. He sent the Lord Jesus to save us, to make us good and right for Him. The Lord Jesus Christ died on the cross for our sinful ways (Rom. 8:3). If you will just believe in the Lord Jesus Christ, you will be made clean and fit to go to heaven (1 John 1:7)."

John did that day what I surely hope you, if you have never believed in the Lord Jesus as your Savior, will do—believe on the Lord Jesus Christ (Acts 16:31). Now, John knows and you can know it also, that when the sin nature has had its way, you can be made clean by telling God your sins (1 John 1:9).

While we bow our heads and close our eyes, let's let God "search" us. Will you decide to believe in the Lord Jesus today?

Lesson Review

Let's play a question and answer game. Listen to my questions and see if you can answer them. God is omniscience means: God keeps a secret? God is all knowledge? or God tells us what to do? Yes, all knowledge. God knew that: Eliab, Samuel, Jesse, or David would be king some day? That's right, David. Samuel knew that: one of Jesse's sons, all of Jesse's sons, or none of Jesse's sons would be king? Yes, one of Jesse's sons would be king. Jesse knew that: David was God's chosen king or that David was out with the sheep? Out with the sheep. God knows: all our thoughts? some of our thoughts? or none of our thoughts? God knows all our thoughts. Who has "searched" and knows us: our parents? teachers? or God? God.

Will you say your last memory verse with me? "O LORD, You have searched me and known *me*" (Ps. 139:1, NKJV). And, can you tell me where this verse is found in the Bible? Psalm 139:1. Can you say it all alone?

Memory Verse

"O LORD, You have searched me and known *me*." (Ps. 139:1, NKJV)

LESSON TWO
GOD REVEALS A SECRET

*D*o you know who wrote Psalm 139:1? David did; in fact, he wrote all of Psalm 139. We will learn about some of it today and also finish our story.

Have you ever had a secret and did not tell it to anyone, not even to your best friend? No matter how hard you try, you cannot keep it a secret from God. Why not? Because God is omniscient. God is really the only One who can have a secret; did you know that? God had a secret for many, many years—from all eternity past, for that matter, and that secret was that He had chosen David to be the next king of Israel.

God had shared a part of His secret with the prophet Samuel, but not all of it. So Samuel must trust God's omniscience when he looked at Jesse's sons. Already he had seen seven of them. And what had God told Samuel every single time? "No, not this one; no, not that one either." At last Samuel asked Jesse a question. Can you still remember what that question was? Have you any more children? And what did Jesse answer? And now, Samuel was waiting for the young shepherd boy, David.

Jesse Sent for David

God's Word does not tell us whom Jesse sent out after David; maybe it was one of David's brothers. But I am sure of one thing—whoever went to call David must have told him to hurry because the prophet Samuel must not be kept waiting.

David did not have time to go home and wash up or put on his finest clothes. He stood before Samuel just as he had come in from the hills. David was tanned as brown as a berry and healthy from being out in the fresh air all the day long. He was a good looking boy indeed, and the Lord told Samuel, "Arise, anoint him; for this is he" (1 Sam. 16:12).

What God Saw in David

Can you remember what I told you God saw in David? That David loved God and would obey God's Word (Acts 13:22). God just does not look at the outside of people; He looks right into their souls! David had learned early to obey in the little things. He had been faithful in taking care of his father Jesse's sheep, and God knew that David would be just as faithful in looking after the Israelites.

But God also knew that sometimes David would sin. God hates sin; He does not want any of His children to sin (Gal. 3:26). And, God knew how soon David would confess his sins to Him. That was one thing God really liked about David—that most of the time David did not hide his sins from God. Yes, God liked what He saw in David (Ps. 103:14).

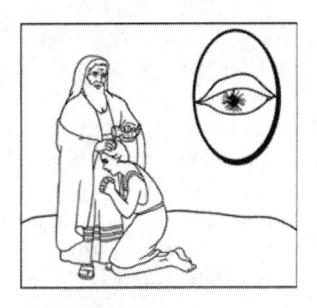

David Anointed

As soon as Samuel had heard the Lord's voice, he took the horn of oil right then and there, in front of all his brothers, and anointed David the new king of Israel (1 Sam. 16:13a). Let me show you how this was done.

Let's pretend that you are David and I am Samuel. I'll roll up a piece of paper into a cone and make believe it is Samuel's horn with the oil in it. Samuel raised the horn of oil and gently poured it out over David's head.

When the old prophet had done this, a very wonderful thing happened to young David. The Bible says that "The Spirit of the LORD came mightily upon David from that day forward" (1 Sam. 16:13b). The reason God gave David the Holy Spirit was so that David would know how to be a good king. Samuel's work was finished. He could return to his own place at Ramah now.

David Trusts in God's Omniscience

David did not begin to rule as a king immediately. God knew that David was not yet ready to be a king. Instead, Jesse sent David back to the hills to look after the sheep; David did not even argue. He never said, "Now just a minute, Father, I am a king now, so you cannot tell me what to do." He did not whine like so many boys and girls I know and say, "Oh, Father, must I?" Not David; he had learned to obey his parents. Do you know what Ephesians 6:1 says to all children? "Children, obey your parents in the Lord, for this is right." Do you obey like David did?

David was back with his sheep in the field. Do you think he sat and pushed out that lower lip and pouted because he was not allowed to sit on his throne and live in a palace? He did not! He simply trusted in God's wisdom and omniscience. Surely God must have a good reason to keep David waiting; God knew when it was David's time to be king.

What God Knew about David

God in His omniscience could tell exactly when David would actually wear his crown—fifteen more years had to pass until the day when David was crowned king of the land (2 Sam. 5:4). Do you know how old that makes David at the time of his anointing? Approximately fifteen years old. But, until the day he would be crowned, David, knowing that God knew best what was good for him, was content to wait on the Lord.

When David was a grown man and king, he often thought of God's omniscience. How wonderfully well God knew him; how well God knew *all* things! Like the time when David said he would go out to fight the giant, Goliath. Why, God had known all the time that David would win that fight, or else He would have stopped David from going to meet the giant (1 Sam. 17). Or the time when David had disobeyed God and had counted the people in his country when he was told not to count them, just to see if God had really kept His Word (1 Chron. 21).

God had known what went on in David's soul. Yet, God had not stopped David, for He had given David volition and only David could say whether he would obey God or not. Now, King David took a pen and a scroll and wrote, "O LORD, You have searched me and known *me*" (Ps. 139:1, NKJV). David wondered, "You have known all my badness and disobedience; how can You love me still?"

What God Wants Me to Know

The Lord has searched us and knows us, too. He knows when we are good and pleasing to Him and when we are bad and disobedient. How can He always love us, even when we are hateful and unloving? Because God *is* love.

He knows us because He is what? Omniscient! What does He know about us that David tells us God knew about him? Let's hear what David said (Ps. 139:2–5). God knows when we sit down or get up; He understands our thoughts. He knows whether they are kind and helpful thoughts or ugly and mean thoughts which will hurt someone. God knows our words before they are spoken. Yes, He knows much better what you are trying to say and what you mean than even you know! God knows all that has ever happened to us or that ever will happen. Do you remember that day when you had planned to go swimming, but company came and you could not go? You were disappointed, weren't you? God knew what might have happened had you been able to go. God kept you from it, for He did not want to see you get hurt (Ps. 139:5).

Can you see right through a glass of water? That's what God does when He looks at things, at people, at our lives. Night or day, darkness or light, all are transparent, clear as a glass of water to God's omniscience (Heb. 4:13; cf., Ps. 139:11–12). If you drop some dirt into the glass of water, what happens to the nice clean water? It gets dirty, muddied up. That's what sin does in our lives. It makes us unfit to please God. Can we hide sin from omniscient God? No more than the dirt can hide in a glass of water.

What's the easiest way for us to have fresh, clean water in our glass once more? That's just what God wants us to do about sin in our lives—spill it out to Him, that is, tell him what you thought, or said, or did wrong (1 John 1:9). Right away God will cleanse you and forgive you. It's no use trying to fool God. We may try to fool our friends or our parents. We may even get away with it. But we cannot ever fool God. Will you remember that?

Yes, God sees right through us. He sees your volition. He knows which way it is deciding. But because I do not see it, and because I do not know, I can only remind you that God's way to heaven is to believe on the Lord Jesus Christ. There is no other way to heaven (Acts 4:12) and no other Savior. Now, you know how wonderful God is and how sinful we are. Like David, only you can decide to obey or not to obey God. Listen to God's Word: "And this is His commandment, that we believe in the name of His Son Jesus Christ" (1 John 3:23a). What will you do?

Lesson Review

See if you know the answers to this Bible quiz. Who said, "Are these all your children?" Samuel. Who said, "I have yet another son. He is out keeping the sheep"? Jesse. Who said, "I have not chosen these"? God. Now, watch this one; it is a trick question: Who was sent out to fetch Jesse's youngest son? The Bible does not say who went after him. Who came rushing in from the hills to stand before Samuel? David. Who said, "Arise, anoint him; for this is he"? God.

What did Samuel say they would not do until Jesse's youngest son came? Sit down. What did David's father and brothers see Samuel do to David? Pour oil on his head. What two things did the pouring of oil on David's head show? One, that he was God's chosen new king; and two, that God would help him do this job. What wonderful thing happened after David was anointed? The Holy Spirit came upon him. What did David do after Samuel returned to his own town of Ramah? Went back out to keep his father's sheep.

How did God know that David would make a good king? God is omniscient. How many years did David have to wait until he got his crown and began to rule? Fifteen years. How did David know that God would call him to the throne when the right time came? He trusted in God's omniscience. How did it happen that David wrote Psalm 139? He remembered all the things God had known about him. And, God knows all about you and about me as well.

Memory Verse
"O LORD, You have searched me and known *me*." (Ps. 139:1, NKJV)

Chapter Fourteen

Omniscience: The Plan of the All-Wise God

OVERVIEW

A. Subject: Omniscience: The Plan of the All-Wise God—Genesis 37–45

B. Lesson Titles:
1. Lesson One: The Story of Joseph
2. Lesson Two: What God Always Knew Would Happen to Joseph
3. Lesson Three: God Knows
4. Lesson Four: How "All Things" Worked "Together for Good"

C. Story Objective:

Omniscient God, who tells the number of the stars and calls them by name (Ps. 147:4), who knows when a sparrow falls (Matt. 10:29–31), is concerned with our every need (Matt. 6:8). Because of His omniscience, His plan for us is perfect in every detail. Our lives are in His hand (Ps. 31:15) and He is ever ready to direct our steps (Ps. 37:23). We can be happy only when we trust His better knowledge and leave the future in His hands (Job 24:1), especially when seemingly bad circumstances come into our lives (Prov. 3:5–6; Rom. 8:28).

The better the believer knows "the depth of the riches both of the wisdom and knowledge of God" (Rom. 11:33*a*), the more he studies "the mind of Christ," His Word, "in whom are hidden all the treasures of wisdom and knowledge" (Col. 2:3), the greater will be his own relaxed mental attitude and grace toward others (1 Cor. 2:16; Col. 2:3; cf., Gen. 50:19–21; Ps. 57:1–2). The story of Joseph and his brothers has been selected as it best illustrates the preceding principles of doctrine and their application.

D. Vocabulary and Doctrinal Concepts:
1. Vocabulary: all-knowing, dream, message, sheaves, wise
2. Doctrinal Concepts:
   a. The extent of God's knowledge (1 Sam. 2:3; Job 28:20, 23–24; Ps. 44:21; Prov. 3:19; Isa. 40:13–14; 42:9; Acts 15:18)
   b. The extent of God's concern (2 Chron. 16:9; Job 34:21; Jer. 32:19; Matt. 6:25–34; 2 Tim. 2:19; 1 Pet. 1:2*a*)
   c. Believer's application of the knowledge of God's omniscience (Job 23:10; 31:4; Prov. 3:26*a*; Isa. 28:29; Jer. 20:12*a*; John 13:7; James 1:5; 3:17)

E. *Source Book* Keywords: essence of God (omniscience), Joseph

F. Activities:
1. Suggested Visuals: Joseph in coat of many colors
2. Games, Songs, Worksheets
3. Memory Verses:
   a. "Lord, You know all things." (John 21:17*b*)
   b. "And we know that God causes all things to work together for good to those who love God." (Rom. 8:28*a*)
4. Opening and Closing Prayer

Lesson One
The Story of Joseph

We all know a few things. Perhaps some of us know more than others; but none of us knows *all* things. Only God is omniscient. I told you last time about some of the all things God knows. Now, hear what else God knows. He knows exactly how many stars are up in the sky, for He has counted them. He even knows every one of them by name (Ps. 147:4–5). He knows how many handfuls of water there are in the oceans. Do you wonder why? The Bible tells us in Isaiah 40:12 that He measured them "in the hollow of His hand." And, I'll tell you what more He knows: He knows every grain of dust on earth and the weight of every mountain and hill.

He knows not only *what* happens, but also *where* and *why*! He knows, because He is omniscient. God is all knowing. Today, we will begin to hear a story of God's omniscience, His plan, and how it all worked together for good in the life of a man named Joseph.

God Knows the Love, Envy, and Hatred in Jacob's Family

There never was a time when God did not know all things—even thousands of years ago when Jacob lived. God's omniscience was the same then as it is today and as it will be thousands of years from now. God knew that Jacob would some day have twelve sons; not just eight sons, as Jesse had, but twelve. What a big family that was! I wonder if the boys' parents ever got their names mixed up? God never did. He knew each one of them perfectly well. There were Reuben, Simeon, Levi, Judah, Zebulon, Issachar, Dan, Gad, Asher, Napthali, Joseph, and baby Benjamin (Gen. 49). Now as we have already learned, God's love is perfect and He has not more, not less, but the same amount of love for all His children. But Jacob loved one of his sons more than all the others. Which one? Joseph, for he was the "son of his old age" meaning that Joseph was very smart or brilliant beyond his years (Gen. 37:3). And, I think that second best, Jacob must have loved baby Benjamin (Gen. 42:36).

When Joseph had his seventeenth birthday, his father gave him a very special present—a coat, woven of many beautiful colors (Gen. 37:2–3). What made this present so very special was not just that the coat was pretty and new, but what wearing the coat meant. It meant that Jacob thought more of Joseph than of his older brothers; Jacob had made Joseph to be his chief shepherd. Oh, how jealous the brothers were of Joseph—so jealous that they could not speak kindly to him any longer (Gen. 37:4)!

Have you ever been so jealous of your sister or brother that you almost hated her or him? That's how jealous Joseph's brothers were. They would rather turn away from Joseph than speak to him; and if they did speak to him, they were gruff and ugly to him. And God, who knows all things, looked down from heaven, right into their souls, and saw those awful sins of envy and hatred there. In fact, God knew that it would not be long until those sinful thoughts would become sinful actions, and the brothers would try to do a terrible thing to Joseph.

The First Dream, a Message and Promise from God

Did Joseph know this, too? Not until very much later; but surely he must have been sad to think that his own brothers hated him. Because God knew what would soon happen to Joseph, He wanted to share His own all-wise plan with Joseph. So, this is how He did it. God showed Joseph a wonderful dream of what His plan for Joseph would be.

As Joseph slept that night, it seemed to him that he and his brothers were out in the fields binding bundles of cut grain. All of a sudden, Joseph's bundle or sheaf stood straight up while his brothers' bundles stood round about it and bowed down low before it. Yes, God was promising Joseph that some day he would surely be a great and important man, so great that even his hateful brothers would bow before him (Gen. 37:6–7).

Did you ever have a strange dream you just had to tell someone? That's how Joseph felt about his dream. He told his brothers what he had dreamt. As you might know, they were not one bit happy. They asked him angrily, "What makes you think you will be greater and rule over us?" You see, in those long ago days before the Bible was written, dreams were very important. Joseph's brothers understood well that God was promising Joseph some wonderful things to come, and they envied him and hated him even more than ever (Gen. 37:8).

The Second Dream

So, God sent Joseph another dream. This dream was much like the first, and this time Joseph told not only his brothers but also his father, Jacob, about it (Gen. 37:10). "Listen," he said, "I had another dream: The sun and the moon and the eleven stars bowed down to me." Though his father was a little put out with Joseph, he, too, knew what the dream meant: someday, Joseph would be greater than his father, represented by the sun, his mother, represented by the moon, and his brothers, represented by the eleven stars. Jacob said no more about the dream, but I am sure he often thought about it as time went by (Gen. 37:11).

Then one day, while the brothers were out with the sheep in a far-off place, Jacob sent Joseph to go and see how his brothers and their flocks were getting along. Joseph was to hurry back home to report to his father. Joseph did as he was told and quickly set out for Shechem (Gen. 37:12–14). There he searched all the fields, but he saw no sign of his brothers or their sheep. "What had become of them?" Joseph asked a stranger. The stranger knew. He nodded and pointed: "This is the way they went, for I heard them say, 'Let us go to Dothan.'" So Joseph went on in the direction the stranger had shown him. Sure enough, there they were. Joseph could see their tents (Gen. 37:15–17).

The Brothers' Wicked Plan

The ten brothers saw Joseph coming (Gen. 37:18–20). I say "ten" because Benjamin was still a baby and he was safely at home in his nursery. The ten brothers poked fun at Joseph. Can't you just hear them? "Here comes the dreamer. Here comes Mr. High-and-Mighty; let's bow down to his Highness," they called. But then they put their heads together and began to whisper: "Let's get rid of him. All we need to do is to kill him and throw his body in a deep hole. We'll tell Father that a wild animal killed and ate Joseph. Then we will see what will become of his dreams."

What God Wants Me to Know

Weren't those wicked plans? Who would ever think that brothers could be so hateful? Did God know what they planned? Indeed He did! Listen to our new memory verse. It is found in John 21:17 and says, "Lord, You know all things." Can you say it with me? "Lord, You know all things." The Lord knew all about Joseph and his brothers. That was why He sent those two wonderful dreams to Joseph. Now, it was up to Joseph to remember these dreams as he finds out what his brothers are planning to do to him.

Today, God no longer speaks to us in dreams, but speaks to us from the pages of the Bible. However, God's promises to Joseph in those dreams were every bit as real as God's promises are to us today. Do you know any of God's promises? God wants you to trust His promises—believe them. And, even if you know only a very few of them now, will you just remember that He knows all the bad things and all the good things that are coming into your life? Now, if God lets these things happen, He must surely have a much better plan. So trust our all-wise God, no matter what!

Can you still remember what God promised Joseph in his two dreams? Might and power; he would be a great man some day. God could promise Joseph these things because Joseph had trusted God for his salvation. God also has a wonderful promise for you who have not believed in His Son. "Believe in the Lord Jesus Christ, and you shall be saved," is His promise to you (Acts 16:31*a*). He promises you life forever with the Lord in heaven (John 10:28). If you will do that, listen to what else God promises you: "But you shall receive power" (Acts 1:8*a*). What kind of power? The Holy Spirit's power; God's very own power inside of you to make your life count greatly for Him. Will God keep His promises? Of course He will! Right now, you don't have to say a word; just think and mean it: "Father in heaven, I do want the Lord Jesus to save me. I do believe in Him now." God, who knows all things, knows your thoughts. He will save and keep you just as He did Joseph. Make your decision now. In our next lesson we will find out what God always knew would happen to Joseph.

Lesson Review

How many things do you know about God? Righteousness, justice, love, eternal life, omniscience. Now let's see if we can still say the verses which tell us what God is like.

What did we learn about Joseph in our lesson? Did God know any of this? Of course He did. Does He know anything about us? All things. Now, shall we talk about the things Jacob did not know? He did not know what his sons planned or where they had taken the sheep. He thought the sons were at Shechem, but they had gone to Dothan. What things didn't Joseph know? He did not know what his brothers were going to do to him or what they planned to tell their father. But God knew all the time, didn't He? God knew, for He is omniscient.

Memory Verse
"Lord, You know all things." (John 21:17*b*)

Lesson Two
What God Always Knew Would Happen to Joseph

Do you know what I have in my purse? Now, I don't want you to guess; I want you to know every bit of what is in there—even to the exact amount of money I carry in my billfold. You don't know, do you? I know Someone who does though—God. But to you, the things I carry in my purse are shut away from sight.

Our lives are like that. All the things that will happen are shut away and hidden from our sight. We can only guess that some things will be good and others bad. God planned it that way so we would learn to trust Him. Had Joseph known what would happen to him that day, he might have stayed home and missed out on God's plan for his life. But Joseph did not know, and now he came closer to his brothers.

The Oldest Son's Selfish Plan

Reuben, Jacob's oldest son, had been thinking about his brothers' plan to kill Joseph (Gen. 37:21–22*a*). Maybe that wasn't such a good idea after all. "Let's not kill Joseph," he suggested, "let's just throw him into this deep, dry well in the wilderness." Was Reuben being kind to Joseph? Did he want to save Joseph's life because all at once he felt sorry for his young brother? It would seem that way to us, but God knew what Reuben was thinking (Gen. 37:22*b*). God tells us in His Word that Reuben had a plan all his own; he would come back later on and rescue Joseph out of that deep hole. Then Reuben would take Joseph home to their father and tattle on his bad, bad brothers. After that, surely his father would love him best.

What does John 21:17 say? "Lord, You know all things." The Lord knew; He had "searched" Reuben and had "known" him (Ps. 139:1). God searches us and knows us. He knows if we do nice things just to be praised or to please Him. He knew that Reuben was acting out of selfishness, not out of love.

Joseph Thrown into the Dry Well

Now, Joseph had reached his brothers. They nodded their heads, and before Joseph could even say "hello" to them, they grabbed him, pulled off his coat of many colors, and threw him into the deep hole where once a water well had been (Gen. 37:23–24). Then Joseph's ten brothers sat down to have their lunch (Gen. 37:25*a*).

What did poor Joseph do? He cried bitterly. He begged his brothers to pull him out and not let him die in the wilderness; but his brothers pretended they did not hear him (Gen. 42:21).

Joseph Sold as a Slave

God was already working out His own perfect plan to spare Joseph's life. What a pity that Joseph had forgotten his dreams and God's promise to make a great man of Joseph! Had he remembered to trust God, he would have turned to the Lord rather than to his hateful brothers. He would simply have said, "Lord, You know all things. I am trusting You to do what is best for me." For that was what God was doing right now. While the cruel brothers laughed at Joseph's cries, God made a caravan, a group of travelers, pass by. They were merchants with their camels loaded heavily with spices, medicines, and oils, going down to the land of Egypt (Gen. 37:25*b*).

Of course, Joseph could not see them, way down in that deep, dark hole. Oh, how miserable he was! He was sure he would die, but God knew better. That was why God had promised Joseph what He did in those two dreams. It was just as if God had said to Joseph, "Joseph, everything is going to come out all right!"

Joseph's brother, Judah, had a new thought (Gen. 37:26–27). "Brothers," he said, "killing Joseph won't really help us; after all, he is our brother. Why not sell him as a slave to these travelers? Then, we can divide the money we get for him amongst ourselves." The brothers agreed, all except Reuben. Remember, Reuben had his own ideas and he seemed to have gone away for a little while, perhaps to look after a stray sheep, or to fetch that long rope he would use to haul Joseph out of the pit.

It was no sooner said than done. The brothers lifted up Joseph out of that deep hole and sold him to the Ishmaelites for twenty pieces of silver. Joseph was now a slave and he was taken into the land of Egypt (Gen. 37:28). Couldn't God have done something better for Joseph than let him be sold into slavery in Egypt? Couldn't God have let Joseph dig a tunnel and escape to run home and tell his father what awful brothers he had? Sure, God could have done all sorts of different things. But God knew the future, the things to come, and God wanted Joseph in Egypt.

Now, you just keep on remembering Joseph's two dreams. Soon, we will find out how those dreams came true. But right now, let's hear what happened when Reuben came back.

The Brothers Tell a Lie

When Reuben returned, the brothers had already split the money nine ways; Reuben did not get a share. In fact, the brothers never even told Reuben what they had done. Joseph told him many years later (Gen. 42:22; 45:4). Reuben looked down into the deep hole and it was empty! Now Reuben was really afraid. Instead of praising and loving him, Jacob, his father, would hate him for not protecting Joseph. Whatever should he do now? He dared not go home to his father unless, unless—"Yes," thought the brothers, "that is just what we shall do, and Father will believe every word we say."

Quickly the brothers took Joseph's coat of many colors. They killed a baby goat and dipped the coat in the blood (Gen. 37:31). When they came home, their faces looked sad. "Look, Father," they said, "we found this coat along the way. We think it might be Joseph's coat. See if you think so, too" (Gen. 37:32).

Jacob examined the bloody coat. He cried, "It *is* my son's coat! Surely a wild animal has torn Joseph in pieces and eaten him." Jacob sobbed with sorrow. He tore his clothes and put on sackcloth; he mourned and grieved over his best-loved son who he was sure was dead (Gen. 37:33–34). "Don't cry so hard," said Jacob's sons and daughters. Yet, his sons did not tell him the truth. How sad they had made their poor father! Still, Jacob shook his head: "I will miss him and cry for him as long as I live" (Gen. 37:35). Jacob would not be comforted.

God Knows All Things

Sad as it is to see such hateful, lying brothers, and such an unhappy father, our story does not end here. God knew that this story would have a very happy ending. But for now, Jacob, too, had forgotten Joseph's dream. What had become of Joseph? We read in the last verse of Genesis 37 that Joseph was bought by the captain of Pharaoh's guard. Next we will see what happens to Joseph in Egypt.

What God Wants Me to Know

Is everything going fine for you today? What about tomorrow? Will all be well then also? Only God knows. Does that mean we should think and fear, "Oh dear me, what if I break a leg next week? Or, what if a car runs into me a year from now? Or, what if all my clothes burn up in a fire? What if my father loses his job and we don't have money to buy food?"

God never wants you to worry or fear (Matt. 6:25–32; 10:29, 31). He says not trusting Him is sin (Rom. 14:23). Once the Lord Jesus told His listeners, "Stop worrying about what you shall eat, or drink, or what you shall wear. Just look at the birds. They neither plant nor gather up harvests into their barns. Yet, your heavenly Father feeds them always. Are you not much better than they?" And then he added, "Look at the wildflowers; they don't work to make their pretty clothes, do they? And yet, I tell you that even King Solomon was not dressed as lovely as God dresses the wildflowers. Don't you think the heavenly Father can take care of you just as well? The heavenly Father knows best what you need," promised the Lord Jesus. "Why, He knows every time a little sparrow falls to the ground, and you are far more important than they."

All who have believed in the Lord Jesus Christ belong to God. They need never fear; they need never worry but can safely trust omniscient God. Next time, when something bad happens to you, and I don't mean getting punished for disobeying your parents, will you remember the verse you have learned? Will you say, "Lord, You know all things. Help me to trust You to make it all come out best for me"?

Even more important than knowing that God is omniscient is "knowing God Himself." What do I mean by that? God wants all people to be saved and to come to the knowledge of the truth (1 Tim. 2:4). The "truth" is really a person—the Lord Jesus Christ, God's own Son. He says to you this very minute, "I am the way, and the truth, and the life; no one comes to the Father, but through Me" (John 14:6). How does anyone come to the Father? By believing in the Lord Jesus Christ. Then, after you have come to believe in the Lord, you can begin to learn what God is like. The Bible says that "the fear of the LORD is the beginning of knowledge" (Prov. 1:7*a*). Here, fear does not mean to be afraid, but to believe in, to trust in the Lord. Why not believe in Him right now?

Lesson Review

At the time when God sent Joseph those two strange but wonderful dreams, God knew that his brothers would soon throw Joseph into a deep hole in the desert. God knew what Reuben planned to do later, but He had a better plan for Joseph's life. Who knows what Reuben was going to do? Pull Joseph out and return him to his father, tattle on his bad brothers, and become his father's favorite son instead of Joseph. What happened while Reuben was gone? Joseph was sold into slavery.

Did Joseph think what happened to him was a good thing? I should say not! He thought it was bad, very bad indeed. And in a way it was bad. Only omniscient God knew that He was going to take a bad thing and make it all come out good in the end. Had Joseph remembered his dreams and God's promise to make of him a great man some day, he could have said, "I know that all things work together for good to me, because I love God; because I know that God knows all things." But he didn't, did he?

Memory Verse

"Lord, You know all things." (John 21:17*b*)

Lesson Three
God Knows

*I*f we know that God is sovereignty, righteousness, justice, love, eternal life, and omniscience, we, too, can say, "And we know that God causes all things to work together for good to those who love God" (Rom. 8:28*a*). Because God is sovereign, His plans are greater than anything people can plan. Because He is righteous and just, He can only be fair to us. Because He is love, He loves us more than anyone else. Because He is eternal life, He is always there to help us just as He helped Joseph thousands of years ago. Because He is omniscient, He can see our lives from start to finish. God knows what is best for us.

In our next lessons we want to learn how God took these bad things in Joseph's life and how He worked them together for good.

God Knows Why Jacob Wept

Jacob wept bitter tears. He sorrowed over his best-loved son, Joseph, whom he thought had been killed by a wild animal. The Bible tells us that Jacob "refused to be comforted" (Gen. 37:35). Instead, he said, "I will weep for my son until I die." I wonder, because I do not know, just what Joseph's brothers told their poor, sad father to try and make him feel better. But God knew, for He knows all things!

Do you suppose they told him, "Please stop crying, Father; Joseph is not really dead; we just lied to you"? I don't think they said that because then they must also admit what they had done—that they sold their own brother as a slave. No, rather than tell the truth, the brothers let Jacob think that Joseph was dead (Gen. 37:33–35).

God Knows How Joseph Was Sold to Potiphar

Now I am going to turn to Psalm 33:13. Can you find that verse? Psalm 33:13 says, "The LORD looks from heaven; He sees all the sons of men." God had seen Jacob weeping, and He saw that long line of men and their camels with goods and spices making their way to Egypt. With the men was a young boy—Joseph. At last the travelers arrived in Egypt. "Who will buy this handsome young slave?" they shouted. "He will make a good and strong servant!"

Did God know who would buy Joseph? Certainly He did! I am sure that God sent Potiphar to the slave market that day so he would be there when Joseph was offered for sale. But, you may wonder, who is Potiphar? Well, Potiphar was the captain of Pharaoh's guard, and Pharaoh was king over Egypt (Gen. 37:36; 39:1).

God Knows Joseph Is in Prison

After Joseph served Potiphar for some time, he was put in prison unfairly (Gen. 39:2–4, 19–20). He was a good and faithful servant to Potiphar, but Potiphar's wife was angry with Joseph and lied about him to her husband. Potiphar believed those lies and punished Joseph.

"Poor Joseph," some may say, "another bad thing has happened to him again." But wait a minute! What did we learn from Romans 8:28? "And we know that God causes all things to work together for good to those who love God" (Rom. 8:28*a*). God knew where Joseph was and that was all that mattered. God also knew exactly how and when He would bring Joseph out again.

About that time, two of Pharaoh's servants had angered the king and were taken to prison. One was the king's cupbearer or wine taster; the other was the king's baker (Gen. 40:1–3). One night both of them had dreams. The next morning they told Joseph. God had shown Joseph the meaning of their dreams so he could explain to them what was soon to happen. "When you get back to the palace in three more days, remember that it was I who told you these things. And remember also that I have done nothing bad to be put in prison" (Gen. 40:14–15).

Joseph still had not learned to trust God's omniscience! He hoped the cupbearer would remember him, instead of trusting in God. Two whole years had to come and go before Joseph learned to look to God alone (Ps. 57:1–2). For although God remembered Joseph and took care of him in prison, back at the palace the cupbearer had forgotten all about him (Gen. 40:23).

Pharaoh's Dream

Now the two long years were over. Pharaoh lay sleeping in his palace. He dreamed he was standing beside the river Nile when suddenly, seven fat cows climbed out of the river and went to feed on the green grass of a meadow close by. Next, seven skinny cows came out from the river. They walked over to the fat cows and ate them up, but you'd have never known this, for the cows were just as skinny as before (Gen. 41:1–4, 21). Pharaoh awoke. "What a strange dream I had!" he thought to himself. It was still night, so Pharaoh went back to sleep.

Again, Pharaoh dreamed. This time he saw seven ears of corn growing on one stalk. How firm and round and strong that corn was. But what was that? Right after the good corn, a stalk of bad, dried-up corn grew in the field! Why, those seven ears of corn were surely the poorest Pharaoh had ever seen. As he watched, the seven skinny, poor ears of corn swallowed up the seven full and good ears of corn. When Pharaoh awoke this time, he was greatly troubled. What could these dreams possibly mean (Gen. 41:5–8*a*)?

Pharaoh sent for his wise men. He told them his dreams, but the wise men just stood there, shaking their heads. They could not tell the king one thing about his dreams (Gen. 41:8*b*). It was then the cupbearer remembered Joseph. "I do remember now a promise I made Joseph two years ago in prison," he said. The cupbearer then told Pharaoh about his own dream and how all that Joseph had explained would happen, actually happened (Gen. 41:9–13). The Pharaoh commanded, "Bring Joseph here." Hurriedly Joseph shaved himself and put on clean, fresh clothing. Then he came and stood before the mighty Pharaoh and listened to his dream (Gen. 41:14).

God Knows All Dreams and Their Meanings

Did Joseph jump up and down excitedly, like some boys and girls do when they know the answer? No, Joseph had finally learned that only God knows all things. And Joseph said, "I cannot tell you, but God shall give Pharaoh an answer which will put the king at peace" (Gen. 41:16).

Do you know why Pharaoh had seen such strange and frightening things in his dream? God was showing him what He was about to do. That was how Joseph explained it to the king (Gen. 41:25). "The dream of the king is one dream," he said. "The seven good and fat cows and the seven good and ripe ears of corn are seven years of plenty. The seven skinny cows and the seven poor and sun-dried ears of corn are also seven years, but they will be seven years of famine when nothing will grow at all. Consequently, there will be great hunger. God showed the king this dream for God knows the future. He knows what will be even though we do not" (Gen. 41:26–31).

Then, Joseph advised the Pharaoh (Gen. 41:32–36). "Now, this is what you should do, Oh king, for what God has shown you will happen very soon. Find a wise man and make him the leader of your country. Send officers to gather all the food of the seven good years, and lay up this food and corn safely in storehouses. Then, when the seven bad years come, there will be food in the land of Egypt."

Joseph Promoted

Pharaoh listened carefully. He was sure that Joseph was telling the truth, and he was pleased with Joseph's good advice. Even the wise men agreed that Joseph must be right. Pharaoh said, "Can we find a man like this, in whom is a divine spirit?" (Gen. 41:38). And all the wise men nodded their heads. Then Pharaoh turned to Joseph once more. "Since God has informed you of all this, there is no one so discerning and wise as you are" (Gen. 41:39).

Where had Joseph gotten his wisdom, his knowledge? God had given it to him. Do you remember what I said at the close of last lesson: that "the fear [or trust] of the LORD is the beginning of knowledge" (Prov. 1:7)? Joseph had trusted God, and now he had learned what God is like; that God knows all things, and that whatever happens, God will work it out for good to them that love Him.

Like Joseph, all believers, and that means you, too, may share in God's knowledge. How do we get such great knowledge? The Bible is "the mind of Christ" (1 Cor. 2:16). In Christ "are hidden all the treasures of wisdom and knowledge" (Col. 2:3). Are you listening when God speaks to you in His Word today?

Pharaoh was not yet through speaking (Gen. 41:40–41). "You, Joseph, shall be over my house and land, and whatever you say shall be done. Only I shall be greater than you." Pharaoh took a ring off his own hand and put it on Joseph's finger. He sent for fine, new linen clothes for Joseph and put a gold chain about his neck (Gen. 41:42). That meant that Joseph was not the greatest man in all of Egypt, but right next to the king; he was ruler over all the land. He rode through the streets in Pharaoh's second best chariot (Gen. 41:43). Wherever he went, the king's servants called loud for all to hear, "Bow down the knee; here comes the ruler of Egypt!" Pharaoh even changed Joseph's name so everyone would know how wise Joseph was; he called him "Zaphenath-paneah"—the one who showed the king the meaning of his dream (Gen. 41:45*a*).

Joseph's dreams had come true, at least in part. Joseph was a great and mighty man, the most important man in the kingdom of Egypt, next to the Pharaoh himself. No doubt he lived in a fine palace. He had all he needed, and more. He had a beautiful wife, the daughter of the high priest of Egypt, and soon God was going to give him two sons (Gen. 41:45*b*, 50–52). How very busy Joseph was now. He traveled all through the land of Egypt, laying up food for the years ahead. At first, he kept count of all the corn which had been stored, but then it could no longer be counted or weighed. God had blessed the land of Egypt so very much that all her storage places bulged with their plentiful harvests. Then the seven years were over (Gen. 41:46–53), and the next seven years of famine began.

What God Wants Me to Know

Did God know that Joseph would rule over a land some day? Did He know that people would bow to him? How did God know these things? God is omniscient. When did God know what would happen to Joseph? There never was a time God did not know! He knew all things, long before He showed Joseph the dreams of the bundles of grain and the sun, moon, and stars bowing down before him. God had kept His promise; the dreams had come true as God knew they would. But something was still missing—Joseph's father and brothers must still come to bow down before him. Yet, how could they? Joseph was in Egypt and they lived far, far away in Canaan. But God knew just how He would bring the family of Jacob back together again!

Some days, everything seems to go wrong for us just like it once did for Joseph. What should you remember then? Perhaps some dream you once had? Oh, no! I'll tell you what you should remember—a wonderful promise from God's Word like Romans 8:28. "And we know that God causes all things to work together for good to those who love God" (Rom. 8:28*a*). Can you say it with me? Do you believe it? You can and you should! But you cannot remember something you do not know! So be sure to learn your Bible verses, and pay attention to what God shows you from His Word!

We can never have God's omniscience, but we can and should have knowledge of God's Word. God's Word says to every believing boy and girl, and to every believing man and woman, "But grow in the grace and knowledge of our Lord and Savior Jesus Christ" (2 Pet. 3:18*a*).

Can we grow up if we are not even born? Of course not! Likewise, until we are "born again," that is until we have believed in the Lord Jesus Christ and have entered God's family (Gal. 3:26), we cannot grow in the knowledge of the Savior. We cannot even understand what the Word of God tells us (1 Cor. 2:14). So listen very carefully to what I am going to say now: God the Father is omniscient. God the Son is omniscient. God the Holy Spirit is omniscient.

God the Father made a very wonderful plan. In His plan, God the Son, the Lord Jesus Christ, left heaven to die for your sins and to make a way whereby you can go to heaven. Now, God the Holy Spirit takes this plan and shows it to you. He tells you that "all have sinned" (Rom. 3:23), and all need to be saved. Jesus Christ is ready to save you, if only you will believe in Him.

God has always known that you would hear those important words: "Turn to Me, and be saved" (Isa. 45:22*a*).

There is only one Savior—Jesus Christ; there is only one way to heaven—by believing in Him. God knows how you will decide or whether you will decide. Think it over, and then make up your mind while we close our eyes and bow our heads in prayer.

Lesson Review

Was it a good thing that Joseph's brothers threw him into a deep hole in the desert? Was it a good thing they sold him as a slave and told their father a lie? No, these things were not good in themselves; nor was going to prison a good thing. I am sure Joseph must have wondered many times why God allowed these terrible things to happen to him.

But, God knew exactly what He was doing and why. And, as time went by, Joseph learned that God takes bad things and works them together to make them come out good. What verse did we learn that taught us this same truth? Romans 8:28*a*. Will you say it for me? "And we know that God causes all things to work together for good to those who love God" (Rom. 8:28*a*). What good thing did God work out for Joseph and how did He do this? What was Joseph doing for the first seven years as the king's most important helper?

Memory Verse
"And we know that God causes all things to work together for good to those who love God." (Rom. 8:28*a*)

LESSON FOUR
HOW "ALL THINGS" WORKED "TOGETHER FOR GOOD"

What would you do if your sisters and brothers were real mean to you and treated you in an ugly way? Would you try to get even with them as soon as possible? Would you never speak to them again? Or would you do what Joseph did—love them and forgive them? I cannot say what you would do, but God knows. He knew what Joseph would do; that's why God wanted Joseph in Egypt, even if getting there was so hard and sad. Are you ready to listen as I finish the last part of our true story from God's Word today?

God Knows How to Keep Them Alive in Famine

The seven years of plenty had ended, and the seven bad years of want when nothing would grow had begun. All was just as God had shown Pharaoh in his dream and just as Joseph had explained it would happen (Gen. 41:53–54*a*). All through the world the rain had stopped falling and the land had dried up. Soon what little food had been left over from the years before was eaten up, and people everywhere began to be very hungry. Only in the land of Egypt could food and bread be found (Gen. 41:54b), for remember, Joseph had used the knowledge God had given him. He had stored up corn for this terrible time of famine.

Even in Egypt, the farmers could grow nothing in their fields. But they still had to feed their hungry children, so they came to Pharaoh to ask him for bread. Pharaoh said, "Go unto Joseph; whatever he says to you, you shall do" (Gen. 41:55). Joseph was ready to help all who came. He opened up the storehouses and sold food to the Egyptians (Gen. 41:56). When it became known that there was food in Egypt, men came from near and far to ask Joseph if they might buy corn. It was not long until there was much money in the king's treasury, I'm sure, and still there was more than enough corn left (Gen. 41:57).

By now Joseph's own faraway homeland, Canaan, was in great need. People were starving. His father, Jacob, had heard of all the grain which was stored up in Egypt also (Gen. 42:1–2). "Don't just sit here, looking sadly at one another," he said to his sons. "Look, I've heard that there is corn in Egypt. Go to Egypt, buy some food for us there, that we may live and not die!"

A Dream Comes True

Jacob handed his sons several bags of money. His ten oldest sons were ready to leave, but Jacob kept young Benjamin home with him (Gen. 42:3–4) because he just could not bear parting from his youngest son.

At long last the brothers came to the palace in Egypt. The sons of Jacob had to wait their turn like everyone else, and now they stood before the great Prince Zaphenath-paneah. He sat upon a throne; how mighty and fearsome he looked! The ten brothers bowed down before him with their faces to the ground (Gen. 42:5–6).

Do you know who this great and mighty prince was? God knew, for He knows all things. God had placed Joseph on Egypt's throne to be Pharaoh's first helper. Would Joseph recognize his brothers after so many years? He certainly did! But his brothers did not know him! Joseph pretended he did not know who they were. He spoke roughly to them and asked, "Where do you come from?" They answered, "From Canaan, to buy food"; and still they were bowing and bowing.

Suddenly Joseph remembered his two dreams from long ago (Gen. 42:9–13). Why, they *had* come true; his brothers *were* bowing down to him! Was Joseph going to be proud now and say, "Ha, ha, you didn't feel sorry when I cried and begged you to save my life; and now you are here asking me to help you. Well, I am not going to do it; so scram!" At first it almost seemed like that, for Joseph was asking the brothers a lot of questions. He even told them they might be spies sent to Egypt. "Oh, no, sir," the brothers assured him, "*We* are not spies. We are Jacob's sons. There are twelve of us. We left our youngest brother at home with our father, and our other brother is no more."

Joseph had found out what he wanted to know. His father and Benjamin were still alive! Oh, how he longed to see them again. Joseph's voice sounded gruff when he spoke: "I will believe your words when I see your youngest brother. I will keep one of you here to make sure you will bring him; you others may return home with some food." The brothers put their heads together and spoke quickly to each other. They remembered how badly they had treated Joseph some twenty years ago, and now, bad things were happening to them, too. "We certainly have it coming to us!" they whispered. But they did not know that Joseph had understood every word, for he had spoken to them in the language of the Egyptians.

Joseph's Nobility—He Rewards Evil with Good

Joseph kept Simeon, his second oldest brother, in prison while all the others went home with heavy bags of corn. The first night they stopped at a roadside inn. One of the brothers opened the sack to feed his donkey. My, how surprised he was! Right at the very top of the sack, with food Joseph had given them for their journey, lay Jacob's bag, full of money.

The brothers were really frightened. What would the ruler of Egypt say? Would he think they were thieves? They hurried home and told Jacob all that had happened to them (Gen. 42:24–28). But, as they opened their sacks to put away the corn they had bought, there were all the other bags of money, too—not one coin was missing! The ruler of Egypt had not let them pay for the food! Jacob and his sons looked at each other with puzzled faces. Whatever should they do?

Jacob did not want to let Benjamin out of his sight. "I have lost Joseph, and Simeon, and now you want to take away Benjamin also?" he sighed. "If anything should happen to him, I would die" (Gen. 42:36–38). But Reuben had made a promise to the ruler of Egypt; so in the end, when all the food had been eaten up, the brothers went back to Egypt, and Benjamin was with them. This time they brought double the money to pay for the corn they had bought before, as well as for the corn they wanted to buy now. And again they came to bow down before Joseph (Gen. 42:36—43:15).

Joseph Makes Himself Known to His Brothers

Joseph looked at Benjamin. Benjamin had been a little baby when he last saw him. He was a young man now. Joseph could stand it no longer. He sent out all his servants and said to his brothers, "I am Joseph whom you sold as a slave" (Gen. 45:1, 4). The brothers were afraid. "What would he do to them now?" they wondered. Joseph had become a man of great power and importance. He might have them punished to get even with them. But no, Joseph's voice was kind and loving. "Come near to me," he said; "do not be grieved nor angry with yourselves because you sold me here, for God sent me before you to preserve [or save] life" (Gen. 45:5).

Then, Joseph began to tell them that the famine would continue for five more years (Gen. 45:9–13). "And God sent me before you that our family might be kept alive. So you see, it was not you but God who brought me here. God made me great in Pharaoh's palace and in all Egypt," he said (Gen. 45:6–8). "Now, hurry back home to our father and tell him these things. Then bring our father here, and your wives, and your children that you may live here, near me."

When Joseph had finished speaking, he hugged his brothers lovingly and promised to take care of them for as long as he lived. Pharaoh, too, was pleased to hear the good news Joseph had to tell him. He gave gifts to Jacob and his sons and families and told them they might live anywhere they wished in the land of Egypt. So Joseph's entire family was taken care of by omniscient God.

All Things Work Together for Good

Many years later the brothers asked Joseph to forgive them their awful thoughts, their unkind words, and the bad things they did to him (Gen. 50:15–18). However, Joseph had already forgiven them long before they even asked him. Joseph had learned what God is like. It did not matter that his brothers had been cruel and hateful to him. What mattered was that God is omniscient! He knew all along what was best for Jacob and his large family. All things in Joseph's life had not been good, had they? But God had worked them together for good (Rom. 8:28; cf., Gen. 50:20). God had known them all from the beginning. Don't you think Jacob, Joseph, and all his brothers were thankful for the plan of the all-wise, omniscient God?

What God Wants Me to Know

Sometimes we do not see or understand why things happen the way they do. Should we say, "Oh, no! Why did this have to happen to me? Doesn't God know I wanted to go on a picnic today? Now just look at all that rain!" Does God know? Why, yes, He does! And, because He knows what is best for you, He may just have specially ordered that rain for you, perhaps to keep you from getting hurt, or from getting sick. Wouldn't it be much better for girls and boys who know the Lord Jesus as their Savior to say, "Lord, I don't know why it happened, but I know that You know all things. I'll just keep right on trusting You."

When the Lord Jesus was on the earth, He told His friend, Peter, "What I do you do not realize now; but you shall understand hereafter" (John 13:7). That is God's promise to you and to me. Some day, we will know all the answers! Until then, we must simply know that God knows best, for He knows all.

God is just as omniscient today as He was in those long-ago days when Joseph lived. We learn from Psalm 33:18–19 that "The eye of the LORD is on those who fear [or trust] Him, On those who hope for His lovingkindness [or unfailing love], To deliver [or save] their soul from death, And to keep them alive in famine."

Now, if the Lord knows those who belong to Him, do you think He also knows those who do not? Oh, yes, He does! Do you belong to Him? God knows. Even though He knows that some of you may never believe on the Lord Jesus Christ, He cannot and will not force you to change your mind. He gave you a volition.

Like Joseph, God is ready to forgive your sins. Just as Joseph said to his brothers, "Come near to me," so God says to you right now, "Come unto me" for He wants to take care of you like He took care of Joseph. Will you let Him? He wants to save your soul forever and ever. Yes, omniscient God can be your own heavenly Father. How? "Through faith in Christ Jesus" (Gal. 3:26). "But as many as received Him, to them He gave the right to become children of God, *even* to those who believe in His name" (John 1:12).

Lesson Review

Today I want to ask you some questions. Who dreamed the dream that the sun, moon, and stars were bowing down before him? Joseph. Who dreamed that the skinny cows ate up the seven fat cows? Pharaoh. Who dreamed that the brothers' sheaves bowed down before his own? Joseph. Who dreamed he saw seven large and seven scrawny dried-up ears of corn? Pharaoh. Today, does God show us knowledge through His Word or through dreams? Through His Word. What do we call God's all-knowledge? Omniscience.

Now listen carefully. I will tell you four things that God knew, but one of them will have a mistake in it. Tell me which one. God in His omniscience knew that: there would be a famine; Joseph would be a great man some day; Joseph had not been killed by a wild animal; Joseph would bow down before his brothers. The last statement is wrong. Can you tell me what I should have said? Joseph's brothers would bow down to him.

What did God do with some very bad things that happened in Joseph's life? He made them come out good. Can you tell me what verse in the Bible tells us that God will work all things together for good for some people? Romans 8:28. For whom? For those who love Him—believers. Let's say that verse. "And we know that God causes all things to work together for good to those who love God" (Rom. 8:28*a*).

Memory Verse

"And we know that God causes all things to work together for good to those who love God." (Rom. 8:28*a*)

Chapter Fifteen

Omnipresence: The Ever-Present God

OVERVIEW

A. Subject: Omnipresence: The Ever-Present God—Genesis 28; The Book of Jonah

B. Lesson Titles:
1. Lesson One: Jacob Learns of God's Omnipresence
2. Lesson Two: A Lesson for Jonah
3. Lesson Three: God's Loving Care

C. Story Objective:
God is omnipresent. He is neither limited by time nor space. The heavens cannot contain Him (1 Kings 8:27). Heaven is His throne, the earth His footstool (Isa. 66:1). Man cannot escape the presence of God (Ps. 139:3*a*, 7–10). It is both comforting and sobering to realize this great truth about God. Believers of all times have found peace and reassurance in the knowledge of God's loving presence (Ps. 23:6*a*; Matt. 28:20).

In ages past, God was said to have been "among" or "with" His people (Ex. 25:8; 33:14). In the present dispensation, the Church Age, He indwells every believer forever (John 14:17, 23). Therefore, the believer in the Lord Jesus Christ can never and will never be separated from God's love or presence (Rom. 8:35–39) for as long as he lives on earth. Then, upon his death, the Christian immediately enters into God's presence in heaven to be forever with Him (John 14:3; 17:24; 2 Cor. 5:8).

D. Vocabulary and Doctrinal Concepts:
1. Vocabulary: desert (verb), everywhere, flee, forsake, presence, sulk
2. Doctrinal Concepts:
    a. The omnipresence of God (Jer. 23:24)
    b. The promise of God's presence (Gen. 28:15; Ex. 33:14; Deut. 33:27; Joshua 1:5, 9; Ps. 121:4–5; Matt. 18:20; 1 Cor. 3:16; Heb. 13:5)
    c. The result of His omnipresence (Job 26:6; 34:22; Ps. 4:8; Prov. 15:3)
    d. The reality of His presence (Acts 17:27*b*)

E. *Source Book* Keywords: essence of God (omnipresence), Jacob and Esau, Jonah

F. Activities:
1. Suggested Visuals: Jonah, omnipresence symbol, Trinity
2. Games, Songs, Worksheets
3. Memory Verses:
    a. "Lo, I am with you always." (Matt. 28:20*b*)
    b. "The eyes of the LORD are in every place, Watching the evil and the good." (Prov. 15:3)
4. Opening and Closing Prayer

Lesson One
Jacob Learns of God's Omnipresence

Today we will find out one of the reasons why God knows all things; and in finding out, we will learn the second word about God which begins with the letter "O"—in fact, with the same four letters—o-m-n-i.

The first word, beginning with an "O" was what? Omniscience. That word means—? All knowledge. God knows all because He is OMNIPRESENCE. Now let's see what omnipresence means: "Omni" means all. "Presence" means here, there, and everywhere; all places. God is in all places at the same time. He is everywhere at once.

Can you be at school and at home all at once? Can I? Of course not, but God can. "How can He?" you may ask. He can because He is God! And because He is in all places at all times, we are never alone. If we think we are all alone, it's just because we haven't learned that God is omnipresent. Here, let me teach you a very wonderful promise the Lord Jesus left for us before He went back to heaven: "Lo [that means "See"], I am with you always [for as long as we live]." And where is His promise? In Matthew 28:20. Don't you think that is a good Bible verse to learn and remember?

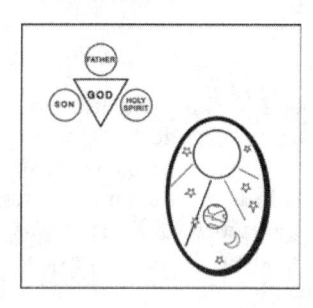

You just heard that God is in all places at all times. Would you like to know how Joseph's father, Jacob, learned of God's omnipresence?

Background to Genesis 28

Jacob and his twin brother, Esau, did not know what it was like to live in a house, like you and I, until they were grown men. Together with their parents they lived in tents. You think that would be fun, do you? Well, perhaps it was, but Esau and Jacob had their problems just the same. They had their spats and quarrels from the day they were born (Gen. 25:22–26*a*); and now that they were grown young men, their quarrels became more serious.

More often than not, Jacob was to blame, for he liked to cheat. But in spite of his cheating, Jacob loved the Lord, while Esau did not like the things of God or trust God (Heb. 12:16–17). Esau began to hate his brother, Jacob, and as time went by their mother, Rebekah, feared for Jacob's life. If there was only some way she could think of to help Jacob get away from home until Esau forgot his anger. At last she knew what Jacob must do. Quickly she went and talked to Isaac, his father (Gen. 27).

Jacob Leaves Home

Jacob stood in his father's tent. "Son, you are a grown man now," said Isaac; "it is time for you to think of taking a wife. But do not marry one of the girls of Canaan, where we live, for they do not know nor love the true God. Go instead to my own people, to Padan-aram, to your uncle's house. Choose one of his daughters to be your wife" (Gen. 28:1–2). Then Isaac blessed his son asking that God Almighty bless him and give him many children, and that He might give him the land which God had promised (Gen. 28:3–4).

After many loving good-byes, Jacob set out on his long journey (Gen. 28:5). He had traveled all day long without a break. It was late in the afternoon and the sun had already set when Jacob at last stopped. There was no place nearby where he might find lodging for the night, but Jacob was used to camping out. The place where he had stopped was just perfect; he would sleep under the stars that night. Jacob looked around for some smooth, flat stones. He thought they would make a fine pillow. He stretched himself out on the ground and covered himself with his robe. He yawned and fell asleep (Gen. 28:11).

Alone in the Dark?

Would you have been lonesome, perhaps even afraid all by yourself in a dark, open field? Would you have thought of all those wild animals, prowling about in the night? Would you have cried yourself to sleep away from home and mother and father? Would you have thought that you were out there—all alone? I think that Jacob never thought of anything like that. He was much too tired to stay awake long. Perhaps he looked up into the starry sky, thinking how far away God must be. But that very night he was going to find out differently—that God is *not* far from any of us; for that night God showed Jacob that He is omni—what? Yes, omnipresent.

The Ever-Present God

All around Jacob, the night had been dark. Above him, the stars had twinkled merrily as he drifted off to sleep. But what was that? Was Jacob dreaming? It was a dream, and yet it was oh, so very real! Jacob could have reached out and touched what he saw. Right there next to him stood a bright and shiny ladder. Where did it lead to? Jacob looked up in his dream; to his surprise, the ladder reached all the way up into heaven. Now, angels began to go up and down that shiny ladder between heaven and earth. Wouldn't that have been a lovely sight to see (Gen. 28:12)?

In his dream, Jacob kept looking up and up and up, as far as he could see. There, at the very top of the ladder stood the Lord Jesus Christ, God's Son, Himself. Listen to what He said to Jacob: "I am the LORD, the God of your father Abraham [your grandfather] and the God of Isaac [your father]; the land on which you lie, I will give it to you and to your descendants [your children]. And behold, I am with you, and will keep you wherever you go, and will bring you back to this land; for I will not leave you" (Gen. 28:13, 15a).

Jacob heard every word God spoke to him. What great things God was promising him—the land, many children—but best of all, God was saying that He would always be with him wherever he went. God would keep him; that means He would watch over him, guarding Jacob's life in all places, and bring him back safely once again. Yes, Jacob could be sure God would keep His promise to him, for God's Word is always true.

Jacob Has Learned His Lesson

As sudden as the heavenly sight had come, it also disappeared. The night was over and the morning sun rose bright and clear. Jacob opened his eyes. He jumped up and looked about him. All seemed the same as it had the day before, and yet, Jacob knew something was different! Yes, he knew something he had not known yesterday. Happily he called out, "Surely the LORD is in this place, and I did not know it" (Gen. 28:16b).

Because Jacob knew so much less about what God is like than you and I know, he wondered, "Is this the house of God? Is this the gate to heaven?" (Gen. 28:17). He wanted to be sure to remember this special place where God had promised him so many wonderful things. So he took one of the stones which had been his pillow the night before, set it upright, and poured some oil over it, almost like Samuel did when he anointed David king over Israel. After God brought him safely back home again, he would build a place where people might come and thank God and praise Him for all that He is and does (Gen. 28:18–22).

God kept His Word. Some twenty years later Jacob and his large family of twelve sons and his daughters returned home. I should not wonder that Jacob's own wonderful dream is the reason why he knew that God had indeed spoken to Joseph in his dreams.

What God Wants Me to Know

Wherever Jacob went, there was God. Throughout those long years, God never for a moment left Jacob. Day in, day out, night after night, God looked after him and blessed him. Doesn't something God said to Jacob remind you of your own memory verse which is God's promise to you and to me, to all who have believed in the Lord Jesus Christ? What did that verse say? "Lo, I am with you always" (Matt. 28:20b). Who said these words? The Lord Jesus Christ. "But, you don't see Him!" you say. No, you don't, and that does not matter. What matters is His Word. He says it, so you can believe it!

The reason why God is with us always is that He is *in* us. You cannot see your soul, but it's in you just the same, wherever you go! Our great God is in everyone who has believed in Jesus Christ. He will never leave us, day or night. God never sleeps, so He can watch over us always. Daylight or midnight are all the same to Him. Aren't you glad to know that God is everywhere, that He is omnipresent? Now you know you are never really alone!

Do you know what happens to God's children (John 1:12) once they leave this world? They go to be with our great God, to be with Him always. Would you like to have God be with you and in you? Would you like to go to be with Him some day? Would you like God's promise, "Lo, I am with you always" for yourself? You may have it. All you need do is to believe in the Lord Jesus Christ, and you will be safe for all time, safe with the ever-present God (Ps. 9:10).

Lesson Review

What was the last thing we learned about our great God? Omnipresence. What does that word mean? It means that God is everywhere, in all places, at all times.

How did Jacob learn that God is omnipresent? Through a dream. Do you remember what Jacob was to Joseph? His father. What is God to all who believe in His Son, Jesus Christ? The heavenly Father. To those who do not know the Lord Jesus as their Savior, God is their Creator or Maker, but not their Father. Though they may not know this, God is in all places at all times and can see the good and bad things they do, even as He watches those who belong to Him.

Memory Verse
"Lo, I am with you always." (Matt. 28:20b)

Lesson Two
A Lesson for Jonah

When you awoke this morning, sunlight filled your room. Do you know what? This same sunlight filled my room also. It shone in every part of this city and also in Dallas, New York, and all over in this part of the world. There was enough light for all of us. God's presence is even greater. He can be all over the world at once and at the same time, He is in heaven too. We know this from the Bible; even though we cannot see God's presence, He sees us (Gen. 16:13). Wouldn't it be foolish to try to run away from what we know God wants us to do? Wouldn't it be foolish to think if we run far enough God would forget us and forget His plan for our lives? Let's see today how someone once tried to hide from God's omnipresence, and how he found out it just could not be done.

God Sends Jonah to Nineveh

Jonah was God's prophet. Do you remember what a prophet does? He takes God's message where God sends him. Samuel was a prophet. I am sure you can still tell me where God sent him, and with what message? God sent Samuel to Bethlehem, to anoint David king.

Well, God had chosen Jonah to go to Nineveh with a very important message. We find that message in the Book of Jonah. If you start at the end of your Old Testament and count back eight books, you will come to Jonah. Let's see if you can. In Jonah 1:2, we read what God told Jonah: "Arise, go to Nineveh the great city, and cry against it, for their wickedness has come up before Me."

We have learned that it says in the Bible, "hear the word of God and do it" (Luke 8:21b). Is that what Jonah did? No, although that's what he should have done. Instead, we read, "But Jonah rose up to flee to Tarshish from the presence of the LORD [God's manifest presence in the Temple in Jerusalem]" (Jonah 1:3). What was the matter with Jonah? Didn't he know that God is omnipresent? I am sure that he did; but Jonah was out of fellowship through disobeying God's Word. He wanted to run away from what God wanted him to do. He fooled himself into thinking that God would not bother with him if he went as far away from Nineveh as he possibly could.

Jonah Flees

Jonah was on a sinful path wasn't he? He ran away from God down to Joppa, which was in the opposite direction from Nineveh. Joppa was a busy harbor town. Jonah looked for a ship that was ready to sail. There was one ready to go all the way to Tarshish, in southern Spain. That was the one Jonah would take. He paid his ticket and went aboard (Jonah 1:3b). Now, he noticed how very tired he was from running away. He would go down into the ship and stretch out on his bunk and sleep. Perhaps Jonah thought, "God will never look for me here." But, oh, how wrong he was! God does not have to go and look for any of us. He is omnipresent. Listen to what Proverbs 15:3 says: "The eyes of the LORD are in every place, Watching the evil and the good."

Does that mean that God has many, many eyes? No, of course not. It just tells us that He is everywhere at the same time. Was what God saw good? It was not. Disobedience to God is sinful and must be punished. God would have to remind Jonah what He is like: that He is sovereign, and His will must be obeyed; that He is righteous and just, and that Jonah cannot get away with sin; that He is love, and He cares very much what Jonah does; that He is eternal life, and He wants to share His life with the people of Nineveh (Jonah 4:2, 11); that He is omniscient, and He knows where Jonah is right now and what he is doing; and that He is omnipresent, and therefore Jonah cannot get away from God.

A Lesson for Jonah

God had to teach Jonah the hard way what He is like. Yet God would much rather have us learn the easy way—that is, learn His Word and then do it! Now, we shall learn our memory verse, Proverbs 15:3, so we will never try to hide ourselves or our sins from omniscient, omnipresent God? "The eyes of the LORD are in every place, Watching the evil and the good."

When God spanks us, He always does so in love and grace. Jonah did not deserve God's loving care in the least, nor do any of us for that matter. Yet, God sent a storm and a fish to bring back His run-away prophet. Do you know how it happened?

The Storm

"Where did this terrible storm come from so suddenly?" wondered the captain and the sailors. They had never been in a storm like this before. "If we do not do something soon, the ship will sink, and we shall all drown," they said. "Let's throw the cargo overboard," someone suggested. No sooner said than done! Now the ship was much lighter (Jonah 1:5); but still it seemed that the waves would dash it to pieces. The sailors prayed to their false gods, and of course, that did no good at all. They wondered about their passenger, Jonah. Surely he must be very much afraid. The captain went down to talk to him. Wasn't he surprised to find Jonah fast asleep?

"Wake up," called the captain; "how can you sleep in this terrible storm? Get up and pray to your God; maybe He will help us and keep us from going down" (Jonah 1:6). Don't you think Jonah felt ashamed of himself now? Even if he had prayed, his prayers would not have been heard! Why not? Because Jonah had an unconfessed sin in his life (Ps. 66:18). No, Jonah could not pray now, nor did he. But he did know why the storm had come up. It was all because of his sin of disobedience; he was to blame for their dangerous journey (Jonah 1:7).

"Tell us, where do you come from, and what is your job; who are your people, and what is the name of your country?" the sailors wanted to know (Jonah 1:8). Jonah answered all their questions (Jonah 1:9). He told them that he was a Hebrew, one of God's people—in fact, God's own prophet. He told them that he had trusted in God who had made heaven, the sea, and the dry land. Then, Jonah added shamefacedly, "I am running away from God."

Running away from the God of heaven, earth, and sea? The captain and sailors could not believe they had heard right. "Why have you done such a thing?" they asked. What a sad thing to see that unbelieving people were more upset over Jonah's sin than Jonah was (Jonah 1:10)! They were afraid of Jonah's great God. "What should we do to you that the sea may become calm for us?" they said fearfully (Jonah 1:11*a*).

Do you know what Jonah told them to do? Right! He said, "Pick me up and throw me into the sea. Then the sea will become calm for you, for I know that on account of me this great storm *has come* upon you" (Jonah 1:12). Throw Jonah into the stormy sea? Why, that would mean certain death for him! The sailors felt sorry for Jonah. They tried harder than ever to row and bring the ship near to the shore, but it was no use. There was nothing else they could do but follow Jonah's advice.

"We beg you, Lord, don't let us die because of Jonah's sin," they called. Then they picked up Jonah and threw him into the sea. At once, the storm stopped blowing, and the sea was still (Jonah 1:13–15). Now the sailors knew how great Jonah's God really was. They promised God all sorts of things if He would only get them safely to Tarshish (Jonah 1:16).

The Fish

And what about Jonah? What happened to him? Well, he did not drown at all, though he thought he would. It was a good thing for Jonah that God is omnipresent. Even before Jonah plunged headfirst into the sea, God was already there. He had prepared a great fish to swallow up Jonah and save the run-away prophet's life (Jonah 1:17).

Now, Jonah was really out of sight, inside the belly of a great fish and way down near the bottom of the ocean. He must stay there three days and three nights. Jonah had plenty of time to think. What was he thinking about? I think I know. Most likely he remembered some Bible verses which King David had written about God's omniscience and omnipresence: "Where can I go from Your Spirit? Or where can I flee from Your presence? If I ascend to heaven, You are there; If I make my bed in hell, behold, You are there. If I take the wings of the morning *and* dwell in the uttermost parts of the sea, Even there Your hand shall lead me, And Your right hand shall hold me" (Ps. 139:7–10, NKJV).

How dark it was inside that fish! Jonah could not even see his hand before his eyes. He must have thought, "Though no one can see me now, God can; darkness hides nothing from God, not even my sin of disobedience. How good God is to me; how glad I am that He is in all places at all times!" (Prov. 15:3; Jonah 2:1–9).

Jonah knew just what he must do. What would you do if you had been in Jonah's place?

What God Wants Me to Know

While we leave Jonah in the stomach of the big fish to think about what he has learned, let's think of what God has taught us in this lesson. We found out that no one, no one at all can run away or hide from God! It's just no use. Wherever we go, God is there! God knew where Jonah went when Jonah ran off to go to Joppa. God knows where we are and whether we are in fellowship or not.

Have you ever thought that you were all by yourself, so it did not matter if you disobeyed instructions? Once Moses thought so, too. The Bible says that Moses was angry at an Egyptian who was beating up a Hebrew slave. Moses "looked this way and that, and when he saw that there was no one *around*, he struck down [or killed] the Egyptian and hid him in the sand" (Ex. 2:12). What had Moses forgotten? He had forgotten that God is everywhere and that He sees the evil and the good.

God saw "the evil and the good" in Moses' day, in Jonah's day, and He sees it in our day. He sees our obedience and rewards us for it. Best of all, because He is omnipresent and omniscient, He can surround us with His loving care.

Many, many years have passed since Jonah went his own way instead of God's way. Yet, nothing has changed since then. God tells us in His Word that people are much like sheep; they want their own way. They wander away and get lost. They think and hope, maybe this is the right way or maybe that. But all the time they get farther and farther away from their flock.

We are all lost in sin (Rom. 3:23). Since God knew that we could never come to heaven by ourselves, He sent the Good Shepherd to find us. The Lord Jesus is that Good Shepherd. He gave His life for His sheep (John 10:15) when He died for our sins. That's how He made a way to save our souls from eternal death.

Still, some people do not want God's way of salvation. They think they'll try their own way. But it will do no good (Prov. 14:12). The only way to heaven is through believing in the Lord Jesus Christ. Will you let Him save you?

Lesson Review

How would you like to spend three days and three nights inside the stomach of a great fish? You would not? Jonah really had not wanted it either. All he thought of doing was to run away. Can anyone run away from God? No. Why not? Because He is omnipresent. Jonah knew that; yet Jonah had tried it and it did not work. What did God do to teach Jonah what He is like?

Memory Verse

"The eyes of the LORD are in every place, Watching the evil and the good." (Prov. 15:3)

LESSON THREE
GOD'S LOVING CARE

How do you suppose Jonah felt while he was inside the fish's stomach, way down there at the bottom of the ocean? All around him was darkness; perhaps seaweeds were still wrapped around his head, and—phew! What a smelly place it must have been (Jonah 2:5–6)? I know exactly how Jonah must have felt. Why? Have I ever been inside of a fish? No, but I have been out of fellowship! When I have sinned against the Lord and I know I did, and still I have not confessed my sin, I am miserable, especially if the Lord has already begun to spank me. That's how Jonah must have felt—miserable and unhappy.

Then Jonah remembered some wonderful things about God—God's omniscience and omnipresence. Jonah knew now what he must do. What would you have done had you been in Jonah's place? Confessed your sin? You are right; that's what Jonah did. He saw that there was no use hiding his sins from God who was right there and knew what he had done. Jonah might as well admit them. Do you know what happened to Jonah then? The same thing that happens to us when we tell God the Father all the sins we have thought, said, or done—He forgives us and cleanses us (1 John 1:9). Let's pick up Jonah's story here and see how it ended.

God Delivers Jonah

Will you say our memory verse with me? "The eyes of the LORD are in every place, Watching the evil and the good" (Prov. 15:3). God was pleased when He heard Jonah confess his sin of disobedience. God had always known Jonah would confess his sins, just as He had always known Jonah would run away. Now He could also hear that Jonah was thanking and praising Him. What might you have thanked the heavenly Father for, had you been Jonah? That He had saved Jonah's life and not let him drown? And would you not have thanked Him for having the big fish ready on the very spot where he went down?

Yes, Jonah thanked God for all those things, but especially for being so loving and kind and for being right there when Jonah needed Him (Jonah 2:2, 7, 9). Then God spoke to the fish and the fish spat out Jonah upon the dry land close to Nineveh (Jonah 2:10). Don't you think Jonah was glad to get away from the presence of the fish? And don't you think, too, that he was glad to have learned that God is everywhere? If God were not omnipresent, Jonah would have surely drowned.

God Speaks Again to Jonah

Jonah had barely picked himself up off the ground when God was already waiting to speak to him. For the second time God was saying, "Arise, go unto Nineveh, that great city, and preach. Yet forty days, and Nineveh will be overthrown [or destroyed]" (Jonah 3:1–2, 4). Jonah was ready to go now. He came to the gate which led into Nineveh. What a big city Nineveh was! It would take him three days to walk around it.

Everywhere Jonah went he cried out, "Forty days from now your city will be destroyed! Forty days from now your city will be destroyed!" What terrible news that was! The news had come straight from Jonah's God, the true God of heaven and earth. The people of Nineveh heard what Jonah had to say, and they understood. They knew that they were sinful and that their worst sin was that they had not wanted the Lord to be their Savior. Now, they changed their minds. From the youngest person to the oldest, from the king in his palace to the beggar in the street, all believed in God's promised Savior (Jonah 3:5–6). Would God see their faith and perhaps save them and their city?

Nineveh Spared

Can you give me two reasons why God knew that the people of Nineveh had truly believed in the Lord Jesus Christ? He is omniscient and omnipresent. He was in all places of Nineveh when the people believed in Him. And God did save them; He decided not to wipe out their city (Jonah 3:10). How happy the angels in heaven must have been to see so many, many new believers! But there was one person who wasn't happy in the least. Who was he? Jonah.

Jonah Sulks

Whatever is the matter with Jonah now? Well, I'll tell you; Jonah is hopping mad. He hates the Ninevites and would much rather see them wiped out than saved. He thinks they are too bad to be saved. Is anyone too bad to be saved, or too good to need salvation? Of course not! God doesn't think so. God came down from heaven in the Person of the Lord Jesus Christ to save anyone from sin and death who will believe in Him so that anyone can come into His presence to live with Him forever (1 John 4:14; 5:11).

You and I, who are already saved, should always be glad over anyone new who has come to believe in the Lord Jesus. Jonah should have been, but he was not. See if you can find the fourth chapter in the Book of Jonah and tell me the first word of Jonah 4:1. What is it? "But!"

Do you sometimes talk back to your mother or dad? That's what Jonah now did to God. Of course, you know you cannot talk back to someone who is not there! But God *was* there because He *is everywhere*! Jonah complained, "Lord, didn't I tell you this would happen? I told you so when I was still in my own home town!" Ah! What does that tell us about God again? Yes, that He was with Jonah all the time.

"I knew it! I knew you would save them!" Jonah said. Do you wonder how Jonah knew? What did Jonah know about God? The same things you know about Him, that He is sovereignty, righteousness, justice, love, eternal life, omniscience, and omnipresence (Jonah 4:2).

Pouting, Jonah walked away from the city of Nineveh. Secretly, he was still hoping that God would change His mind, that He would destroy Nineveh and her people after all. And just in case God did destroy Nineveh, Jonah wanted to be sure to see it. So he found a lookout place, just opposite the city and built himself a shelter (Jonah 4:5).

Oh, oh! Jonah was out of fellowship again. Do you think God will leave him now? Who remembers what God promised all His children? Think of your memory verse: "Lo, I am with you always" (Matt. 28:20*b*). He promised to be with them always, didn't He? God did not leave Jonah, even then (Heb. 13:5*b*). God knew it would be a hot day and so He made a gourd plant, a tall, fast growing plant, to grow out of the ground overnight (Jonah 4:6). Guess what! At last Jonah was happy. He was glad to have a shade tree all to himself. I am sure he slept well that night.

How good God was to take care of Jonah so lovingly. Yet Jonah did not want God to take care of the Ninevites who had also believed in Jesus Christ. It seems that God must teach Jonah another lesson. How would He do it?

Jonah's Last Lesson on What God Is Like

Early next morning Jonah opened his eyes. He looked up to see the shady leaves of the gourd plant. They were gone! Why, the whole gourd plant was gone; it had withered away. What had happened? God had sent a hungry little worm to gnaw away at the plant just before Jonah woke up. Now Jonah's shade tree had wilted, and oh, how that sun beat down on his head! Now, the awful east wind began to blow hot as fire. It was too much for Jonah. He fell down in a faint and wished he might die (Jonah 4:7–9).

But, God did not let Jonah die. He was right there with His disobedient prophet (Jonah 4:10–11). It was God who had sent the hot sun and the east wind; and now God said, "Jonah, should you be angry with Me for saving the people of Nineveh? You were sad that a plant died which you neither put there nor made to grow. But I, God, made these people. Look at all the little children in the city; look at all the men and women, and at the many animals. Should I not save and spare them?"

Surely Jonah must have hung his head in shame. God's care of him had never stopped. God's presence had never left him. Shouldn't God do as much for others who trusted Him?

What God Wants Me to Know

Has God ever stopped taking care of you? Has He ever broken His promise and left you? He has not! Think how much He is doing for you every day. He saved you when you believed in the Lord Jesus Christ, and now He keeps you. He is with you wherever you may go and says "I will never desert you, nor will I ever forsake you" (Heb. 13:5*b*).

God wants to do as much for others who still do not know Him. He needed Jonah to go to Nineveh, and He needs you to go to your friends and to your family. What should you tell them? Tell them the good news that "Christ Jesus came into the world to save sinners" (1 Tim. 1:15*b*). Have you ever told anyone that God will save them from the penalty of sin and care for them if only they will believe on the Lord Jesus Christ? Remember, God will go with you and help you as He has promised (Joshua 1:5*b*).

Although we cannot see Him, the Lord is here with us and in us. Just like He once sent Jonah to talk to the people of Nineveh, so He brought you and me here to hear what He wants us to know. God does not want anyone to die in his sins—neither the Ninevites, nor you (2 Pet. 3:9). Jonah's news was bad news, but I have good news for you: "For the wages of sin is death, but the free gift of God is eternal life in Christ Jesus our Lord" (Rom. 6:23). Will you receive His gift—eternal life in the presence of our omnipresent God—today? Anyone may have His wonderful gift. How? "Whoever believes in Him should not perish [or die], but have eternal life" (John 3:16*b*).

Memory Verse

"The eyes of the LORD are in every place, Watching the evil and the good." (Prov. 15:3)

Chapter Sixteen

Omnipotence: The Greatness of God's Power

OVERVIEW

A. Subject: Omnipotence: The Greatness of God's Power—Exodus 14—15

B. Lesson Titles:
1. Lesson One: God's Power to Help
2. Lesson Two: God's Power over the Sea

C. Story Objective:
God is omnipotent, limitless in ability and authority. By His power He rules forever and upholds all things (1 Chron. 29:11–12; Ps. 66:7a; Heb. 1:3). God is almighty to save and to keep to the uttermost (Neh. 1:10; Heb. 7:25; 1 Pet. 1:5). To those who believe He makes known "what is the surpassing greatness of His power toward us who believe. *These are* in accordance with the working of the strength of His might" (Eph. 1:19b).

The Lord God Omnipotent challenges believers of all times: "Behold, I am the LORD, the God of all flesh; is anything too difficult for Me?" (Jer. 32:27). Once the believer learns to apply this doctrine to his daily experience, he will respond along with Job of old: "I know that Thou canst do all things" (Job 42:2a), and he will relax in the knowledge that "nothing will be impossible with God" (Luke 1:37b).

D. Vocabulary and Doctrinal Concepts:
1. Vocabulary: defeat, nations, power, powerful
2. Doctrinal Concepts:
   a. The omnipotence of God (Ps. 147:5; Rev. 19:6).
   b. There is nothing too hard for God (Gen. 18:14; Matt. 19:26).
   c. The Word of His power (Ps. 33:9; Heb. 1:3).
   d. The manifestation of His power (2 Chron. 16:9; 25:8; Ps. 74:13; John 10:28–29).
   e. The power of God the Son (Matt. 28:18).
      1) To forgive sins (Matt. 9:6)
      2) To lay down His life and take it up again (John 10:18)
      3) To give eternal life (John 17:2–3)
      4) To judge (John 5:30)

E. *Source Book* Keywords: essence of God (omnipotence), Israel, Jacob and Esau, Moses

F. Activities:
1. Suggested Visuals: omnipotence symbol, Trinity
2. Games, Songs, Worksheets
3. Memory Verse: "For God has power to help and to bring down." (2 Chron. 25:8b)
4. Opening and Closing Prayer

Lesson One
God's Power to Help

To be strong and powerful means to be able to do something very great and mighty. Let's talk about some great and strong things, shall we? See whether you can help me tell about them. I'll give you the first one—light. Light can be so powerful as to blind you. That's what the light of the sun is like. Water is also very powerful. When water is put to use rightly, it can give us electricity and many other wonderful things. Yet water can also do terrible things; it can wash away entire cities. Who knows of another very powerful force? Yes, the wind. The wind can blow so mightily that it can tumble down great big buildings as if they were matchboxes. Fire? Yes, fire is very powerful also. It can burn things into ashes and melt hard metals into liquid. Atomic power is another great force, isn't it?

Sometimes we read about mighty men of strength who can do very great and unusual things. Samson, in the Bible, was such a man. I want you to think of all these powers put together. That's how powerful God is! All power in heaven and on earth belongs to God because He is OMNIPOTENT! Do you know what omnipotent means? Omni means what? Yes, all. Potent means strong, powerful. God is not only strong and powerful, He is omnipotent. Om-ni-po-tent.

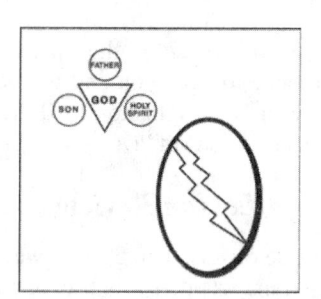

We see God's omnipotence every day and night, yet we never pay much attention to it, do we? It is God's power that keeps the sun, moon, and stars in the sky. It is God's power that keeps the earth hanging in space (Job 26:7). God's omnipotence keeps you and me; His power protects us as it has protected believers in long-ago days. God wants us to know that He is omnipotent so that we will trust Him to help us. Our new memory verse tells us that "God has power to help and to bring down" (2 Chron. 25:8*b*). He helps some and makes others fall down. Let's find this verse and learn it. Then, I will tell you a true story from the Bible about God's power to help His people and His power to make their enemies fall down. "For God has power to help and to bring down" (2 Chron. 25:8*b*).

How the Israelites Came to Egypt

More than twenty years had passed since Jacob found out that God is omnipresent. Remember, God had promised to be with Jacob always and that He would bring him safely back home again (Gen. 28:15). Well, God kept His Word, and now Jacob was on his way home with all his family and their many servants. One night, when Jacob was all alone, God said to him, "Your name shall no longer be Jacob, but Israel" (Gen. 32:28). I think Jacob must have been glad to have this beautiful new name, for "Israel" meant Prince of God, while his old name, Jacob, had meant "Cheater." And who would want to be called that all of his life?

God had also kept another promise He had made to Jacob, whose new name was now Israel—to give him many, many children (Gen. 28:14). The Bible calls them "the children of Israel" (Deut. 1:3) or "the Israelites" (Ex. 35:29). Jacob had twelve sons. Do you remember the name of one of them especially? Yes, Joseph. We learned all about Joseph and his dreams, and how God knew all along that Joseph would become a mighty ruler in Egypt.

Now, when the great famine came over all the earth, Israel and his sons came to live in Egypt where there was food for them all (Gen. 45:17–21). As long as kind Pharaoh and Joseph were alive, all went well for the Israelites. Although they were far away from their own home country, they now lived happily in Egypt. They knew that some day God would bring them back home once more (Gen. 50:25).

A Family Becomes a Nation
Exodus 1:7a

The children of Israel "increased greatly, and multiplied" (Ex. 1:7*a*). What does "multiplied" mean? Let's take a number and see if we can make it increase and multiply, shall we? One and one makes two; two times two makes four. Now let's double the four. What number do we get? Eight? You see, that was just what happened to Israel's great family in Egypt. Jacob's, or Israel's, sons had so many children that before long this big family became a mighty nation. The Bible tells us that the Israelites became very great and that the land of Egypt was filled with them.

About that time a new king began to rule over Egypt. He had never known Joseph, and he was concerned about the Israelites (Ex. 1:10). So, the new king said to his people, "The Israelites are greater and stronger than we are. Some day they might go to war against us and win over us. We must do something so this will not happen; we must act 'wisely.'" So the Egyptians made the Israelites their slaves, and forced them to build great cities for the new Pharaoh (Ex. 1:11).

Did the Egyptians act "wisely" by mistreating the Israelites? They did not, for God had said that He would bless those who were good to the children of Israel, and punish those who would treat His people badly (Gen. 12:3).

Meantime, the Israelites' lives were made harder and harder. Cruel men, whipping them to make them work faster and harder, watched over them. There was nothing the poor Israelites could do to help themselves; they were powerless against the Egyptians. Already, four hundred years had passed, and still there was no way out of slavery for the children of Israel. But, if the Egyptians had hoped that the Israelites would become fewer in number, they were very much mistaken. No matter what the Egyptians tried to do to them, their number grew and grew and grew. Do you know why it did? Because God in His omnipotence, His all-power, watched over them and helped them.

What was our memory verse? "For God has power to help and to bring down" (2 Chron. 25:8*b*). God helped His people by giving them many promises. When the Israelites were sad, they reminded one another of God's promise that the day would come soon when God would bring His people back to their own land. They knew that God could do all things, and that nothing is too hard for Him. He would set them free when the right time came. And so He did.

God's Power to Deliver, Exodus 14

God sent Moses to lead the Israelites out of the land of Egypt, but Moses was only a man. It would take more than man's power to free the people of God from cruel Pharaoh. Yes, it would take the very power of God Himself. And that is exactly what happened—God's omnipotence brought the Israelites out of Egypt, and God's all-power guided them all the way. The Lord went before them in a pillar or column of cloud by day, and in a pillar of fire, to give them light, by night (Ex. 13:21). It was God's omnipotence that gave them strength along the way.

One day, God told Moses that the Israelites were to put up their tents right between the high mountains, close to the Red Sea ahead of them and Egypt behind them. Perhaps it did not seem a very safe place for camping out, but God had a special reason for wanting His people right there, and He had let Moses in on a secret. "Pharaoh will come after you to try to bring you all back to Egypt with him," God said to Moses; but Pharaoh would not get away with this. Instead, God would show His might and power in a wonderful way (Ex. 14:1–4).

How did God know what would happen? Why, He knows all things, doesn't He? God is omniscient. And, what God said would happen, really did happen. As soon as the Israelites had left Egypt, Pharaoh began to think: "Why have we done this; why have we let the slave people go? Who will build us cities now? Go quickly after them, for they are still in the wilderness, in a trap where we can easily catch them." It was but a short time later that Pharaoh's army was chasing the Israelites. The horses galloped as fast as they could go; the chariot wheels rolled and crunched over the sand, and a dust cloud rose up for all to see. Pharaoh's army was catching up with the Israelites and blocking the way behind them.

The Trap

Maybe the Israelites hoped that what they heard was only thunder, but we know better, don't we? What do you think they did when they saw that all the soldiers of Egypt were coming after them? Do you think they said, "We will trust God, for we know that God has power to help us and to cast down our enemies"? They did not. Instead, they looked at the high mountains and sighed, "We will never be able to climb these to escape our enemies." They looked at the sea and wondered which was worse, to die of drowning or to die by the sword. Then they blamed Moses for bringing them into this trap and complained and whined that he had brought them there to die in the wilderness (Ex. 14:5–12).

What God Wants Me to Know

Isn't that just like us? When something scares us, we are like that only too often. We go to pieces and try to blame others for what has gone wrong. Why, we even blame God and think He no longer cares for us. But our Lord cares for us more than we will ever know. When we know that God is love, when we know that He can do all things and knows all things, we can safely trust Him and need not be afraid.

But, have you ever trusted in the Lord Jesus Christ? He has the omnipotence to save you and to keep you forever. Will you believe in Him right now? "Believe in the Lord Jesus, and you shall be saved" (Acts 16:31).

Lesson Review

Let's play a true or false game, shall we? Listen to what I will say and tell me whether it is true or false.

God has no power to help. False. God is omnipotent means that God is perfect goodness. False. God is omnipotent means that He can do all things. God can save us and keep us always. True. If we will trust in God's omnipotence, we need not be afraid. True. Moses took the Israelites out of Egypt by his great power. False, God's all-power showed the Israelites which way they must go. God has power to make our enemies to fall down. True.

Memory Verse

"For God has power to help and to bring down." (2 Chron. 25:8*b*)

Lesson Two
God's Power over the Sea

*D*o you wonder why God had led His people right into a trap? Well, I'll tell you why He did—to teach them to trust in His great power. Remember, on two sides of the Israelites were mountains, to the back was the army of the Egyptians; and what was before the them? Yes, the Red Sea. And, by now the Egyptians had caught up with them. They were trapped and so afraid they hardly knew what to do other than cry and blame Moses for bringing them there. But it wasn't really Moses who had brought them to this place. Who was it? Right! God. God was planning to do something very great that day. I want to tell you about it.

God Fights a Battle

Let's hear what Moses told the frightened Israelites. "Do not fear! Stand by and see the salvation [or deliverance] of the LORD, which He will accomplish for you today; for the Egyptians whom you have seen today, you will never see them again forever. The LORD will fight for you while you keep silent" (Ex. 14:13–14). Moses believed God's Word, did he not? He knew God had power to help them. In fact, God alone would fight the whole army of Egypt while they would watch His great power.

How do you think God fights? Does He send for all the angels to help Him? No, God needs no help; He is all-power. Can you tell me the big new word we learned for God's all-power? Yes, that He is omnipotent. Moses had said, "The LORD will fight for you." He can do everything. Surely it would be easy for God to do what the Israelites could never do for themselves (Ex. 14:13–14; cf., 2 Chron. 14:11*a*). But what was that? The Israelites thought they had not heard right. Had Moses really meant what he said—"Go forward"? Were they to march right into the sea (Ex. 14:15)? Yes, they were, for that was what God said they must do.

The Israelites obeyed; and while they marched forward, Moses, with his rod in his hand stretched it out over the sea, just as God had commanded him to do (Ex. 14:16). And, what do you think happened? When the first Israelite had reached the edge of the water, the sea parted and the dry ground appeared. All that night "the LORD swept the sea *back* by a strong east wind all night, and turned the sea into dry land, so the waters were divided" (Ex. 14:21). As the Israelites marched through the sea on dry ground, the waters were "a wall to them on their right hand and on their left" (Ex. 14:22).

You have probably seen the ocean. Now, imagine, if you can, that right down the middle of the sea was a dry path, perhaps as wide as a street, with water standing up like high walls on each side. What was holding back the sea? Had God suddenly built a dam of steel and concrete thick enough to withstand a flood like men can build today? Of course not. Only God's omnipotence held back the waters. It must have looked like a huge, blue-green wall of shaky Jello® piled many feet high on each side.

Now, while all the Israelites, men, women, boys, and girls, walked along this path, the Lord stood between the Israelites and the Egyptians. He gave light to the Israelites and darkness to the Egyptians: "Thus the one did not come near the other all night" (Ex. 14:19–20, 22). Do you know why it took a whole night for every last one of the Israelites to cross the sea? More than two million people had to make their way to the other side, and God's great power protected every one of them. No one was left behind! "There was not one who stumbled" (Ps. 105:37).

The Egyptians Defeated

When the Egyptians discovered what had happened, they followed the Israelites right into the sea; horses, riders, chariots, and all the soldiers (Ex. 14:23). It was almost morning when God began His fight against the enemies of His people. His omnipotence made the wheels fall off the chariots so that they came to a screeching halt. The Egyptians looked at each other in fear. They knew that God was fighting against them (Ex. 14:24–25). Already the last soldier stood in the dry path God had made for the Israelites that night. "Let us flee from Israel, for the LORD is fighting for them against the Egyptians" (Ex. 14:25). But it was too late. God had said to Moses, "Stretch out your hand over the sea so that the waters may come back over the Egyptians, over their chariots and their horsemen" (Ex. 14:26).

So, the Lord's power brought back the waters once more. The watery walls collapsed on top of the Egyptians, and every last one of them was drowned (Ex. 14:27–28). They sank to the bottom of the sea "like a stone" (Ex. 15:5). That day God showed His people again that He "has power to help and to bring down." Will you say the verse we learned about God's great power? "For God has power to help and to bring down" (2 Chron. 25:8*b*).

Yes, now it was easy for the Israelites to trust the Lord and say the Lord is of "great power" (Ex. 14:30–31; 15:1–21). They had seen His power with their own eyes; but would they keep on trusting in His omnipotence? Sad to say, they did not! They soon forgot all about it.

What God Wants Me to Know

Isn't it too bad that the Israelites did not believe that God has power to help until after He had brought them safely through their troubles? Very often we are like that. We believed that God has power to save us, for we trusted in the Lord Jesus Christ. But somehow, when bad things come our way, we will not believe that He can and will help us if only we will trust in His omnipotence. God has given us many promises in His Word. He wants us to know that He keeps every one of them. God says, "Do not fear, for I am with you" (Isa. 41:10). "I will help you and make you strong; just trust Me." The Israelites did not know just *how* God would help them, and neither do we know. It is enough for us to know *that* He has power to help.

God's Word tells us much about our great and powerful Lord. God Himself says, "I am God Almighty" (Gen. 17:1*b*). He made our world by just speaking a word. He made you and He made me. He made a way out for His people when no one else could help them; and He will most certainly take care of your troubles and mine. Next time you just don't know what to do when a problem comes your way, will you try to remember that "nothing will be impossible with God" (Luke 1:37)?

Perhaps you would like to talk about how some things frighten you, and how God can help you in your times of fear. Some boys and girls are frightened of the dark—are you? Who made the darkness? God did. He did not make darkness to frighten you, but that you might rest better. He is omniscient and can see right through the deepest darkness, even though you cannot (Ps. 139:11–12). He is omnipotent and can keep all harm away from you; just trust Him. We will hear in our next lessons how God's omnipotence helped His people time and time again.

Lesson Review

Listen carefully to what I will say, then tell me which part of my sentence is right. God is omnipotent means: God is all present, all powerful, or all knowledge? Yes, all powerful. Here is another one for you. Who divided the Red Sea: Moses, the Egyptians, or God? God. Who fought for the Israelites: the Lord, Moses, or the soldiers? The Lord.

Tell me whether the next three things I am about to say are true or false: God built a dam to hold back the sea. False. God's omnipotence held back the waters. True. A cloud stood between the children of Israel. False. The Lord stood between them. The Lord tests us to see whether we will trust Him. True.

How did the Lord test the Israelites at the Red Sea to see if they would trust Him? God has power to help us also, but we must trust Him.

Memory Verse
"For God has power to help and to bring down." (2 Chron. 25:8*b*)

Chapter Seventeen

Omnipotence: Letting God Fight Our Battles

OVERVIEW

A. Subject: Omnipotence: Letting God Fight Our Battles—Joshua 6 and 10

B. Lesson Titles:
   1. Lesson One: The Walls of Jericho
   2. Lesson Two: God Fights a Battle

C. Story Objective:
   The Word of God cites many incidents of the Lord's omnipotence in action on behalf of His own. All these were recorded for our benefit and instruction (Rom. 15:4). However, learning to lean personally on God's strength alone, and trusting solely in His power is often a hard lesson. Once the believer fully understands and appreciates the fact that "Great is our Lord, and abundant in strength; His understanding is infinite" (Ps. 147:5), he will find comfort and perfect peace (Phil. 4:6–7; 1 Pet. 1:7). It is wonderful to know that when we are weak, He is strong and ever ready to manifest His power (2 Chron. 16:9*a*; 2 Cor. 12:9).
   The Bible stories used to illustrate the application of the omnipotence of God are both taken from the Book of Joshua, chapters 6 and 10.

D. Vocabulary and Doctrinal Concepts:
   1. Vocabulary: hailstones, walled city, wars and battles

2. Doctrinal Concepts:
   a. "I am God Almighty" (Gen. 17:1*b*).
   b. "The LORD strong and mighty" (Ps. 24:8*b*).
   c. "The LORD is the defense of my life" (Ps. 27:1).
   d. "The greatness of His might and the strength of *His* power" (Isa. 40:26*b*).
   e. "He gives strength to the weary" (Isa. 40:29*a*).
   f. "Have I no power to deliver?" (Isa. 50:2).
   g. "By My great power" (Jer. 27:5*b*).
   h. God's strength released through prayer (Jer. 33:3).
   i. "There is no authority except from God" (Rom. 13:1).
   j. "Lord God, the Almighty" (Rev. 4:8*b*).
   k. "The Lord God omnipotent reigneth" (Rev. 19:6*b*, KJV).

E. *Source Book* Keywords: Gideon, Joshua, Tabernacle

F. Activities:
   1. Suggested Visuals: none
   2. Games, Songs, Worksheets
   3. Memory Verse: "Great is our Lord, and abundant in strength." (Ps. 147:5*a*)
   4. Opening and Closing Prayer

Lesson One
The Walls of Jericho

Have you ever said, "I just cannot do this; I don't know how"; or, "This is too hard for me"? Well, there is One who never says this, One who never gets tired or weary. That One is God Almighty. He says instead, "Behold, I am the LORD, the God of all flesh [or living things]; is anything too difficult for Me?" (Jer. 32:27). No, nothing is too hard for God to do: "For nothing will be impossible with God" (Luke 1:37). He has omnipotence; His strength is everlasting strength. He never sleeps, but watches over us always and keeps us by His great power (Ps. 121:4–5) just as He watched over the Israelites and kept them so very long ago.

In our last lesson we talked about God's power over the sea in the days when Moses was the leader of the Israelites. Today, we want to begin to hear how God helped His people after Moses had died, and about a man who truly trusted in our all-powerful God. That man's name was Joshua.

Joshua, Israel's New Leader

After the death of Moses, Joshua became the new leader of the Israelites. God had chosen him to lead His people into the promised land (Joshua 1:1–2). God had made Joshua a very wonderful promise, a promise very much like the one God gave Jacob. It went like this: "And the LORD is the one who goes ahead of you; He will be with you. He will not fail you or forsake you" (Deut. 31:8a). Joshua need not fear his enemies in the Land. He was to be strong and of good courage—not strong in his own power, but in the power of God (Deut. 31:6; cf., Joshua 1:6–7; Eph. 6:10). "Joshua," God promised, "every place on which the sole of your foot treads, I have given it to you . . . No man will *be able to* stand before [or against] you all the days of your life" (Joshua 1:3a, 5a).

Yes, even before Joshua went into the Land, God had already as good as given it to him. All Joshua needed to do was to walk right in and take the Land. Joshua could count on God to keep His promise, for God has the power to make all His promises come true (Rom. 4:21). Suppose that I told you, "When you go out after church, I promise to give you every place in this country that your foot touches," could I keep my promise to you? Why not? That's right, because our land does not belong to me to give away, and I do not have the power to keep my word. But when God says He will do something, you can be sure that He will.

A Walled City

Already the Israelites under Joshua's leadership had crossed the river Jordan, and now they were coming near the great city of Jericho. Some must have wondered how they would ever get into that city, for a great, thick wall surrounded Jericho and the gates were tightly shut and locked. Joshua looked up. Perhaps he blinked his eyes, for all at once a man blocked his path. The man held a sharp sword in his hand. Joshua was brave and strong because God had told him to be; he did not back away in fear but asked, "Are you for us or for our adversaries [our enemies]?" (Joshua 5:13b).

"No," said the stranger, "I am the captain of God's angel armies." Can you guess who Joshua was talking to? Yes, the Lord Jesus Christ, God the Son Himself. Just as God had promised He was going before Joshua, ready to fight Joshua's battles in His omnipotence. Joshua dropped to his knees. He wanted to know what God's orders for him were (Joshua 5:14).

"And the LORD said to Joshua, 'See, I have given Jericho into your hand . . . And you shall march around the city, all the men of war [the soldiers] circling the city once. You shall do so for six days. Also seven priests shall carry seven trumpets of rams' horns before the ark [not Noah's ark, but the special golden box which stood inside the Tabernacle in which God's Word was kept]; then on the seventh day you shall march around the city seven times, and the priests shall blow the trumpets. And it shall be that when they make a long blast with the ram's horn, and when you hear the sound of the trumpet, all the people shall shout with a great shout; and the wall of the city will fall down flat, and the people will go up every man straight ahead'" (Joshua 6:2–5).

Do you think that if God can make water stand up like two high walls, He can also make a thick wall tumble down flat? Why, of course He can. Listen to what Psalm 147:5a says: "Great is our Lord, and abundant in strength." Can you say that with me? Psalm 147:5a is our memory verse for this lesson, but let's not only learn it, let's believe it because it is true.

Joshua Believed It

Although Joshua was a general and knew how to fight a war, he did not question God. He did not ask, "But why?" like some boys and girls I know who want to argue with their parents about what they are told to do. Maybe it did not seem the right way to fight against a city to some, but Joshua obeyed God's order. Everything was prepared for this strangest of all fights. No doubt God was pleased with Joshua and the Israelites. The Bible tells us that God is looking around all through the world and waiting to show those who trust Him how strong He really is. Listen: "For the eyes of the LORD move to and fro [they look up and down] throughout the earth that He may strongly support those whose heart is completely His" (2 Chron. 16:9a). Can you think of another verse about the eyes of the Lord? Yes, Proverbs 15:3. Let's all say it together. "The eyes of the LORD are in every place, Watching the evil and the good."

The "Battle" of Jericho

Joshua had called the priests and the soldiers and the people together. He passed on to them God's orders. Once every day, for six days, they must march around the walled city. But on the seventh day they were to march around the city seven times. No one must make any noise; no one must speak a word until Joshua would tell them when to shout. Then they must shout with all their might (Joshua 6:6–7).

Early the next morning, the Israelites were ready to do what God asked them. It must have seemed strange to the people of Jericho to watch the Israelites parade all around their city wall day after day, with only the sound of the trumpets and never a word spoken. First came the soldiers, next came the priests with their trumpets, then those who carried the golden ark-box, and all the people followed behind. Surely it was quite a sight to see.

The people of Jericho had shut the gates of the city wall because they had heard of the Israelites and feared them. Yet, no Israelite had tried to break down their wall, and they did not force open the gates. Surely the Israelites were acting foolishly. Who ever heard of anyone's taking a city by merely walking around it? Maybe the people of Jericho looked over the wall and laughed at the Israelites and made fun of them.

Do you want to know why God waited six days before He made the wall fall flat? Because He was willing to show the people of Jericho His great love and goodness. The golden ark was a picture of God's grace in saving all who will believe in the Lord Jesus Christ. If the people of Jericho would trust in God's Son, they would be spared; if not, they would not feel the greatness of God's love, but the greatness of His power in judgment.

"So he had the ark of the LORD taken around the city, circling *it* once . . . Thus the second day they marched around the city once and returned to the camp; they did so for six days" (Joshua 6:11, 14b).

God's Victory at Jericho

Then came the big day, the seventh day. It was barely beginning to get light when all the Israelites got up. This was going to be a busy day for them. Who remembers how many times they must walk around the wall of Jericho? Yes, seven times. Once, twice, three times, four, five, six times they had come. Surely they must have been really excited. I am sure it was hard for the girls and boys to keep from talking, or even whispering to each other. But now, the seventh round was completed. The priests raised the trumpets to their lips and blew them with all their might. Then Joshua, their captain, commanded, "Shout! For the LORD has given you the city" (Joshua 6:16b). Think what a shout that must have been! No doubt, the boys and girls must have shouted the loudest. And what happened then? The thick wall around the city of Jericho fell down flat, and the Israelites marched right in and captured the city (Joshua 6:20).

What was it that made the wall fall over? Was it the shouting of the people, or the blowing of the trumpets? No, it was the omnipotence of God. His might and power, not the might and power of the Israelites, toppled the thick wall. You see, just as once before at the Red Sea, so now God fought for His people. They had only to believe His Word and power and they would see great and mighty things happen.

What God Wants Me to Know

Do you wonder why God does such great miracles as those we read about in our Bible? He does them to prove His omnipotence. When God's children (Gal. 3:26) find out what God can do, they will trust Him all the more.

Once, many thousands of years ago, a man said to God, "I know that Thou canst do all things" (Job 42:2a). That man had just lost all that he had ever owned, even all of his children. His name was Job. Still he trusted in God's power. God saw this man's great faith and showed him that He is all-powerful indeed. In the end, God gave Job twice as much as Job had at the beginning of the story. And, do you know what? God is still looking up and down throughout all the world for believing boys and girls, men and women, who are ready to take Him at His Word. Are you such a boy, such a girl? Can you truly say, "I know that God can do everything"? Then believe God's promises, no matter what! Be like Joshua, and trust the Lord always.

But, do you know what the greatest miracle is that God can do? It is the miracle that makes you and me, who are sinners, into children of God. Now, this greatest of all miracles is one that only you can help bring about. In spite of God's omnipotence, He cannot save you unless you are willing to let Him. And, how can you show God that you want to be saved? By believing in the Lord Jesus Christ and in His power to save you forever. Will you make up your mind right now and believe in God's Son? He alone is able to "save forever" all who come to God by Him (Acts 4:12; Heb. 7:25).

Lesson Review

Can you tell me *how* and *where* God showed His omnipotence? Yes, at the Red Sea, when He made a path right through the water. He showed that He has power to help and to bring down. *How* and *where* else did God prove that He is a great God with great power? Right! At Jericho, where God made the thick wall of the city fall down flat so the Israelites could march in and take the city.

I want to see how well you remember your lesson. Joshua was to pick out how many priests? Yes, seven. What did the priests carry in their hands? Trumpets. Can you pretend you are carrying a trumpet in your hands? Four more priests were to carry the golden ark of the covenant, where God's Word was kept. They were to carry it carefully, for the ark is a sign that God is among His people and that He will surely fight for them as He has promised. The priests marched around the city wall, right behind the soldiers. Then came the priests who carried the golden ark. Who comes next? All the children of Israel. How often did they march around the wall the first six days? Yes, once. The priests blew their trumpets!

How many times did they go around the city on the seventh day? Yes, seven times. At the end of the seventh time around, Joshua commanded the priests to blow their trumpets and the Israelites to shout. God knocked down the wall by His great power, didn't He?

Memory Verse

"Great is our Lord, and abundant in strength." (Ps. 147:5*a*)

LESSON TWO
GOD FIGHTS A BATTLE

Do you think that if God can make a way through the sea, if He can make a thick wall fall down flat, He could also make the sun stand still in the sky and not let it go down? Certainly He can, for remember "nothing will be impossible with God" (Luke 1:37). In this lesson we will find out about the longest day in history, and about how God fought for His people to win a great victory for them.

Who remembers what God promised Joshua when he became the new leader of the Israelites? He promised to give Joshua every bit of land on which his feet would stand. He had told Joshua to be brave because no one would be able to stand against him as long as he lived (Joshua 1:5). Watch that promise come true.

God Repeats His Promise

With Joshua for their leader, the Israelites won victory after victory. Soon word got around that no one could hope to stand against Joshua and his soldiers. Had God kept His promise? I should say He had! Now Joshua was marching toward Gideon. The Israelites were not going to destroy Gideon for they had made a friendship agreement with them.

Near Gideon were five great cities. Each of these had a king ruling over it. When the kings heard that Joshua was on his way, and that the Gideonites had made peace with him, they were very angry at the Gideonites (Joshua 10:1–4). "Let's put all our soldiers and weapons together and fight the Gideonites. That'll teach them not to be friends with the Israelites," they said.

The people of Gideon were afraid. Quickly they sent messengers to Joshua to ask for help. "Come up to us quickly," they said, "and save us and help us, for all the kings of the Amorites that live in the hill country have assembled against us" (Joshua 10:6). Joshua was ready to help them, just as he knew God was ready to help him in his time of need. All that night Joshua and his brave soldiers marched so that they might fight the Amorites the next day (Joshua 10:7, 9). They did not stop to rest along the way; but that did not matter to them, for God had repeated the promise He had made Joshua some time ago. "Do not fear them," God had said, "for I have given them into your hands; not one of them shall stand before you" (Joshua 10:8).

Could God win a battle before it was even fought? Of course He can. He can do everything, remember? He is omni—what? Yes, omnipotent. All powerful. And, when God makes a promise, He has the power to keep it. Joshua knew this, and God wants us to know it also.

The Longest Day and the Shortest War

Often wars and battles last a long time, but when God fights a battle, you can be sure He makes quick and thorough work of it. The war against the five enemy kings lasted only one day, but yet, the day was the longest day of all time. Do you know how many hours are in a day? Right! Twenty-four hours. But this day lasted forty-eight hours, and on this long day a most unusual battle was fought—not with planes and cannons, not with bombs, but with weapons of God's own making.

The long night of marching toward Gideon was over. Joshua and his army had arrived, but God was there before them (Deut. 31:8). He had already begun to fight. "How?" you ask. God made the enemy panicky. He confused them;

He got them all mixed up in their minds and made them afraid of Joshua so that they turned around and fled as fast as they could get away. All Joshua and his soldiers had to do now was to chase them. Yet God was not through fighting for His people. Suddenly, as the Amorites tried to escape, the Lord bombarded them from the air with great big hailstones. Those hailstones fell from the sky and killed the enemy soldiers, but not one of them touched the soldiers of the Israelites (Joshua 10:10–11).

This is what God's Word tells us about this war: "*There were* more who died from the hailstones than those whom the sons of Israel killed with the sword" (Joshua 10:11*b*). Why was that? Think back to what God had promised: "I have given them into your hands." Joshua and his men had chased the enemy, but really it was God's battle and God's victory. Before that day was over, God once more proved His might and power. "Lord, we are not through yet chasing the enemy," Joshua prayed; "don't let this day end until all the battle is won." Joshua knew that God could do everything—even make the sun and moon stand still, high up in the sky (Joshua 10:12*a*). He called out, "O sun, stand still at Gideon, And O moon in the valley of Aijalon!" (Joshua 10:12*b*).

Could Joshua command the sun and moon? No, but he knew that God could, and that was enough for him. Joshua trusted God to do a miracle. Why, such a thing had never happened before! Everyone knows that the sun comes up early in the morning and goes down in the evening. Then the moon rises. But Joshua was sure that God who made the sun and moon could just as easily order them to stand still. And wonder of wonders, omnipotent God did as Joshua asked. There was daylight for another twenty-four hours.

Do you know why we have night and day? Let me see if I can explain it to you. God hung our earth in the heavens upon nothing. There it turns slowly around by itself. It takes twenty-four hours to make one complete turn. The earth also makes a circle around the sun, so that the sun shines on our earth at all times. Now, as the earth turns, the sun can only shine on one side of the earth. The bright side is called daytime, and the dark side is called night. When the earth has made one-half turn, daytime is almost over. The shadows lengthen, and soon darkness comes over the land.

We do not see too well in the dark, do we? Joshua knew that some of the enemy might escape once darkness came. But God is omnipotent. He can see through the darkness as easily as through the light (Ps. 139:11–12). He knew just what to do to make the day last for another twenty-four hours—He stopped the earth from turning! Did God do this just to please Joshua? Oh no, God did it to show His omnipotence, so that all might see and know of His mighty power. He did it also to reward Joshua's faith that nothing is too hard for the Lord. "And there was no day like that before it or after it . . . for the LORD fought for Israel" (Joshua 10:14). So God gave five great cities and their kings into the hands of the Israelites and Joshua that one day. Truly, "Great is our Lord, and abundant in strength" (Ps. 147:5*a*).

What God Wants Me to Know

Are you as sure of God's omnipotence as was Joshua? Maybe you say, "I would be, too, if God gave me such a wonderful promise as He gave Joshua—that no one can stand against him!" Well, He did! Listen to His promise: "If God *is* for us, who *is* against us?" (Rom. 8:31*b*). God is always on the side of His children. In fact, He is in us! The Bible says, "Greater is He who is in you [in us] than he who is in the world" (1 John 4:4*b*).

That's right! God's omnipotence is much greater than any trouble that can come into our lives. Have you forgotten that God has taken care of you up to this moment? Surely, God in His omnipotence won't find it too hard to keep on looking after you and after me if He can make the whole earth stand still. If He can chase away the enemies of His people, can He chase away your worries and fears? Maybe you just haven't thought to ask Him to fight for you. But now that you have learned of His power, you can safely trust Him. Will you?

But for all God's power and might, there is one thing He cannot do and still be righteous and just. Do you want to know what that is? He cannot force you to believe in Jesus Christ as your Savior. He cannot make you believe in His Son. God gave you volition so that you can choose for or against Him. Are you for God? Decide right now and watch God's omnipotence go to work for you. The Lord Jesus Christ said, "All authority has been given to Me in heaven and on earth" (Matt. 28:18*b*). He has power to save you. He has power to forgive your sins (Matt. 9:6) because He died for them on the cross. He has power to keep you forever and take you to heaven with Him. But, to be righteous, just, and fair, God must give you the freedom to make up your mind about Him. While we close in prayer, think this over very carefully. There will never be a better time for you to believe in the Lord Jesus Christ and be saved.

Lesson Review

I am thinking of two verses we have learned. Both of them have the word "power" in them. Both of them speak about our great God. Can you say those verses for me and tell where they are found? "For God has power to help and to bring down" (2 Chron. 25:8*b*). "Great is our Lord, and abundant in strength" (Ps. 147:5*a*). What kind of power does God have? Yes, all-power. What did we call God's all-power? Omnipotence, that's right.

We learned how God showed His omnipotence at the city of Jericho and at Gideon. God had won the battle before it started. His weapons killed many more of the enemy of His people than did the swords of the Israelites. Only God could have stopped the earth from turning; only He could have made the sun stand still in the sky.

What else can you remember about God? Listen to the clues I will give you and tell me the words from the Essence Box: God is always fair to everyone. Justice. He is the highest King. Sovereign. He has no favorites, but loves all of us the same. Love. He is in all places at the same time. Omnipresent. He is perfect goodness. Righteous. He has no beginning and no ending. Eternal life. He knows all things. Omniscient.

Does God prove to us that He is all these wonderful things we have already learned about? Or did He show it only to believers who lived long ago in the days of the Bible? Yes, He proves to us over and over what He is like, in caring for us and loving us and protecting us. He does as much for us as He did for all who loved Him long ago. And He will continue to do so as long as this world will last. He is eternal life, remember? More than that, He is unchangeable.

Memory Verse
"Great is our Lord, and abundant in strength." (Ps. 147:5*a*)

Chapter Eighteen

Immutability: God Keeps His Promises

OVERVIEW

A. Subject: Immutability: God Keeps His Promises—Genesis 6—8

B. Lesson Titles:
1. Lesson One: God Never Changes
2. Lesson Two: Noah and the Flood

C. Story Objective:
God is immutable. He is neither capable of, nor susceptible to change (Mal. 3:6). "The unchangeableness of His purpose" (Heb. 6:17b) "stands forever" (Ps. 33:11b). His sovereign decisions, His omniscience, and His holiness (His integrity—righteousness and justice), as well as all of His other characteristics, are always the same. He will keep His promises without fail, for there is "no variation, or shifting shadow" with God (James 1:17b). He "does not become weary or tired" (Isa. 40:28b), and His great faithfulness extends to all generations (Ps. 119:90; Lam. 3:23b).

D. Vocabulary and Doctrinal Concepts:
1. Vocabulary: change, promise, unchangeable
2. Doctrinal Concepts:
   a. The immutability of God stated (Heb. 1:12).
   b. God's thoughts are unchanging (Num. 23:19).
   c. The connection between eternal life and immutability (Ps. 102:24–27).
   d. God's unchanging Word (Ps. 119:89; Isa. 40:8).
   e. God's unchangeable works (Eccl. 3:14).
   f. The faithfulness of the indwelling Holy Spirit (John 14:16).
   g. The faithfulness of God to forgive (1 John 1:9).
   h. The faithfulness of God as Creator (1 Pet. 4:19).
   i. The faithfulness of Christ (Heb. 13:8).
      1) His immutability, veracity, and love are the basis for His faithfulness (Heb. 13:8).
      2) His faithfulness preserves us in time as well as in eternity (Lam. 3:21–24).
      3) All of God's promises for the believer's life on earth are based on Christ's faithfulness (Heb. 10:23).
      4) His faithfulness makes it possible for us to be victorious in times of testing (1 Cor. 10:13).
      5) His faithfulness is the basis of our stability (2 Thess. 3:3).
      6) His faithfulness continues even when we are unfaithful (2 Tim. 2:13).
      7) His faithfulness to the Father in the execution of the divine plan (Heb. 3:2).

E. *Source Book* Keywords: essence of God (immutability), Jonah, Noah, promises

F. Activities:
1. Suggested Visuals: immutability symbol, Trinity
2. Games, Songs, Worksheets
3. Memory Verse: "For I, the LORD, do not change." (Mal. 3:6a)
4. Opening and Closing Prayer

Lesson One
God Never Changes

Do you and I change? We certainly do. You have grown and learned to read and write. What's more, you will keep on changing as long as you live. We all change not only in size and looks, but we also change in our moods and in our behavior. Some days we are sweet and good and kind and obedient. Other times we are mean and naughty and grouchy, are we not?

Did you ever notice how things change around us? Why, just yesterday I picked a flower. When I picked it, it was a beautiful flower. But today it has changed, for it has wilted.

Can you help me think of some other things that change around us? Yes, the weather. Day changes into night and night into day, spring turns to summer, summer changes to fall, then to winter. There is only One who never, ever changes—and that is God. We want to learn about our unchanging God. As we do, we will learn another new word to add to the Essence Box. God is IMMUTABLE. Say our word with me—im-mu-ta-ble. That means God is unchangeable. How do we know that God is immutable? Why, He tells us so Himself: "For I, the LORD, do not change" (Mal. 3:6a). Malachi 3:6a is our memory verse for this lesson. Now, let's learn a story from the Bible that tells us of one of God's promises and shows us God's great faithfulness and immutability.

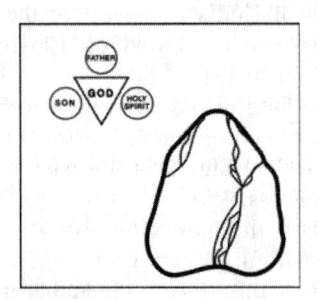

God Keeps His Promises

Did anyone ever make you a promise and then break it? Were you very disappointed? That happens to all of us, doesn't it? We, too, make promises and intend to keep them, but we don't always live up to our word, do we? The Bible is full of God's precious promises. Do you remember what the first promise was that God gave mankind? Yes, to send a Savior. Adam and Eve were the first people to hear this wonderful promise. But, it was given to us as well (Gen. 3:15).

Did God keep His promise? Did He send His Son to be the Savior of the world? Indeed, He did. We can trust God to keep all of His promises. He will never let us down or go back on His Word, because God's promises come from God's unchangeableness. What is our new word? Yes, immutability. Everything we have learned about God and what He is like backs up God's promises. First, God is sovereign. When He decides to make a promise, He means every word He says. God is righteousness. His promises come from His perfect goodness. God is perfect justice. His promises are always fair. He is love. All of God's promises come from His great love for us. He is omniscient. That means He knows exactly what promises we will ever need. He is omnipotent; therefore, He is able and has all power to make all His promises come true. He is eternal life. That means His promises are every bit as good today as when God first made them. Finally, God is immutable. He does not change like you and I change; so He will most certainly do what He said.

But, there are some places in God's Word where it seems like God changed His mind or that He repented about something that had happened. Does that mean God suddenly changed? No, God never changes, God is immutable; only His treatment of us changes depending on how we change, for good or bad. Do you remember the lesson we had about God and Jonah? Let's think back to it for just a moment so we will understand what the Bible means when it says that God changes His mind. God had sent Jonah to Nineveh with a warning that in forty more days He would overthrow the city and all who lived in it. But then God "did not do *it*" (Jonah 3:10). Remember how angry Jonah was about that? He went outside the city and sat, sulking. Why did God not put an end to the city of Nineveh as He said he would? Had God changed? No, the people of Nineveh had changed; they had trusted in the Savior and now had God's perfect righteousness. God could no longer treat them in judgment; He must treat them in grace! God's righteousness and justice will always punish sin and bless His righteousness because God is immutable. He never changes.

In the Garden of Eden, did God change when Adam and Eve sinned against Him? No, God did not change; Adam and Eve changed. They became sinners. Our story begins sometime after Adam and Eve left the beautiful Garden. By now they had many, many children and grandchildren, so that before long many people lived on the earth. Sin passed down from Adam to all of them (Rom. 5:12), and sin changed mankind from bad to worse as time went on. God, who is omniscient, looked down from heaven. He saw all the bad things that were done on the earth. More than that,

He knew the terrible thoughts man was thinking. And so we read, just three chapters after Adam and Eve became sinners, that "the LORD saw that the wickedness of man was great on the earth, and that every intent of the thoughts of his heart was only evil continually" (Gen. 6:5).

Was God going to close His eyes to all this wickedness? Would He pretend He had seen nothing bad? Never! God is righteousness and justice; He must punish sin wherever it is found. We read in the next verse that "the LORD was sorry [or sad] that He had made man on the earth" (Gen. 6:6a). Was God sad because He made man? No! God can never be sad because He is perfect happiness. This verse explains to us that God always punishes sin and wickedness in mankind. God is immutable; He never changes. God must punish those wicked people; He must treat them in judgment and justice. "And the LORD said, 'I will blot out man whom I have created from the face of the land, from man to animals to creeping things and to birds of the sky'" (Gen. 6:7a).

God meant exactly what He said. He would destroy, not just one city, but all living things on earth! Had God forgotten His first promise to send a Savior to save us from sin? If no one was left upon the earth, there would be no need for a Savior, would there? There would be no one to be saved! God remembered His promise perfectly well, and His judgment was fair and just. God can do no wrong. And because He is omniscient, He knew that none of the people whom He would destroy would ever believe in His Son (Isa. 46:10).

God had another plan waiting for the earth. He would spare one righteous man and his whole family; He would spare some of the animals, creeping things, and birds; and He would wash away the wickedness from the face of the earth and make a clean, fresh start. Do you know the man's name? Yes, Noah. And do you know the story? Right, about the flood. Do you remember our memory verse? "For I, the LORD, do not change" (Mal. 3:6a). Because God is immutable, He is faithful to do as He has promised. In our next lesson we will see how God made a promise and kept it.

What God Wants Me to Know

The fact that you and I are here should prove to you that God has been faithful to His promise. Jesus Christ came into the world to die for our sins, and God's promise to save all who will believe in the Lord Jesus Christ still stands. The only thing that can possibly keep God's promise of salvation from coming true for you is if you do not believe in Him.

I have taken the Lord Jesus Christ as my Savior. I know that some day I will live in heaven with God forever. I know it because God promised it, and because I took God at His Word (1 John 5:11–12). Perhaps you do not know where you will go after you die. Here is what God says: "He who believes in the Son has eternal life; but he who does not obey the Son shall not see life, but the wrath of God [God's judgment of the lake of fire] abides on him" (John 3:36). Do I mean to scare you? No, I just want you to know that God means what He promises—the bad and the good. Now it's up to you. "Believe in the Lord Jesus, and you shall be saved" (Acts 16:31).

God must not only punish the unbelievers, He must also discipline His children, believers in the Lord Jesus Christ (Gal. 3:26; Heb. 12:6). He must punish sin wherever sin is found, remember? When you have disobeyed your parents and they have to discipline you, does that mean they no longer love you? No, their love for you hasn't changed, but their treatment of you has changed. Do you know of a good way not to get disciplined? I do—obey your parents!

God, too, wants His children to obey Him and His Word. Because God is immutable, we can count on Him to be faithful to discipline us when we have disobeyed His Word and are out of fellowship with Him. But God promises us a way to recover that fellowship. "If we confess [name] our sins, He [God] is faithful and righteous to forgive us our sins and to cleanse us from all unrighteousness" (1 John 1:9). Whether God disciplines us or not, His treatment of us can only be fair and loving because God is immutable. Isn't it good to know that He will never disappoint us nor let us down, because He is the same, yesterday, today, and forever? Let us thank Him for it, shall we?

Lesson Review

God never changes. He tells us so in the words of Malachi 3:6a. Can you say that verse? Let's say it together. "For I, the LORD, do not change" (Mal. 3:6a). What word in the Essence Box tells us that God is unchangeable? Immutability. Can you recall some of the many ways in which God shows His immutability and faithfulness to us daily? Day and night, seasons, His promises, salvation, etc. When we read in the Bible that God changed His mind, does that mean God has changed? No. God is immutable. What does it mean then? That God changes His treatment of us because we have changed. What did God see happening on the earth? That the earth was filled with wickedness of thought and deed. What did God decide to do about that? God would destroy every living thing on earth except Noah, his family, and some of the animals.

Was it mean of God to promise to do this? No, God is perfect goodness, righteousness, justice, and love. The Bible says that with God there "is no variation [or change], or shifting shadow" (James 1:17b). The God about whom we read in the first verse of the Bible (Gen. 1:1) is the same, yesterday, and today, and forever!

Memory Verse
"For I, the LORD, do not change." (Mal. 3:6a)

Lesson Two
Noah and the Flood

Let's play a word game now. It's a game about God's immutability. Just remember these two words: "always" and "never." I will show you how it is done. Then, when you understand, you can pick up and go through the Essence Box and say it all by yourselves. Ready? God is *always* the same; He will *never* change. He is *always* sovereign; there will *never* be a time when God is not sovereign. God is *always* righteous; He will *never* be unrighteous. God is *always* perfect justice; there will *never* be a time when God is not just. God is *always* love; there will *never* be a time when God is not love. God is *always* eternal life; there will *never* be a time when God is not eternal life. God is *always* omniscient; there will *never* be a time when God is not omniscient. God is *always* omnipresent; there will *never* be a time when He is not omnipresent. God is *always* omnipotent; there will *never* be a time when He is not omnipotent. God is *always* immutable; there will *never* be a time when He is not immutable. He will *never* change. Very good; now just be sure to remember that, will you? Now, let's look at our story about God's immutability and His faithfulness to Noah and to all of us.

The Coming of the Flood, Genesis 6:8–22

"The eyes of the Lord are in every place, Watching the evil and the good" (Prov. 15:3). God looked down from heaven and saw the evil—all the badness of man, but He also saw the good—Noah and his family. Noah loved God and walked with God; that means Noah was in fellowship with God always (Gen. 6:8–9). Yes, Noah, his wife, and their three sons, as well as the ladies they had married, had all believed God's promise of the Savior. There were eight believers in the Lord Jesus Christ. Just eight in all the world! I am sure that Noah often talked to God in prayer; but don't you think Noah must have been surprised and happy to hear God speak to him one day?

"Noah," God said, "the wickedness of man is great on the earth" (Gen. 6:5a), and "the earth is filled with violence because of them . . . I am about to destroy them with the earth" (Gen. 6:13b). But God promised Noah and his family that he would be spared. He told Noah to build an ark; to make it just as He told him, and for Noah to bring animals and food enough for all. Noah listened carefully in order not to miss one word. All God was saying was so very important (Gen. 6:14–21).

Now, Noah was very busy building the ark, the first boat ever to be made! God had called it an "ark." Surely Noah's three sons must have helped their father cut down trees and trim them into planks for the boat, while their wives may have helped Mrs. Noah prepare the food. One could plainly hear all the hammering and sawing. What a busy home theirs was!

Their neighbors came rushing out to see what Noah was doing now. "What are you making, Noah?" they asked. "A boat?" They shook their heads. "Why, Noah, you must be crazy. What would anyone want to do with a boat? There's no water for miles around!" Every time they asked, Noah told his neighbors about God's coming judgment, about the rain and the flood. He also told them how to be spared—believe on the Lord Jesus Christ. But they just shook their heads and thought, "Noah has gone crazy; he even thinks God talked to him! Ha-ha, ha-ha!" Oh, how they must have teased Noah and made fun of him and his family! But Noah carried right on. He knew that God meant what He said. God was not a liar, nor did He change, and God had said that He would send rain and a flood. Surely He would do just that! For years and years, Noah kept right on building the ark and warning everyone about the flood. No one listened to or believed him. "Rain?" they laughed; "who ever heard of rain? It has never rained before (Gen. 2:6). There is no such thing as rain," they mocked.

Little by little, the ark was completed. The first, second, and third floors were now finished; the window and the door were properly placed. Noah had waterproofed the ark inside and out, and now all that was left for Noah to do was to take his family and the animals and enter the ark, with enough food for all their needs. All that Noah had done was exactly as God had commanded him (Gen. 6:22).

The Rains Came, Genesis 7

Again God spoke to Noah. "'Enter the ark, you and all your household; for you *alone* I have seen *to be* righteous before Me in this time. You shall take with you of every clean animal by sevens, a male and his female; and of the animals that are not clean two, a male and his female; also of the birds of the sky, by sevens, male and female, to keep offspring alive on the face of all the earth. For after seven more days, I will send rain on the earth forty days and forty nights; and I will blot out from the face of the land every living thing that I have made.' And Noah did according to all that the Lord had commanded him. Now Noah was six hundred years old when the flood of water came upon the earth. Then Noah and his sons and his wife and his sons' wives with him entered the ark because of the water of the flood. Of clean animals and animals that are not clean and birds and everything that creeps on the ground, there went into the ark to Noah by twos, male and female, as God had commanded Noah" (Gen. 7:1–10). Seven days before the rains came, the eight believers entered the ark and took with them the animals and the food. The Lord closed them in, safe and secure. How the people on the outside must have laughed! The first day had come and gone, and it had not rained. The second, third, fourth, fifth, and sixth days—still no rain. Maybe they said, "We knew it all along, Noah was out of his mind." But, oh, oh—then came the seventh day, and according to God's Word the rains started. It rained forty days and forty nights. The waters rose from below and came down from above until even the highest mountains were covered (Gen. 7:11–19).

Today we measure our rainfall. We think that if we have as much as four inches of rain, we've had a regular flood. Do you know how much water there was covering the earth when God at last stopped the rain? Thirty thousand feet, or six miles, all the way up. It looked as if the whole earth was only a sea. Even the mountaintops were covered with water (Gen. 7:19)! God had kept His word—every living thing had drowned in the waters of the flood. Only Noah and his family and the animals in the ark were saved (Gen. 6:16), for the Lord had shut them in safely, and the ark floated on top of the waters.

A New Beginning, Genesis 8

"But God remembered Noah and all the beasts and all the cattle that were with him in the ark" (Gen. 8:1a). You mean to tell me that God suddenly said, "Oh, my goodness, I had almost forgotten about Noah. I'm so glad I thought of him"? No, God never forgets! He is immutable. God is just reminding us that He did not forget that He had promised safety for Noah and his family; He would keep Noah in the ark until it was time for him to come out without danger. After one hundred and fifty days, the waters had begun to go down. After seven months, the ark came to rest on top of Mount Ararat. Still the waters continued to go down so that after ten months the mountaintops were again visible (Gen. 8:3–5). Finally, after forty more days God said to Noah, "Go out of the ark, you and your wife and your sons and your sons' wives with you. Bring out with you every living thing of all flesh that is with you, birds and animals and every creeping thing that creeps on the earth" (Gen. 8:16–17). What do you think was the very first thing Noah did? Yes, he thanked God for His goodness and for His immutability. Wouldn't you have thanked Him for keeping His promise?

God promised Noah that never "shall there again be a flood to destroy the earth" (Gen. 9:11b). And, so that Noah could be sure of God's promise, God added, "This is the sign of the covenant [or agreement] which I am making . . . I set My bow [My rainbow] in the cloud . . . and it shall come about, when I bring a cloud over the earth, that the bow [the rainbow] shall be seen in the cloud" (Gen. 9:12–14). How long would God's promise last? For as long as the earth remained. When God says "never," He means "never." Now hear what else God promised Noah that day, and then tell me whether God kept that promise or not. "While the earth remains," God said, "Seedtime and harvest, And cold and heat, And summer and winter, And day and night, Shall not cease [or end]" (Gen. 8:22). Indeed, God is true to His promise. Even though He does not have to prove it to us, He shows us His great faithfulness over and over, many times a day.

Have you ever seen the sign that God has not forgotten His promise to Noah and to us? It is a beautiful sign. What do we call God's "bow in the cloud"? Yes, the rainbow. Next time you see a rainbow, will you thank God that He is immutable?

What God Wants Me to Know

A rainbow is made of light. It appears to be made of seven beautiful colors. The light of the rainbow speaks to us of our wonderful God. Do you know what the Bible says about God? See if you can find 1 John 1:5. Can you read the last part of that verse with me? "God is light, and in Him is no darkness at all." The rainbow reminds us of God's goodness and love, of His sovereignty and justice. But most of all, the rainbow reminds us of God's unchangeableness—His immutability.

The rainbow we see today is exactly like the one Noah saw thousands of years ago. It is God's promise to you that no matter how hard the rain may pour down, there will never be another flood to destroy the whole earth. Just as Noah trusted God, so you can trust Him, too. Just as God kept His word to Noah, so He will keep His many promises to you. God's promises are all found in God's Word. God does not change; He cannot change. God's Word, the Bible, does not change. In His Word God tells us, "Everything God does will remain forever" (Eccl. 3:14a). That tells us that God is true to His Word. If He gave us the gift of eternal life through Jesus Christ, He will never take it away from us; if He promises us anything, He is faithful to His promises. You can count on Him!

Let's remember that it was God who found a safe place for Noah and his family. It was God who invited all the Noahs to come into the ark; it was God who shut the door after them so that the waters could not hurt them. He had promised Noah safety. Noah had believed God's promise, hadn't he? The greatest of all of God's promises is safety forever in the Lord Jesus Christ.

Why do we need a safe place? Because we are all born spiritually dead, and because the punishment for spiritual death is eternity in the lake of fire, when the last judgment comes. Even now if you have not believed on the Lord Jesus Christ you are dead to God even though you are alive and move about in your body. We all need to be saved. Some of us have believed God's promise of salvation already; some have not. While the rainbow reminds us of God's immutability and promises, the cross reminds us of His love. "For God so loved the world, that He gave His only begotten Son, that whoever believes in Him should not perish, but have eternal life" (John 3:16).

Right now God invites you to the only safe place from judgment—to safety in His Son (Rom. 8:1). Will you come to Him by believing He is your Savior?

Lesson Review

Shall we play a word puzzle game about God's immutability? Let's call it "missing words from our story." There will be twelve missing words, for that is the number of letters in the word "immutability." By the way, what does immutability mean? Yes, it tells us that God never changes. He cannot change, for He is "the same yesterday and today, *yes* and forever" (Heb. 13:8). Now, listen to my sentences, and see if you can fill in the missing words. Call out the answers to me. Here we go.

Our first missing word has four letters and the first letter is "r." The sentence goes like this; After Noah and his family entered the ark, God sent the *rain*. Second, Noah was told to take his family and the *animals* into the ark. Third, God always keeps His *promise*. Fourth, every *mountain* was covered with water. Fifth, the ark came to rest on top of Mount *Ararat*. Sixth, Noah and those with him were safe in the *ark*. Seventh, the sign of God's promise to Noah was the *rainbow*. Eighth, this word means God will never change, *immutability*. Ninth, Noah and his family trusted in the *Lord*. Tenth, there was one door and one *window* in the ark. Eleventh, the *water* remained on the earth for one hundred and fifty days. And now for the last sentence. Twelfth, when the right time had come, Noah and his *family* were allowed to leave the ark.

Memory Verse
"For I, the LORD, do not change." (Mal. 3:6*a*)

Chapter Nineteen

Veracity: God Is Truth

OVERVIEW

A. Subject: Veracity: God Is Truth—Psalm 12:6; 33:4*a* and John 8:45–46

B. Lesson Titles:
1. Lesson One: God's Word, Ways, and Works Are Truth
2. Lesson Two: God's Truth and Satan's Lies

C. Story Objective:

God is veracity or truth (Deut. 32:4). He stands for absolute truth, which is manifested in all His ways (Rev. 15:3), in all His works (Ps. 33:4), and in all His Word (John 8:45). Upon this very attribute of God and upon His immutability depend all certainty and assurance in life. God means what He says, whether it be by way of revelation, command, promise, or warning. His faithfulness backs up His Word of truth (Heb. 10:23; cf., 1 Kings 8:56*b*), making it the inerrant guide and the divine standard of right and wrong for every believer taught in the truth (1 John 4:6*b*).

The knowledge that God abhors all untruths (Prov. 6:16–19) should motivate us to truthfulness always (Matt. 5:37).

D. Vocabulary and Doctrinal Concepts:
1. Vocabulary: liar, right and wrong, true, truth, untruthful
2. Doctrinal Concepts:

a. The veracity of the Godhead:
1) The Father (Ps. 31:5*b*; Isa. 65:16; Jer. 10:10*a*; John 3:33; 17:1, 3; Rom. 3:4)
2) The Son (John 1:14; 8:32; 14:6; 1 John 5:20; Rev. 16:7; 19:11)
3) The Holy Spirit (John 14:17; 15:26)
b. The veracity of God makes Him a faithful and true witness (Jer. 42:5*a*; John 5:32, 37).
c. God's paths are mercy and truth (Ps. 25:10; 86:15).
d. All God's works are done in truth (Ps. 111:8; Dan. 4:37).
e. God's counsels are faithfulness and truth (Isa. 25:1).
f. God keeps faith forever (Ps. 146:6).
g. God makes known His truth and the truth of His salvation (Isa. 38:19*b*; Ps. 69:13).
h. The veracity of God's Word (2 Sam. 7:28; 1 Kings 17:24; Ps. 19:9; 138:2; John 17:17; 2 Cor. 6:7; Eph. 1:13).

E. *Source Book* Keywords: essence of God (veracity), Satan

F. Activities:
1. Suggested Visuals: Trinity, veracity symbol
2. Games, Songs, Worksheets
3. Memory Verse: "Teach me Thy way, O Lord; I will walk in Thy truth." (Ps. 86:11*a*)
4. Opening and Closing Prayer

Lesson One
God's Word, Ways, and Works Are Truth

Now we have come to the last word in the Essence Box. Do you think you can learn one more big new word? Of course, you can. And what is that word? Veracity. Can you say it with me? Ve-rac-i-ty. God is VERACITY. That means that God is truth.

Do you know what the very opposite of truth is? Yes, lies, and oh, how God hates lies! They are right at the very top of God's "hate list." Do you always tell the truth, no matter what? Can you truly say, "I have *never* yet told a lie"? I think not! Have you never pretended you did not do something just to get out of being punished? Have you never cheated in a game or in a test? Oh, there are so many ways in which we can be untrue—in our ways, in our words, and in our works.

Let me tell you about a little girl and what she did one afternoon. She had gone over to her best friend's house to play. My, but did they have fun playing together! She hated to think that it was soon going to be dark and she must be going home. Then something dreadful happened—she had not meant to do it, but she had broken her friend's favorite toy. She was too scared to admit it. While her friend's head was turned away, she carefully put the two pieces together, laid down the toy so that it would appear to be all in one piece, and excused herself. She said that she must be running on home because mother was expecting her before dark. Secretly, she hoped that her friend would pick up the toy and think that she, herself, had broken it.

She had not said one untrue word; yet she had acted in untruthfulness. There was untruthfulness in her, and God knew it all the time. He was not pleased, and He did not let her get away with it. Although nothing was ever said about the broken toy, this little girl lost her best friend. Why? Because she was too cowardly to go back and admit what she had done. To this day she remembers what she did, even though she is a grown lady now, and she knows that the Lord Jesus had to die for our sins so that we could come to know the true God.

No wonder the Bible says about us, "All have sinned and fall short of the glory of God" (Rom. 3:23). And, then the Bible points to God and tells us that He "cannot lie" (Titus 1:2). His ways are truthful always; His works are true, and so are His words. Do you remember learning a Bible verse about God's pure words? Can you still say it? Yes, "The words of the LORD are pure words" (Ps. 12:6a). They are true from beginning to end. As we study God's veracity, pay good attention; do not miss a single word. Then, when you find out how true God is and how He hates anything untrue, you will surely say, "Teach me Thy way, O LORD; I will walk in Thy truth" (Ps. 86:11a).

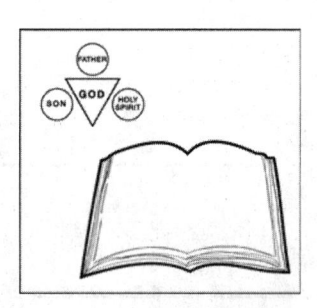

God Is Truth

Do you remember in our lesson about the rainbow, I told you that it is made of light? And, then I said that the rainbow reminds us of God, for "God is light, and in Him is no darkness at all" (1 John 1:5)? Light shows up what a person or a thing is really like, doesn't it? Darkness covers up things and hides them. Because God is light, He can see right through all our untrue ways, our untrue words, and our untrue works. He says that those who have nothing to hide from Him come to Him eagerly and gladly (John 3:21).

God stands for everything that is true. When He says that He will do something, you can count on it, for He means exactly what He says. Over and over and over in our Bibles we read these most important words: "Thus says the LORD!" (Ex. 4:22; 8:1; Judg. 6:8; 1 Sam. 2:27; 2 Sam. 7:8). And, once the Lord Jesus came to walk on the earth as a Man, He often said, "Truly, I say to you!" (Matt. 5:18, 26; 17:20), so that we could know some very important doctrine was coming up. Let's listen to the Lord Jesus, who is God and therefore veracity, speak words of truth.

"I am the light of the world; he who follows Me shall not walk in darkness, but shall have the light of life," He said (John 8:12). Do you think the Lord Jesus had spoken the truth, or had He lied to them by pretending He was someone He was not? Of course not; He had told them the truth, for God is truth. The Bible says that "God is not a man, that He should lie" (Num. 23:19a). The Bible also says that it is "impossible for God to lie" (Heb. 6:18). God could not tell a lie if He tried! But people who listened to the Lord Jesus had angry faces and didn't believe His words. They thought He was lying to them (John 8:13).

So, the Lord Jesus answered them: "What I said is true, and My judgment is true. That's why I tell you that if you do not believe I am He [God's Son, the Savior], you shall die in your sins! He that sent Me is true, and His Word is true" (John 8:14, 16, 24, 26, 32). Yes, every word the Lord Jesus had said to them was true. Yet, they did not believe Him (John 8:45). But there was someone whom they were ready to believe—not God the Father, but their father, the devil (John 8:44). That's what Jesus was telling them now, and oh, were they ever mad at Him! What did Jesus mean—their father, the devil? Wasn't God the Father the father of all the people in the world?

Let's see what God's true Word has to say about that. I read in Galations 3:26, "For you are all the sons of God through faith in Christ Jesus." The verse doesn't stop after "sons of God"; it goes on to say that God is only the Father of those who believe in His Son (John 1:12). All of us are either on God's side because we believe in the Lord Jesus, or we are on Satan's side because we do not. God is truth; Satan is the very opposite. He is a liar—the first liar who ever lived. Listen to what Jesus says about the devil: "He was a murderer from the beginning, and does not stand in the truth, because there is no truth in him. Whenever he speaks a lie, he speaks from his own *nature*; for he is a liar, and the father of lies" (John 8:44*a*).

The Father of Lies

There is truth in God the Father, God the Son, and God the Holy Spirit. Do you remember what I told you at the beginning of our lesson—God's *ways*, God's *words*, and God's *works* are all truth? But, now let's look at Satan, the devil. What is he like? Does he have truth in his ways? Once he did, but that was long, long ago, when God first made him, and when his name was not Satan, but Lucifer, the shining one. God had made this super-angel to serve Him and to praise Him. Lucifer walked in God's truth, obeying and loving God for a while (Ezek. 28:12–14). He was perfect in his ways because God had made him so (Ezek. 28:15*a*). So, we see that his ways were truth then, and so were his works and his words.

What had happened to change all this? One day Lucifer did not want to obey and serve God any longer. He had become proud of himself; he wanted to please himself, not God. In fact, he wanted to be God—not perfect in goodness and truth, but to have all the power that belonged to God alone. Well, just like the Lord Jesus had said that day to those who were listening but not believing His words, Lucifer "does not stand in the truth." Along with sin, untruthfulness had come into his life; and now "there is no truth in him" (John 8:44).

Now think, if Satan has no truth in him, will his ways and works and words be true? I should say not! I want to tell you some of the ways and works and words of our wonderful and truthful God, and how Satan lied about them. Perhaps you can think of a terrible lie Satan said to two people at the beginning of time.

What God Wants Me to Know

While Satan's ways are false and untrue, God's ways are always truth. Where can God's ways be found? In God's Word, the Bible. God wants us to know what He says in His Word. But He does not just want us to be hearers of His Word; He wants us to become doers. He wants us to pray, and mean it, too: "Teach me Thy way, O LORD; I will walk in Thy truth" (Ps. 86:11*a*).

All of God's Person—that is, all that He is and can do stands behind God's Word. By His Word, through the Lord Jesus, God made the heavens and the earth and all that is in them—even you (John 1:1–3). Then God made His promise of salvation. His beloved Son would come down to earth to die for sinners. Was God's promise true? Indeed, Jesus came to earth to save us. Those who saw Him and believed in Him said, "And the Word became flesh, and dwelt among us, and we beheld [saw] His glory, glory as of the only begotten from the Father, full of grace and truth" (John 1:14).

His ways are truth, His works are truth, and His words are truth. Listen to them speaking to you: "I am the way," He says to you, "the truth, and the life; no one comes to the Father, but through Me" (John 14:6). Do you believe Him? Then tell God the Father right now that you are putting your trust in the Lord Jesus Christ.

Lesson Review

What word in the Essence Box tells us that God is truth? Yes, veracity. God stands for truth, He acts in truth, and He speaks the truth. He hates every false thing, every lie, no matter how small it seems to be to us. When God speaks to us through His Word, His whole Person backs up what He says. What do I mean? Look at our Essence Box. God is the Highest King. When He makes a plan, no one can question Him and say, "But why?" His plans can only be good and right for us because God is righteousness and justice. His plans come from His great love, and His love for us is true. He doesn't just pretend that He loves us; He means it and has proved it by sending His Son to take the penalty for our sins. Because God is eternal life and immutability, His love is forever and unchangeable, true love. It isn't here-today-and-gone-tomorrow love.

God is omniscient. He can detect any little or big untruthfulness in us. So, be sure not to try to hide your sins from Him (Prov. 28:13)! He is omnipresent, right there with you while you act or speak untruthfully, even though you thought you were all alone and no one saw you, or heard you. He is omnipotent. His truth is all-powerful and can help you to be calm in trouble (John 16:33). And when God's children stand up for the truth of God's Word and God's Person, God is pleased and honored.

Now, who is it that stands up for everything that is untrue and false? Yes, Satan, the devil. Do you remember what the Lord Jesus had said about him? Right, that he, Satan, is the father of lies. I hope you did some thinking and are ready to help me tell how he turned God's true words into a terrible lie.

> **Memory Verse**
>
> "Teach me Thy way, O LORD; I will walk in Thy truth." (Ps. 86:11*a*)

LESSON TWO
GOD'S TRUTH AND SATAN'S LIES

Lucifer had become a sinful angel. It was true, he still had his beauty and power and his wisdom, which God had given him in the beginning, but now he had no more truth in him. God had to punish him. Lucifer could no longer be the greatest angel in heaven, and some day, so God had promised, he would be thrown into the lake of fire forever (Matt. 25:41*b*).

Lucifer or Satan did not like his punishment one bit. He flew off immediately to tattle on God to the other angels. "God is unfair," he claimed. Of course, that was an awful lie, since God is righteousness and justice. "See what He did to me?" Satan said, "Now, if you will come and serve me, I'll never be unfair to you, and together we can get even with God." Sad to say, many of God's good and holy angels became sinful angels, enemies of God (Rev. 12:4). They hated God and tried to hurt Him, but God was too strong for them. Their lies could not stand up to God's truths. So what do you think they did? Why, they turned against God's people whom He had just created and whom He loved so very much.

God's Truth and Satan's First Lie

In the Garden of Eden, Adam and Eve knew perfectly well what God's will and way was for them. God had told them truthfully what would happen to them if they disobeyed His rule about the tree of the knowledge of good and evil. Do you know what God's true word about this was? "If you eat of this tree," God had warned, "you shall surely die!" (Gen. 2:17).

For as long as Adam and Eve walked in God's way, all was well for them. God had taught them His way, and now they were to walk in His truth. But then Satan, the devil, came along, slipped inside the shiny serpent, and began to talk to Eve. "Didn't God tell you, 'You shall not eat from any tree of the garden'?" he asked in the voice of the serpent (Gen. 3:1). Eve shook her head; the truth was that God had forbidden them to eat of only one tree. Which tree? Yes, the tree of the knowledge of good and evil.

Eve had been so happy in the beautiful Garden that she had not even thought about the forbidden tree. But now Satan made it sound as if God were trying to keep something good from her and from Adam. She began to wonder about that, and that was just what Satan wanted her to do. "From the fruit of the trees of the garden we may eat; but from the fruit of the tree which is in the middle of the garden, God has said, 'You shall not eat from it or touch it, lest you die,'" she said importantly (Gen. 3:2–3). Now, turn to Proverbs 30, verse 5, and let's read that "Every word of God is tested; He is a shield to those who take refuge in Him." If only Eve had put her trust in God's pure words, instead of trusting Satan's lies!

Eve had even said more than God had told them—she had added the part about touching the tree. Read on in Proverbs 30, verse 6: "Do not add to His words Lest He reprove you, and you be proved a liar." Satan had Eve well off the path of God's way and onto his own way of untruthfulness. He hoped that she would follow his path and not God's. I imagine that Satan was already secretly rubbing his hands together, inside that serpent, saying, "Oh boy, oh boy, have I ever got her fooled!" Again he opened the serpent's mouth and spoke an outright lie: "You surely shall not die!" (Gen. 3:4). Why, Satan was actually calling God a liar. And, you know very well what happened next. Adam and Eve chose to become sinners. It looked as though Satan had won the first round, didn't it?

How God's Truth Overcame

Too late, Adam and Eve found out that God's Word, not Satan's word had been true. They lost their perfection and could no longer walk and talk with God as friends. But God made a way back for them. Jesus Christ is God's way back, for them and for us (John 14:6). When the right time came, God's promise came true. Jesus was born to be our Savior (Gal. 4:4; 1 John 4:14*b*). Oh, how Satan hated Him, who is full of grace and *truth*!

Remember how Satan tried to overpower the Lord Jesus out there in the desert? You learned how Satan kept throwing his fiery missiles at Jesus. One of his fiery missiles was Satan's lie. He knew that the Lord Jesus was going to do everything God's true Word commanded. Remember how Satan took a Bible verse and tried to make it say something it does not really mean (Matt. 4:6)? "Jump down from this temple tower," Satan tempted the Lord Jesus. "Since you are really the Son of God, jump, for it is written (in God's Word), he shall make his angels take care of you, and they won't even let you hurt your foot on a stone—at any time."

Now, who was adding to God's Word? Satan was, and adding to God's Word made him a liar, didn't he? We know that every time Satan tried to get the Lord Jesus to sin, God's Son showed that the truth of God's Word was stronger than any of Satan's fiery missiles, tricks, and lies. When you and I, who belong to the Lord, hide His Word in our souls we, too, will not sin against God (Ps. 119:11).

What God Wants Me to Know

God wants us to know what He is like. He wants us to learn that He is truth, that He is veracity. When we first know what truth is, we will recognize errors and lies. God's true Word warns us about the wiles, or tricks of the devil—and he has many tricks up his sleeve, believe me! To trick someone is to make him think that something which is not true is true. Tricking is actually cheating. The devil loves nothing better than to cheat us. How does he do it?

Satan is the most beautiful creature that ever came from the hand of God. I am sure that if we could see him, we could scarcely take our eyes off him. When he tricked Eve, he did not choose the ugliest animal in the Garden, but the most beautiful and cleverest one of them all (Gen. 3:1; 1 Tim. 2:14b). When he wants to deceive us, he can change himself into an "angel of light" (2 Cor. 11:14). Then he makes right seem wrong, wrong seem right. He makes television programs, comic books, and video games seem more important than the truths of God's Word. He makes a lie seem an easy way out.

Susan is a Christian; that is, she has believed that the Lord Jesus Christ died for her sins. Susan thinks she loves the Lord and His Word. Susan was looking at pictures in a book she received as a birthday present. Then her mother called from the kitchen, "Susan, honey, come and help me dry the dishes." Susan heard her, only she did not want to put down her book. She pretended she had not heard her mother. All of a sudden Susan remembered God's Word: "Children, obey your parents in the Lord, for this is right" (Eph. 6:1). That was the way the Lord had taught her, and she wanted so to walk in His truth, to please Him. Quickly she put down the book, confessed to the heavenly Father what she had done, and ran to help her mother.

Tom was a fine boy and a believer in the Lord Jesus Christ. All the neighbors liked him, especially Mr. Jones across the street. One day, to Mr. Jones' dismay, the kids playing ball in the neighborhood had broken one of his windows. Mr. Jones called Tom: "Tom," he asked, "do you know which of the kids threw the ball that broke the glass?" Oh, yes, Tom knew only too well—he had been the one. It would have been easy to shrug his shoulders and say, "I am sorry, Mr. Jones, I really don't know." But Tom looked straight at Mr. Jones. He couldn't let the Lord Jesus down. Tom thought, "My mouth will utter [speak] truth" (Prov. 8:7a), so he answered; "I did it." To Tom's surprise, Mr. Jones did not fuss at him. He only cautioned him to be more careful next time. It had paid to be truthful, hadn't it? Mr. Jones was glad about Tom's honesty, but even more important, God was pleased; and Satan? Well, Satan lost another battle.

Do you walk in God's truth? When you know that God's ways, works, and words are true, when you know how much He hates lies, when you know His Word, you can and will want to be truthful yourself. Do you want to know how? Truthfulness begins in the soul. When you think truth, you will speak the truth. Tom did some fast thinking, didn't he? But then he spoke the truth. Susan thought, too. At first she thought untruthfulness; that's why she acted untruthfully and pretended she had not heard. Later she thought of what God expected of her, and she acted as she should.

God says to His children, "Whatever is true, whatever is honorable, whatever is right, whatever is pure . . . let your mind dwell [or concentrate] on these things" (Phil. 4:8). If you do not, you must put all the ugly, false thoughts out of your mind by confessing them quickly. Then your ways will be true and pleasing to the great God of truth (Ps. 51:6). When you are tempted to tell a lie, remember the greatest liar of them all—Satan. Do you want to do his work for him? Then go ahead and lie, and your words will be as false as his own. I am sure that you would much rather please God and open your mouth to speak the truth. God made you, too, to serve and please and praise Him. Will you do it?

And, now, let's go back to that day when the Lord Jesus had finished telling His listeners about the father of lies, Satan. Did they believe the Lord Jesus Christ's words then? Did they put their trust in Him? They did not. They argued with our Lord, first about one thing and then another. And when they got nowhere by arguing, they picked up stones to throw at Him until they would have killed Him (John 8:59). Our Lord Jesus Christ said no more to them that day. Quietly and unafraid of them, He walked out on them, right through their midst. Yes, the Lord was right; all those men died in their sins because they did not believe His words, His ways, nor in the work He had come to do for them, and for all of us—to save us (2 Thess. 2:10).

Today, the Lord Jesus does not speak to us Himself. He speaks to us through His Word of truth. This very minute He wants to know where you stand—on His side of truth or on the devil's side of lies. He says, "Everyone who is of the truth hears My voice" (John 18:37b). His voice says to you, "I give unto you eternal life . . . I am the way, the truth and the life . . . do you believe in me?" Listen to God's Word: He cannot lie; He is veracity. He is offering you eternal life, just for believing in Him. All that He is backs up His offer. Trust Him, won't you, and find out the truth of His Word for yourself!

Lesson Review

When God says something, we can be sure His Word is true and trustworthy. When He does something, we know that all His works are done in truth because we know that God's ways are truth. What did we call the new word which tells us God is truth? Yes, veracity. Who comes along trying to turn God's truth into lies? Satan, doesn't he?

Memory Verse

"Teach me Thy way, O LORD; I will walk in Thy truth." (Ps. 86:11*a*)

Chapter Twenty

Divine Essence Understood and Applied

OVERVIEW

A. Subject: Divine Essence Understood and Applied—Daniel 3

B. Lesson Titles:
 1. Lesson One: The Golden Image
 2. Lesson Two: The Fiery Furnace

C. Story Objective:
  The doctrine of divine essence ascribes the same attributes to the threefold Personality of the Trinity (Deut. 6:4; Mark 12:29). As studied previously, the divine characteristics explain God's attitude and relationships to mankind. God's dealing with the human race where the salvation of man is concerned is the same in every dispensation (Eph. 2:8–9).
  Believers who have a thorough understanding of the doctrine of divine essence and apply it daily will have perfect peace and stability in every experience in life, whether good or bad (Isa. 28:29; Rom. 8:28). A particularly beautiful illustration of the application of this doctrine is given in the third chapter of the Book of Daniel. It is used as the Bible story background for this summary lesson.

D. Vocabulary and Doctrinal Concepts:
 1. Vocabulary: Babylon, divine, fiery furnace, impossible, possible

 2. Doctrinal Concepts:
    a. Sovereignty (Ps. 24:1, 8, 10)
    b. Righteousness (Ps. 97:6; Rom. 3:21)
    c. Justice (Deut. 32:4; Isa. 45:21)
    d. Love (Rom. 5:5; 1 John 4:16)
    e. Eternal life (Deut. 33:27; Ps. 90:2; Rev. 1:8)
    f. Omniscience (Col. 2:3; Heb. 4:13)
    g. Omnipresence (Prov. 15:3; Jer. 23:24)
    h. Omnipotence (Job. 42:2; Matt. 28:18)
    i. Immutability (Mal. 3:6; Heb. 13:8)
    j. Veracity (Deut. 32:4; Rev. 15:3)
    k. Applying what we know (Deut. 29:29; Joshua 1:8–9; Ps. 18:30; 48:14; Prov. 23:12; Eccl. 3:14; Rom. 4:21; 8:31–32, 38–39; 15:4; 1 Tim. 4:15–16; James 1:22; 4:17)

E. *Source Book* Keywords: Daniel; essence of God; Shadrach, Meshach, and Abednego

F. Activities:
 1. Suggested Visuals: none
 2. Games, Songs, Worksheets
 3. Memory Verse: "For nothing will be impossible with God." (Luke 1:37)
 4. Opening and Closing Prayer

Lesson One
The Golden Image

Have you ever wondered why we spent so many lessons learning what God is like? Getting to know someone takes time. We learn about God the Bible way: "Line on line, line on line, A little here, a little there" (Isa. 28:10b). It takes a lot of time to get to know all about God; in fact, it will take all eternity to discover how wonderful God really is! Once we begin to know God, we cannot help loving Him.

Many of you have piggy banks at home. Little by little, penny by penny, whenever you can, you keep adding to what you have saved. Now, why do you save your money? Just so you can say, "I have some money saved up"? No, you will want to do something with your money; perhaps you want to buy something special, or go somewhere special. In any case, you will want to keep it until you need it, won't you? Certainly you will not forget about that money!

Just so, as we learn little by little, we store up knowledge. But, how is knowing what God is like going to help me, you say? It will help you in time of need, just as it helped three young men who faced a terrible time of danger in their lives. They remembered what God is like, they believed what they knew, and they trusted God to make a bad thing in their lives turn out wonderfully well. Listen, and I will tell you about it.

The Golden Idol, Daniel 3:1–7

Far away, in the land of Babylon, ruled a mighty king. His name was Nebuchadnezzar. Do you remember learning about him? He was that king who dreamed one night about a huge tree that was to be cut down. For seven years he ate grass in the fields like an animal. Do you remember what the king's real trouble had been? Yes, pride. At one time he thought he was so great that everyone ought to fall down and worship him as though he were a god. That was why he had ordered a huge golden statue to be made in his likeness. Of course, all these things happened before God had taught him that God alone is most high in heaven and on earth.

The day came when at last the golden idol was all completed. What a sight it was! It was made of pure gold and stood ninety feet tall. It measured nine feet wide, and the king ordered that it be set up on a large, flat stretch of land where it could be seen for miles around. Then the king ordered a special holiday. Messengers were sent throughout the whole kingdom to call the princes, the captains and chiefs, the rulers and judges, and all other important people together. They all came, for the king's orders must be obeyed. "And they stood before the image that Nebuchadnezzar had set up" (Dan. 3:3b).

Suddenly, one of the king's servants called out loud and clear, "To you the command is given, O peoples, nations and *men of every* language, that at the moment you hear the sound of the horn, flute, lyre [harp], trigon, psaltery, bagpipe, and all kinds of music, you are to fall down and worship the golden image that Nebuchadnezzar the king has set up" (Dan. 3:4b–5). Then the messenger raised his voice even louder as he said, "But whoever does not fall down and worship shall immediately be cast into the midst of a furnace of blazing fire" (Dan. 3:6).

He had barely finished speaking when the musicians began to play a loud and shrill tune. What do you think the people did then? Why, they fell down on their faces and worshiped the golden idol, for they feared the king's anger. No one wanted to be burnt to death in the flames of the fiery furnace. It was ever so much easier to obey the king (Dan. 3:7). Only three men dared go against the king's command.

God's Essence and the Events on Earth
Psalm 33:13–14

Did God know what went on down below on earth? He most certainly did. What word in the Essence Box tells us that God knows everything? Omniscience. See if you can find Psalm 33, in the middle of your Bible. Follow along as I read what verses 13 and 14 say: "The LORD looks from heaven; He sees all the sons of men; From His dwelling place He looks out On all the inhabitants of the earth." God sees right into their souls and knows their thoughts long before they themselves know what they will think or say or do (Ps. 139:1).

"All the inhabitants of the earth" included King Nebuchadnezzar, and it included you and me. He knew Nebuchadnezzar's thoughts of pride; He knows our thoughts. Can you say our verse about God's omniscience? "O LORD, Thou hast searched me and known *me*" (Ps. 139:1). That day, God looked right inside all those people bowing before the golden image and He knew they were afraid of the king's law of punishment. But God knew something else. He had seen the three brave young men who had remained standing while all others fell flat on their faces before the golden idol. These young men were Jews who had important positions in Nebuchadnezzar's kingdom. They would worship only the true God, come what may. Their names were Shadrach, Meshach, and Abednego. God knew what a big decision these three young men must shortly make.

The Crisis, Daniel 3:8–15

Someone else had been watching the three men as well. They had noticed that every time the band played, Shadrach, Meshach, and Abednego stood tall and straight and refused to bow down to the golden image of the king. They were the jealous princes of the kingdom who hated the three friends and envied their important places in the land. "Well," they thought, "this will give us a good excuse to get rid of the three Jews." They hurried to the king. Oh, how they bowed and scraped before him to show how well they loved and respected Nebuchadnezzar, and they said, "O, king, live forever!" (Dan. 3:9b).

Would King Nebuchadnezzar live on earth forever? Of course not; his life had a beginning and an end. Only one King has eternal life. Who is that King? God, the Sovereign of heaven and earth. These wicked men went on to say, "You yourself, O king, have made a decree that every man who hears the sound of the horn, flute, lyre, trigon, psaltery, and bagpipe, and all kinds of music, is to fall down and worship the golden image. But whoever does not fall down and worship shall be cast into the midst of a furnace of blazing fire" (Dan. 3:10–11). And now the princes came closer: "There are certain Jews whom you have appointed over the administration of the province of Babylon, *namely* Shadrach, Meshach and Abed-nego. These men, O king, have disregarded you; they do not serve your gods or worship the golden image which you have set up" (Dan. 3:12).

The men had finished speaking. Perhaps they looked at each other slyly and wondered whether the king would even reward them for reporting this case of disobedience to him. They made it all sound as if the king had been so good to those three by giving them a place of rulership over Babylon, and now the three had turned against the king and had broken his law (Dan. 3:8–12).

Nebuchadnezzar was angry. "Bring Shadrach, Meshach, and Abednego!" he commanded. "Then these men were brought before the king" (Dan. 3:13b). Maybe King Nebuchadnezzar remembered how faithfully these three had served him in the past, for he gave them another chance. He asked, "Is it true, Shadrach, Meshach, and Abed-nego, that you do not serve my gods or worship the golden image that I have set up?" He boasted, "Now if you are ready, at the moment you hear the sound of the horn, flute, lyre, trigon, psaltery, and bagpipe, and all kinds of music, to fall down and worship the image that I have made, *very well*. But if you will not worship, you will immediately be cast into the midst of a furnace of blazing fire; and what god is there who can deliver you out of my hands?" (Dan. 3:14–15).

The Decision, Daniel 3:16–18

Fearlessly the three friends looked at the king. They were not the least bit frightened and had their answer ready. "If it be *so*, our God whom we serve is able to deliver us from the furnace of blazing fire; and He will deliver us out of your hand, O king," they said (Dan. 3:17).

What made these three so fearless and brave? They were serving the heavenly King. They knew that He is greater than any ruler on earth. They knew that God's plans were greater than any plans a man might make (Ps. 33:10; Isa. 51:12). Do you still remember learning about how Paul served his heavenly King? All the terrible plans his enemies made to try to get rid of him did not come true, for God's greater plan kept him safe. You and I are just as safe while we serve our Lord. He has His better plans for our lives; and no matter what people may try to do to us, our times are in God's hand (Ps. 31:15). No one can take us out of this life until the Lord is ready to call us home to Him.

But, did you notice two other very important words in the answer of Shadrach, Meshach, and Abednego? Let me say them again: "Our God whom we serve is able" (Dan. 3:17)! Yes, our God is able. They knew that although Nebuchadnezzar was a mighty king, God is mightier than all earthly kings put together. Can you tell me the word for God's all-power? Omnipotence. God has power to save and keep safe, doesn't He? If it pleased God, He could very easily set His three servants free, and all of Nebuchadnezzar's boasting and threatening would not harm them.

Are you sure that God is omnipotent, powerful enough to help you, too? Then, you can safely trust Him, come what may. When David was king, he once wrote, "The LORD is for me [He is my helper]; I will not fear; What can man do to me?" (Ps. 118:6; Heb. 13:6). "If God *is* for us, who *is* against us" (Rom. 8:31b)? Yes, "Greater is He who is in you than he who is in the world" (1 John 4:4b).

But, notice also that Shadrach, Meshach, and Abednego knew that if God was ready for them to die, then no matter what they did, nothing could save them from death. They knew that only God can decide the place, the manner, and the time for each of us to die. They made their decision—nothing or no one would keep them from serving and obeying God. God's plan and Word counted, not the king's. Shadrach, Meshach, and Abednego were sure that "Whatever the LORD pleases," that He would do, "In heaven and in earth, in the seas and in all deeps" (Ps. 135:6)—even in a fiery furnace!

What God Wants Me to Know

Shadrach, Meshach, and Abednego made their decision. It took a lot of courage, didn't it? They knew that their decision would surely send them into the burning flames which King Nebuchadnezzar had prepared for all who disobeyed his rule about worshiping the golden idol.

Do you know that an even greater King, the King of heaven and earth—God, has also prepared a fiery place? He never intended this place for any of us, only for Satan and for his sinful angels (Matt. 25:41b). The true God then made a rule. He would send His Son into the world to die for sinners, to make a new way for us to come and worship Him, the true God (John 3:17; Heb. 10:20). The Bible says that before Him "EVERY KNEE SHOULD BOW, of those who are in heaven, and on earth, and under the earth" (Phil. 2:10). But God gives us a choice: Believe in the Lord Jesus Christ or refuse to believe in Him. Refusing to believe in Him means that you will spend eternity in the lake of fire, with no one to help you (John 3:18).

Shadrach, Meshach, and Abednego made a good and wise choice—to obey God's rule rather than man's (Acts 4:19). Will you make your choice now? "And this is His commandment [His rule], that we believe in the name of His Son Jesus Christ, and love one another, just as He commanded us" (1 John 3:23). Your decision for the Lord Jesus Christ will save you forever.

Lesson Review

'Did they' or 'did they not'? Let me see how much knowledge you have stored up in your soul. I want you to listen to what I say and then decide whether the persons I talk about did or did not do what I said. Ready?

King Nebuchadnezzar put up or did not put up a golden statue of God? Did not. Whose golden statue did he put up? His own. Nebuchadnezzar did or did not call for a special holiday? Did. All the important people in the land came or did not come to see the statue because they loved the king? Did not come to see the statue because they loved the king. Why did they come? Because they were commanded to come. The king sent messengers or did not send messengers to every part of his great kingdom? The king did send messengers to every part of his great kingdom. First the musicians played a tune; then the messenger did or did not tell the people what they must do? Did not. What happened first? The messenger gave the king's rule; then the band played. All the people did or did not bow down to the golden image? They did not all bow down. How many people did not bow down to the image? Three. Shadrach, Meshach, and Abednego knew or did not know the king's command? They knew. Their enemies ran or did not run to tattle on them to the king? They ran. The king said or did not say, "Throw them in the fire at once!" He did not. The three brave men had to or did not have to make a choice? They had to. What was the choice they were given? To bow down to the idol and live, or to refuse to bow down and die in the fire. Shadrach, Meshach, and Abednego decided or did not decide to obey the king's command to worship his own image? They decided to disobey the king and worship God. They knew that God can do as He pleases. Why can He? Because He is sovereign. They knew that God was able to deliver them; why? Because He is omnipotent. They did not say, "O king, live forever," because they knew only one King has what kind of life? Eternal life. What King is that? God. They knew that God knew what was happening to them. How does God know? He is omniscient.

Memory Verse
"For nothing will be impossible with God." (Luke 1:37)

Lesson Two
The Fiery Furnace

*N*ow let's go on with our story, and we will see how knowing what God is like and what He can do made the three friends fearless and brave in a time of great trouble.

Nebuchadnezzar's Command
Daniel 3:19–23

The king had listened to Shadrach, Meshach, and Abednego. He had not expected such an answer. How dare they disobey him and obey their God instead. His face twisted with anger as he ordered that the fiery furnace was to be made seven times hotter than it usually was. He wanted to make sure that the three men knew what he had said so that they would be afraid, terribly afraid of him. No, Shadrach, Meshach, and Abednego would *never* escape death now; the king would make sure of that!

He sent for the strongest men in his army and had them bind Shadrach, Meshach, and Abednego with ropes. The three friends did not put up a fight. They just stood there and let the soldiers bind their hands and feet. They never cried out or struggled as they were carried to the opening of the furnace and thrown into the flames (Dan. 3:20–23).

Now then, tell me, was it fair and just of God to allow His faithful servants to be thrown into the fiery furnace for obeying Him? God is fair and just; He is righteous, perfect goodness. We must always remember that. We don't always know why God does what He does, but in the end we will always find out that God knows best (John 13:7b; Rom. 8:28). Shadrach, Meshach, and Abednego did not know why, nor did they complain and whine, "Why did You let this happen to us, God?" But God gave them an answer, as we will see.

Many people watched as the three faithful servants of God were bound and taken to the furnace. They saw them disappear in the fire. They saw great puffs of smoke and sparks rising up, and flames leaping into the sky. The heat was stifling, and the crowd stepped back. Suddenly everyone stared in horror. Something awful had happened. Flames shot out of the fiery furnace and killed the soldiers who had just thrown Shadrach, Meshach, and Abednego into the pit (Dan. 3:22b). Surely by now Shadrach, Meshach, and Abednego would be burnt to a crisp.

God Is Able, Daniel 3:24–28

The king watched from a safe distance. What was that? He could scarcely believe his eyes. He jumped up from his throne and cried out, "Was it not three men we cast bound into the midst of the fire?" "Certainly, O king," agreed the king's advisers. "Look!" the king insisted, "I see four men loosed [not bound] *and* walking *about* in the midst of the fire without harm, and the appearance of the fourth is like a son of *the* gods!" (Dan. 3:24–25).

Of course, King Nebuchadnezzar did not recognize the true God of heaven—Jesus Christ, God's Son. He just thought that the fourth man was one of the false gods whom he worshiped; or was it perhaps an angel? The king really began to think now. Do you know who the fourth man in the fire was? You are right! It was Jesus Christ, God's own Son indeed. Why was God there in the fire? There are really two reasons why He was there—one, because he is everywhere. What was the word we learned about God's presence everywhere? Omnipresence. The second reason was a promise God had made. See if you can think what that promise was. God first made it to Jacob, but He repeated it many times in the Bible. Yes, it was His promise of Matthew 28:20b. "I am with you always."

God keeps His Word; His Word is truth, for God is veracity. When He promised Jacob to be with him always, He meant it. He tells us, "I WILL NEVER DESERT YOU, NOR WILL I EVER FORSAKE YOU" (Heb. 13:5b). We are never alone, for God is with us always, even when things get really tough in life. God is omnipresent; never forget that! He was right there with His faithful servants, and they walked up and down and talked to each other in those flames.

And, then there was God's omniscience. What does that word mean? Yes, that He knows all things. What does John 21:17b say? Can you say this verse? "Lord, You know all things." God knew all along that no harm would come to Shadrach, Meshach, and Abednego. He only planned to have King Nebuchadnezzar see their faithfulness and love for the true God, and He wanted the king to see a real miracle with his own eyes. You see, God not only loves His children, He also loves the unbelievers—even this unbelieving, proud king. He loves us because He is love. In His love, He sent Jesus Christ to be the Savior of the world. That was how God proved His love for us all (Rom. 5:8). And now He keeps right on showing us His great love in so many, many ways, especially in His loving care of us. We should be like those three men, Shadrach, Meshach, and Abednego; we should trust and obey God always, for we know that He cares for us.

With God Nothing Shall Be Impossible
Daniel 3:28

King Nebuchadnezzar was curious. He came close to the furnace. He did not even think that the flames might burn him to death as they had the soldiers. He walked right up to the opening of the fiery furnace and called, "Come out, you servants of the Most High God, and come here" (Dan. 3:26b). I wonder whether he remembered his foolish bragging: "What god is there who can deliver you out of my hands?" (Dan. 3:15b).

God's three faithful servants heard the king's voice and stepped right out of the fire. The many people who had come to watch Shadrach, Meshach, and Abednego die were amazed when they saw them now. Why, the fire had had no power over their bodies! Not even one hair on their heads was singed, their clothes were not burned—and they did not even smell of fire, although they had been in the very middle of it! How was that possible?

I'll tell you how it was possible, for I know it from God's Word: "For nothing will be impossible with God" (Luke 1:37). God had shown that He *is able* to deliver, had He not? He has shown it many times since. His omnipotence comes to our help when we most need it; we can count on that.

There was no doubt now in King Nebuchadnezzar's mind that God—the God of Shadrach, Meshach, and Abednego—had delivered His servants who trusted in Him (Dan. 3:27–28). The very next chapter in the Book of Daniel tells us how Nebuchadnezzar came to put his own trust in our great God, but you already know that, for we have learned it.

The true story I just finished telling you happened more than twenty-five hundred years ago. Many things have changed since then, but God has never changed and will never change. He is what? Yes, immutable. If He could work miracles then, do you think that He can work miracles now? He certainly can and does. People all over the world are saved every day, and that is the greatest miracle of all. God protects His own, those who have believed in Christ and now belong to God's family. He surrounds them with His loving presence.

He is looking for men and women, girls and boys who will take a stand for Him, no matter what. Would you like to be brave and true to God like those heroes of the Bible we just heard about? Well, you can—not by your own power, but by the power of God the Holy Spirit in you. Yes, God can use you! He can make your life count for Him, for you know now that no one is like our great and wonderful God, and with Him "nothing will be impossible."

What God Wants Me to Know

Maybe you listened like Nebuchadnezzar did so long ago. Remember, he watched from a distance; he was outside of what happened. What happened did not touch him—or did it? It did not matter to him—or did it? Why, of course, it mattered very much. God knew that this proud king was still lost in spiritual death. God let him see His greatness, and His love for His own. Then, the king began to think!

The Lord is here with us now, and though we cannot see Him, we have learned of His presence, His greatness and power, of all that He is and can do. God knows only too well who is still lost in spiritual death—an outsider to God's family. He wants to make you His own. He is "not wishing for any to perish" (2 Pet. 3:9*b*). He wants you to do what Nebuchadnezzar did—believe in the Lord Jesus Christ and be saved (Acts 16:31). Will you trust our wonderful God and Savior (Acts 4:12)?

Lesson Review

Mike was a big fellow for his age. What's more, he had believed in the Lord Jesus as his Savior. He was usually very happy, but something seemed wrong with him today. Nancy noticed it at once in school. On their way home Mike told her why he was so upset—he had to go and see the dentist that afternoon, and he was frightened. Nancy reminded Mike of the promises God had made them in His Word: "Do not fear, for I am with you" (Isa. 41:10*a*); "When I am afraid, I will put my trust in Thee" (Ps. 56:3). Mike only shook his head. "That's fine for you, because you don't have to go to the dentist, but not for me."

Was Mike putting to use what he had learned about God? No. What was the matter with him? He did not put his trust in God to take care of him.

What did Shadrach, Meshach, and Abednego remember about God? That God is the greatest King, more powerful than King Nebuchadnezzar. They remembered God's promise first made to Jacob and repeated many times in the Bible: "I am with you always."

Memory Verse
"For nothing will be impossible with God." (Luke 1:37)

Chapter Twenty-One

Promotion

OVERVIEW

A. Subject: Promotion—1 Samuel 1—3

B. Lesson Title: Samuel's Promotion

C. Story Objective:

The Christian's life knows no plateaus. The believer either progresses or retrogresses. Paul, the Apostle, describes his life's pattern this way: "Brethren, I do not regard myself as having laid hold of [grasped fully or attained] *it* yet; but one thing *I do*: forgetting what *lies* behind and reaching forward to what *lies* ahead, I press on toward the goal for the prize of the upward call of God in Christ Jesus" (Phil. 3:13–14).

The Bible has much to say regarding the intake of doctrine and its application to the daily life (Job 23:12; Ps. 119:16; Jer. 15:16; Matt. 4:4; James 2:21–25). God can use and promote only prepared believers. Without distracting from the desirability of working toward good grades and resulting promotion in school, put across to your child that God's evaluation of their growth and production in the Christian life matters most (2 Cor. 10:18). The thing believers are to strive for is "the measure of the stature which belongs to the fulness of Christ" (Eph. 4:13).

D. Vocabulary and Doctrinal Concepts:
  1. Vocabulary: promotion
  2. Doctrinal Concepts:
    a. Grow in grace and knowledge (2 Pet. 3:18).
      1) Steps toward growth: hear, learn, fear, do (Deut. 31:12).
      2) Reverential trust in the Lord, the beginning of knowledge (Prov. 1:7a).
      3) Hear instruction and do not neglect it (Prov. 8:33).
      4) "Teach a righteous man, and he will increase *his* learning" (Prov. 9:9).
      5) Apply knowledge (Prov. 22:17; 23:12).
      6) "Knowledge increases power" (Prov. 24:5b).
      7) God's desire for us—our knowledge of Him (Hosea 6:6).
      8) Grow up in all *aspects* into Him" (Eph. 4:15).
      9) "Increasing in the knowledge of God" (Col. 1:10b; cf., 1 Thess. 4:10).
      10) "Your faith is greatly enlarged" (2 Thess. 1:3b).
      11) "Continue in things you have learned . . . sacred writings which are able to give you the wisdom that leads to salvation" (2 Tim. 3:14–15).
    b. Promotion.
      1) Promotion comes from the Lord (Ps. 75:6–7).
      2) "Exalt her [Bible doctrine], and she shall promote thee" (Prov. 4:8, KJV).

E. *Source Book* Keywords: priesthood, Samuel

F. Activities:
  1. Suggested Visuals: none
  2. Games, Songs, Worksheets
  3. Memory Verse: "But grow in the grace and knowledge of our Lord and Savior Jesus Christ." (2 Pet. 3:18)
  4. Opening and Closing Prayer

Lesson
Samuel's Promotion

*P*romotion Day in school is very important to you, and also to your mother and father, for they want you to bring home good report cards, with excellent grades in conduct especially! Do you know that in the Christian way of life there is Someone who is also interested in your conduct and "grades"? Who is it? Yes, God. He wants you to increase "in the grace and knowledge of our Lord and Savior Jesus Christ" (2 Pet. 3:18). God's children can only be promoted by pleasing and serving Him as they take in the Word of God and put it to use in their lives. God keeps careful check of our progress and will give us our final reward when we get to heaven.

Remember, He knows all, for He is what? Yes, omniscient. He sees all we do, for He is omnipresent. He judges all, for He is fair and just. He wants to use us all, but He can only use some of us. Would you like the Lord to use you? Would you like Him to promote you to something great and important so that your life will count for Him? Then listen to this true story from God's Word and you can discover how promotion from God can come your way.

Samuel Is Born, 1 Samuel 1:1–23

Elkanah and Hannah loved the Lord and each other. They were happy enough in their neat little house right by the twin mountain peaks in Ephraim, but they would be even happier if God would only give them a son of their own. Every year they traveled to close-by Shiloh to pray and to worship the Lord in the Tabernacle. That year Hannah knew just what she must do: She would ask the Lord God for a son, for surely, the Lord God could do all things! And Hannah prayed, "O Lord, if you will give me a son, I will give him back to you to serve you as long as he lives." Hannah went home happily, for she was sure that God would do as she had asked (1 Sam. 1:1–3, 11, 17–18).

And, Hannah was right; God answered her prayer. He gave her a son, and Hannah called him "Samuel," which meant, "I have asked him of the LORD" (1 Sam. 1:20). When the time came that Elkanah again must go to Shiloh to offer thanksgiving to God, Hannah stayed home. She knew that she must take good care of the boy whom God had loaned her for a little while. She must bring him up to please God, for some day soon he must go to live at the Tabernacle.

Samuel Comes to the Tabernacle
1 Samuel 1:24—2:11, 18–26

Samuel grew bigger and stronger. He could feed himself and dress alone, and Hannah thought he was ready to be taken to the Tabernacle to serve God and the old priest Eli. What an exciting day that must have been for young Samuel! Do you think he cried, or perhaps wondered whether his parents did not love him any longer? I think not. Hannah must have told him why God had let him be born; she must have taught him that obeying and serving the Lord was the most important thing anyone could do!

As the years went by, Samuel had birthdays, just as you and I do. He even had his birthday gifts, for we read that his mother made and brought him a new coat every year, each one a little larger than the one before. Perhaps Hannah joked about that, saying, "Samuel, let me see if I have guessed right this year. My, but how you have grown!" And grow Samuel did, not only in size but more importantly, in grace and knowledge of the Lord. Yes, Hannah and Elkanah were pleased with Samuel's progress, and so was the old priest, Eli. But what mattered most was that God was pleased with Samuel (1 Sam. 1:18, 21, 26). If Samuel had been given a report card, no doubt it would have been straight *"A's"* all the way down, starting with his conduct and obedience, then with his lessons from God's Word, and ending with the work he had been given to do.

Samuel Promoted, 1 Samuel 3

Do you sometimes complain because of your homework from school? If God were to give you a report card today, what would it look like, I wonder? And, do you think that God would be able to promote you? He was able to promote Samuel, and this is how it happened: God did not give him a written certificate of promotion; He did something quite different—He *called* Samuel.

Let me read to you what it says in the Bible. "Now the boy Samuel was ministering to the LORD before Eli. And word from the LORD was rare in those days, visions were infrequent. And it happened at that time as Eli was lying down in his place (now his eyesight had begun to grow dim *and* he could not see well), and the lamp of God had not yet gone out, and Samuel was lying down in the temple of the LORD where the ark of God *was*" (1 Sam. 3:1–3). Samuel had just curled up on his floor mat when he heard someone call his name. Samuel pushed back the covers and answered, "Here I am" (1 Sam. 3:4*b*). Today we would say, "Coming!" Quickly he ran to Eli and said, "Here I am, for you called me" (1 Sam. 3:5*a*). Eli was surprised. "I did not call," he said, "lie down again" (1 Sam. 3:6*b*). Obediently Samuel went back to bed. The voice called again: "Samuel!" Samuel got up without a complaint and went to Eli. "Here I am, for you called me," he insisted. Old Eli shook his head, "No, I did not call you, my son; lie down again" (1 Sam. 3:5–6).

Samuel tiptoed back to his mat. He was sure he had heard his name called. Why, there it was again: "Samuel!" Back flew the covers, as Samuel jumped up for the third time and ran to Eli's bedside (1 Sam. 1:6–8). Now, Eli was sure that God Himself must have spoken to Samuel. He told Samuel what to do if he heard his name called another time; he was to say, "Speak, LORD, for Thy servant is listening" (1 Sam. 3:9).

Eli knew that God had just promoted the boy Samuel to be God's own prophet. God had not spoken to anyone in so many, many years (1 Sam. 3:1); but now He had spoken to Samuel. Samuel was to take Eli's place. He would be the new prophet-priest of God's people.

What a wonderful promotion that was for the boy who had come to do whatever God wished! And, how do you think he came by it? Let's look again at Samuel's life, shall we?

How Samuel Got His Promotion

It says in Proverbs 20:11 that "It is by his deeds that a lad distinguishes himself if his conduct is pure and right." God, who knows all things, knew what Samuel was doing and thinking. What were Samuel's "deeds"? He served unto the Lord before Eli the priest (1 Sam. 2:11, 18).

There were many things to be done in and about the Tabernacle. The golden candlestick had to be lit; its wicks had to be trimmed. The bowls must be filled with pure oil, and the bread must be changed on the table. Wood needed to be cut and laid by the altar; flour and oil must be mixed for the offerings, and many other things besides. Certainly Eli had Samuel help him with these duties. Samuel did all he was told without whining or complaining, "Oh, Eli, must I, again?" What he did, he did to show the Lord his love for Him (Col. 3:17).

And, surely, there were many lessons from the Bible scrolls for Samuel to learn and memorize. He must know the rules God had made for His people, what offerings to bring and when, what judgments to teach the people, what sicknesses he must treat, for in those long-ago days the priests took the place of our doctors today. Then there were God's messages to be remembered and told forth. No, Samuel had little, if any time, to play or loaf. But that did not matter to Samuel. He kept right on doing what he should, willingly, gladly, obediently. So, we read that as Samuel grew up before the Lord, he was in favor with the Lord and men. That was why God had made Samuel the great man he was. God was with him and "let none of his words fail [for all the messages of God delivered by Samuel were fulfilled]" (1 Sam. 3:19).

Before long, the news that Samuel, the boy in the Tabernacle, was God's new prophet was made known in all the land. You remember learning about Samuel being sent by God to anoint David king, don't you? And how did Samuel always know what God wanted him to do? The same way you do: through God's Word (1 Sam. 3:20–21).

What God Wants Me to Know

God spoke directly to Samuel. Today, God speaks to us through the printed Word. God wants us to listen and hear every word He says. Samuel listened. Remember what he said? "Speak, LORD, for Thy servant is listening" (1 Sam. 3: 9). You have learned about God's Word and how important it is for us to know it. When we hear God's Word, we learn what He wants us to know. The next important step is doing what God wants us to do. Doing is the same as obeying. Are you a doer of the Word? Samuel was; that's why God promoted him!

God wants you to keep on growing in grace and in the knowledge of our Savior, Jesus Christ. When you do, you just cannot help pleasing God and people. Then, when the right time comes, God will promote you to do some special things for Him. That is the promotion which really counts!

Would you like all these things to happen to you? And, do you wonder just where to begin? "The fear of the LORD is the beginning of knowledge" (Prov. 1:7*a*). You have been listening to God's Word for some time now. You have heard what God is like. Now will you believe in His Son? Boys and girls who are not yet in school cannot possibly be promoted, can they? Just so, those boys and girls who have not believed in the Lord Jesus as their Savior and are therefore not in God's family cannot hope to grow in the Lord. Right now is your chance to be born into God's family (John 3:7; Gal. 3:26) by believing in Christ. Then you, too, can take in the Word that you might grow in grace (1 Pet. 2:2). Some day, God's promotion plans to have us become exactly like the Lord Jesus will come true. How glad you will be then that you have believed in Him today!

Memory Verse
"But grow in the grace and knowledge of our Lord and Savior Jesus Christ." (2 Pet. 3:18)

Chapter Twenty-Two

Thanksgiving Holiday Lesson

OVERVIEW

A. Subject: Thanksgiving Holiday Lesson—Daniel 6

B. Lesson Title: Daniel Thanks the Lord

C. Story Objective:
   Thankfulness toward God should be a constant mental attitude in every believer. If this attitude is present, it will express itself in praise and thanksgiving. Unhappily, this is not always the case. Man is not thankful by nature. We need to be reminded, and yes, are even commanded by the Word both to be thankful and to give thanks (Eph. 5:20; 1 Thess. 5:18; Heb. 13:15). Just as in childhood we must be taught to say thank you to those around us, so we must be taught to thank God in and for all things He has done and continues to do for us and on our behalf (Ps. 68:19).

   True thanksgiving is not to be confused with "courtesy," but is the outward, and sometimes unspoken, expression of the mental attitude of love. Yet, we are not to love and thank God only for what He has given us, but also for who and what He is. It has been rightly said that thankfulness is *thinkfulness*, and thanksgiving is *thanksliving*. True thankfulness is the response to God's grace in every circumstance of life and always brings about marvelous results. To illustrate true thankfulness, we have chosen the incident of Daniel, chapter 6.

D. Vocabulary and Doctrinal Concepts:
   1. Vocabulary: lion's den, thankfulness, Thanksgiving
   2. Doctrinal Concepts:
      a. "Say continually, 'The LORD be magnified!'" (Ps. 40:16).
      b. "He who offers a sacrifice of thanksgiving honors Me" (Ps. 50:23).
      c. "Enter His gates with thanksgiving" (Ps. 100:4).
      d. "Forget none of His benefits" (Ps. 103:2).
      e. "Let them give thanks to the LORD for His lovingkindness, And for His wonders to the sons of men!" (Ps. 107:8).
      f. "Let the redeemed of the LORD say *so*" (Ps. 107:2).
      g. "Tell of His works with joyful singing" (Ps. 107:22).
      h. "What shall I render to the LORD For all His benefits toward me?" (Ps. 116:12).
      i. "Giving thanks for all things" (Eph. 5:20).
      j. "With thanksgiving let your requests be made known" (Phil. 4:6).

E. *Source Book* Keywords: angels (guardian), Daniel, essence of God (love)

F. Activities:
   1. Suggested Visuals: none
   2. Games, Songs, Worksheets
   3. Memory Verse: "Give thanks to Him; bless His name." (Ps. 100:4*b*)
   4. Opening and Closing Prayer

Lesson
Daniel Thanks the Lord

We have a holiday coming up; do you know what it is? Yes, Thanksgiving. Right away everybody thinks, "Oh boy! No school, turkey with dressing, cranberry sauce, pumpkin pie, and all the other goodies we gobble down that day." Others can hardly wait to watch the ball game. But strangely enough, only a few think of the Lord who has given us good things to enjoy, not just on that day but every day we live (1 Tim. 6:17).

Sure, there will be many people in many churches on Thanksgiving, but will they really mean it when they sing and say their prayers? Not all thanksgiving is true thanksgiving. If we don't mean what we say, it does not count with God (Isa. 29:13*a*). Today we want to find out the difference between true and false thanksgiving and learn of a man whose true thanksgiving had some wonderful results.

False Thanksgiving

Not long ago we learned about two men who went up into the Temple to pray. Let's see if we can remember this man's prayer. Listen to it once more and tell me if his prayer was true or false thanksgiving. This is what he said: "God, I thank You that I am not like other men . . . I fast twice a week; I give tithes [or one-tenth] of all that I possess" (Luke 18:11–12, NKJV). Was he truly thankful? Was he praising God? He certainly was not. He was praising himself and thinking that God should be thankful to him for all he did.

Next, let's think of another person from one of our lessons. This one was King Nebuchadnezzar. One day he strutted about proudly in his palace gardens (Dan. 4:29–30). He said, "Look at my great country; I have built it by my power and for my honor." Was he truly thankful to God who had given him all he had? Why, there was not even one word of thanks; not even one thought of God in what he had said! God had to show him the hard way to be thankful, didn't He? It was not until seven years later that King Nebuchadnezzar praised and truly thanked God as he should have done in the first place (Dan. 4:34–37; cf., Ps. 50:23*a*).

True Thanksgiving

Twenty-six years later, a new king had begun to reign. Daniel who had been King Nebuchadnezzar's first helper was now helping King Darius (Dan. 6:1–3). Daniel was a truly thankful man. Never a day went by that Daniel did not stop at least three times to praise and thank God—at morning, noon, and night (Dan. 6:10*b*; cf., Ps. 55:17). When Daniel thought of God, he just could not help being thankful. How good God had been to him all these years; how wonderfully He had taken care of him and placed him into such an important position in the country.

Daniel not only thanked God for the good things that had happened in his life, but he also thanked Him when bad things came along. That means Daniel did not love God for what he got out of God, but for who and what God was. Daniel was not just giving thanks; he was living thanks so that no one could find fault with Daniel.

King Darius had appointed one hundred twenty princes to see to it that the work of his great kingdom was properly done. Over these princes were set three presidents of whom Daniel was the highest and most important, next to the king. That made the other princes angry and jealous. If they could only find something for which to blame Daniel, but they could not (Dan. 6:4). He had always been faithful, good, and true before God and before the king.

So the wicked princes began to make their plans. They now knew what they would do (Dan. 6:7). Quickly they went to see King Darius and told him, "All the princes and presidents have agreed to ask the king to make a new law. This law should read, 'For the next thirty days, if anyone asks for anything, he may ask it only of King Darius. And if he disobeys, he shall be thrown into the lions' den.'"

The King nodded. It seemed a good law to him. He did not ask if Daniel also had agreed to it, nor did he wonder why Daniel had not come with them. And so, the wicked princes had their way; the new law was signed and could not be changed (Dan. 6:8–9). Oh, how they must have chuckled to themselves, to think it had been so easy to talk the king into signing the new law which was really a trap for Daniel. Whatever Daniel would decide to do, he would most certainly get into trouble. If Daniel obeyed the king's law he would sin against God and His law (Dan. 6:5*b*); and, if he obeyed God, he would disobey the king and must be thrown to the lions (Dan. 6:7*b*). Then they would be rid of Daniel.

"Now when Daniel knew that the document was signed, he entered his house" (Dan. 6:10*a*). What do you think was the first thing Daniel did? Did he shut the wide open windows and pull down the blinds to make sure no one would watch him? Would he mark his calendar to be sure not to pray for the next thirty days? Or maybe he will pray and ask God to strike those wicked princes dead right away?

Let's see what the Bible says: "He continued kneeling on his knees three times a day [in front of the open window where people could see him], praying and giving thanks before his God, as he had been doing previously" (Dan. 6:10*b*).

Daniel went right on praising the Lord and thanking Him three times a day, as he always had done—in front of his open window. "Thank the Lord? For what?" you wonder. "That he would soon be thrown to the lions?" Of course not. I think that Daniel thanked the Lord for being *sovereign*. Daniel knew God was mightier than any human king, and His law was greater. And, surely Daniel thanked God for having a special plan for his life so that he could safely trust the Lord, even now. Don't you think he may also have thanked God for being righteous and just?

God made no mistake. Daniel knew that; God could never be unfair, as the princes had been. God is love. He loved Daniel very, very much (Dan. 10:11); He would be with Daniel no matter what may happen. Yes, Daniel would just trust the Lord to work out his problem. He would not fear the king and the princes (Ps. 118:6).

While Daniel was praying, the wicked princes came to spy on him. This was what they had been waiting for. All they need do now was to run to the king and "tattle" on Daniel (Dan. 6:11–13). What will the king say?

King Darius was angry, very, very angry indeed, but not with Daniel, with himself. Now he knew the princes had tricked him into making a bad law. All day long he tried and tried to think of some way to save Daniel's life. But, King Darius is only a man. There was nothing at all he could do (Dan. 6:14). Daniel must be put into the lions' den, just like the law said (Dan. 6:15). Then, a heavy stone was brought, and the den was tightly shut and sealed (Dan. 6:17).

Sadly the king went to his palace. Only the princes were glad about what had happened that day. And Daniel? Well, let's take a look at Daniel. God was pleased that Daniel had prayed and praised Him (Ps. 50:23*a*). He was going to see to it that Daniel would soon be able to tell of the wonderful thing God was going to do that night (Ps. 107:22). For that night, while the king tossed and turned on his soft pillow, Daniel went to sleep to the purring of lions. God had sent His angel to shut the mouths of the lions and they had become tame as kittens.

Oh, was the king ever glad when he found out that Daniel was still alive on the following morning! Was he hurt? bitten? scratched up? Had he broken any bones in the fall into that deep den? No! "No injury whatever was found on him, because he had trusted in his God" (Dan. 6:23*b*).

What God Wants Me to Know

Don't you think Daniel was glad he had been thankful? Being thankful had really paid off, had it not?

If anyone should be thankful, truly thankful I mean, it should be God's children (Gal. 3:26). God has done so much for us when He saved us from our sins, and He does so much for us every day and night. But do we stop to thank Him? Oh, oh! We forget, don't we? Am I ever glad that God does not forget to take care of us. In fact, the Bible says that God is kind to the *unthankful* (Luke 6:35*b*).

Do you ever have to remind your puppy to wag his tail when you give him his food, or when you play with him? Do you ever have to remind your kitten to purr when he is pleased? You do not! It seems they are more thankful than people. We could certainly learn from them!

Just see if you cannot think of at least five things to thank God for, count them off on your fingers to remind you. Every time you pray, instead of asking Him to do this and that for you, ask Him to remind you to "Give thanks to Him; bless His name" (Ps. 100:4*b*).

Today you have heard what wonderful things God can do for people who love and thank Him. But you have also heard that God is good and kind to the unthankful and evil (Luke 6:35*b*). To be evil is to be bad. The princes were bad, weren't they? We are not bad in the same way, but we are bad just the same. We are all sinners. God showed His kindness and love when He sent the Lord Jesus to die for our sins (Rom. 5:8).

God can do everything. He can shut the mouths of lions when a man like Daniel prayed and thanked Him, and He can open a door in heaven for someone like you. He, too, made a law, and it was a good law which said, "He [meaning anyone] who believes in the Son has eternal life; but he who does not obey the Son shall not see life, but the wrath [the anger, or punishment] of God abides [or remains] on him" (John 3:36). Those who turn away from God's Son unthankfully will not be sent to the lions' den, but to the lake of fire. And there is no way out of that place, for God's law cannot be changed.

But, do not be afraid. No one needs to go there. Like Daniel did so long ago, you can make up your mind right now to believe in the Lord Jesus Christ and trust Him. So, if you want to have a truly wonderful Thanksgiving, just tell God the Father that you believe on His Son this minute. Thank Him for wanting you in heaven and loving you so.

Memory Verse

"Give thanks to Him; bless His name." (Ps. 100:4*b*)

Chapter Twenty-Three

Christmas Holiday Lesson

OVERVIEW

A. Subject: Christmas Holiday Lesson—Matthew 2:1–12

B. Lesson Title: The Christmas Star Gives Light and Life

C. Story Objective:
Christmas had its beginning in eternity past when God so perfectly and so minutely planned man's salvation. However, man's finite mind could only receive the knowledge of this miracle plan of grace through progressive revelation.

We can safely assume that even the stars which God had placed into the firmament of the heavens had their definite part in the overall plan. The "Star out of Jacob," a description of the Lord Jesus Christ at His first advent, was announced in prophecy (Num. 24:17, KJV). Our Lord referred to Himself as "the bright morning star" (Rev. 22:16). Over two thousand years ago, a star guided the Magi to the place where the young Child was.

Today we eagerly wait for the reappearance of our Lord, "the morning star" (a description of the Lord at His second advent; 2 Pet. 1:19). The Word's advice to all unbelievers is that they are to "seek him who" makes the "stars" (Amos 5:8, KJV), "while He may be found" (Isa. 55:6a).

D. Vocabulary and Doctrinal Concepts:
1. Vocabulary: frankincense, gold, Magi, myrrh, resurrection, stars
2. Doctrinal Concepts:
   a. God made the stars (Gen. 1:14–18; Jer. 31:35).
   b. "We saw His star in the east, and have come to worship Him" (Matt. 2:2b).
   c. "The star . . . went on before them . . . they rejoiced" (Matt. 2:9–10).
   d. "By perseverance in doing good seek for glory" (Rom. 2:7).
   e. "I will give him the morning star" (Rev. 2:28).

E. *Source Book* Keywords: Christ (birth, wise men), Christmas, essence of God (eternal life)

F. Activities:
1. Suggested Visuals: none
2. Games, Songs, Worksheets
3. Memory Verse: "God has sent His only begotten Son into the world so that we might live through Him." (1 John 4:9b)
4. Opening and Closing Prayer

Lesson
The Christmas Star Gives Light and Life

Have you ever gone outside to watch the stars at night? Did you notice how high up they are in the heavens (Job 22:12) and how many of them there are? The Bible tells us that God knows their number and calls them by name (Ps. 147:4). No two stars are exactly alike (1 Cor. 15:41). Some seem to twinkle; others shine steadily. Some are brighter than others; and some are large, while others are small. Some streak across the sky, leaving a long tail of light; others look like they are fixed in their places.

We are not the only ones who have looked up thinking how big heaven is and how little we are in comparison (Ps. 8:3–4). Thousands of years ago, King David said, "When I consider your heavens, the work of Your fingers, The moon and the stars, which You have ordained [or commanded], my, how small and unimportant we are! And yet, God thinks of us enough to visit us."

Wouldn't it be terrible if God had not made the stars? How awfully dark the nights would be, and how scary! But God put the stars into the sky, like so many lamps, to shine by night and to bring light into the darkness. Not only for that reason did God make the stars; they are there along with the sun and moon, for signs and seasons, for days and years. That's how we have learned to count time. Today, I want to tell you about a very special star and of the work God had given it to do. God knows that star by its real name, but for now let's call it the "Christmas Star."

Christmas Is a Person

Do you know when Christmas began? Was it when "God has sent His only begotten Son into the world" (1 John 4:9b)? No, that was when Christmas came down to earth, but Christmas was always in heaven. Why do I say that? Because, Christmas is not just a holiday; Christmas is a Person—the Person of the Lord Jesus Christ, God's only begotten Son!

You see, Christmas has no beginning because God has no beginning. God is eternal life. Yet, God, because He is omniscient, had always known that some day Christmas would come down to the earth. Christmas had to come so that you and I and millions of others might have eternal life also.

Lights in the Darkness

Remember learning how beautiful and perfect God's world was when He had finished making it? But after Satan and his angels had sinned, the beautiful sky and the perfect earth became empty and dark (Gen. 1:1–2; Isa. 14:12–14; Ezek. 28:12–17). Would they stay that way? Oh, no! God had always known this would happen. He knew what He would do; "God said, 'Let there be light'; and there was light" (Gen. 1:3). Once more the sun and moon began to shine down on the earth: "*He made* the stars also" (Gen. 1:16b).

Soon, the earth was again ready for the first people to live upon it—Adam and Eve. As you know, they, too, disobeyed God and became sinners. It looked as though sin was in the world to stay (Rom. 5:12). Would the lights in heaven go out again? No, they kept right on shining, even to this day. And as they shine, they remind us of God's goodness, faithfulness, and love. They remind us that God will do what He promised!

The Promised Savior

Of all God's promises, the greatest by far is the promise of One who would save us from sin (1 Tim. 1:15b). Did He keep His promise? Indeed He did! Do you know that sometimes the Lord Jesus Christ is called the "Morning Star," or the "Bright Morning Star"? I wonder why He is called that? Let me help you think this through.

When do the stars shine? By night. God put them there to bring light into darkness (Gen. 1:15). Well, sin has brought darkness into the minds of people so that they cannot understand God (John 1:5; Rom. 1:21). Sin had also brought with it death (Rom. 6:23a). What we all needed was life and light, which only God could give. We needed the brightest Star ever to give life and light into our souls (John 1:4, 9; 8:12).

Stars are in heaven, and so was the promised Savior. Stars come out when the time is just right—at night; and God's Son, our Light from heaven, came when God said the right time had come (Gal. 4:4). He did exactly what He said He would; Who did? God. What did He do? He sent His only begotten Son. Where did He send Him? Into the world. Why? That we might live. How? Through Him. "God has sent His only begotten Son into the world so that we might live through Him" (1 John 4:9b).

We know this, for we can read it in our Bibles and learn how He came. But many years ago before His coming, those who believed God's promise kept waiting and wondering, "Will it be today? Will it be tonight?"

Wise Men Seek the God Who Made the Stars

At the time of the Lord's coming there lived some wise men, the Magi, in faraway Persia. We do not know their names, nor do we know how many there were. The Bible does not tell us. But we are told they were wise, not because of all the learning they had, but because they set out one day to seek and find the God who made the stars (Amos 5:8). This is how it happened.

The Star Appears

Night after night these Magi had looked up into the sky. They had studied the stars and had read of the God who had put them there. Knowing His promise, they wondered just how God would show them when His Son had come down to earth. Might there possibly be some sign in the heavens? (Num. 24:17).

There *was*! A bright new star shone in the sky, brighter than any they had ever seen. Where had it come from so suddenly? Could it be His star? Yes, it must be the star of the promised Savior! Just then, the star moved slowly across the sky. It fairly seemed to beckon to them, to call them without a sound saying, "Follow me, follow me, follow me!"

The Journey of the Magi

The wise men saddled their camels with all they needed for their trip. They took with them gifts for the newborn King. I am sure they did not know how long it would take them to find Him—nearly two years (Matt. 2:7; cf., Matt. 2:16). But had the Magi known, they would have gone just the same for they wanted to find Him, and that was all that mattered to them.

God's promise to those who want to know Him is that they shall find Him (Jer. 29:13). You may find Him by listening to God's Word as it is taught; the wise men found Him by following the star in the sky. They must have traveled by night and rested in the daytime, going wherever the star guided them. At long last, the wise men arrived in the city of Jerusalem (Matt. 2:1). They thought that surely everyone there would know where the new King was. But no, none knew of a newborn King; they only knew of old King Herod in his palace.

Herod's Question

Soon, news of the coming of the wise men from far-off Persia was brought to King Herod's palace. The King was told why they had come, and he did not like the news one bit (Matt. 2:3). Was another King trying to take his place? Quickly he sent for his helpers, the priests and leaders of the people (Matt. 2:4): "Tell me where this new King is to be born," he commanded. The men answered, "God's prophets said that He would be born in Bethlehem" (Matt. 2:5–6; cf., Micah 5:2).

Now, King Herod sent for the wise men. "What time did you say you saw the star?" he asked them. "Two years ago? Hmmmm." He leaned forward in his throne and said, "I'll tell you where to find Him—in Bethlehem. Look everywhere until you see Him, and when you have found Him, come back and tell me where He is so that I can go and worship Him, too" (Matt. 2:7–8). Herod's voice sounded as though he meant every word, but that was not so. The real reason why Herod wanted to know where the promised Savior was located was so that he could kill Him. Yes, Herod's mind was dark with unbelief and sin. He could not see God, nor did he want to.

The Wise Men Find Jesus

The wise men thanked King Herod and left the palace. "Where was the star pointing now?" they wondered. Oh, yes! There it was, moving just ahead of them. How glad the wise men were (Matt. 2:10). On and on went the star; on and on went the wise men, when all at once the star stood still, right over a small house, not over a big palace. Was this where the new King was staying? The wise men knocked softly at the door.

"And they came into the house and saw the Child with Mary His mother" (Matt. 2:11*a*). At last they had found Him—a little Child about two years old—and yet He was God, the God who had made the star which they had followed. God had come down to earth so that they could live forever. The Magi wise men dropped to their knees and worshiped Him. Then, they opened up their treasures which they had brought Him—gold and frankincense and myrrh (Matt. 2:11*b*).

"What strange gifts for a baby," we might think. Why didn't the wise men bring Him a rattle or a squeaky toy? They didn't, because they were truly wise; they knew that this was not just any baby, but the Son of God whom God had sent "into the world so that [they and] we might live through [faith in] Him" (1 John 4:9*b*).

The Wise Men Warned

The Magi could hardly wait to get back to Herod and tell him the good news that they had found the little Lord Jesus. They were only going to lie down and sleep a while and then go to Jerusalem and King Herod's palace once more. But, God knew better. He warned them in a dream not to tell Herod. So, they returned to "their own country by another way" (Matt. 2:12). As long as they lived, they would remember the star they had seen in the east which had led them to their Savior. They had given Him presents, that was true, but the present He had given them was much greater. They had given Him things of the earth—gold, frankincense, and myrrh, but He had given them heavenly gifts—life and light forevermore.

What God Wants Me to Know

If you have believed in God's Son, you, too, have been given these same gifts. How do I know? I know it from the Bible. Listen to what Jesus said: "I am the light of the world; he who follows Me shall not walk in the darkness, but shall have the light of life" (John 8:12). You can do better than the wise men did so long ago; you can follow the Lord Jesus, your own "Bright Morning Star," by listening to His Word and doing what it says.

God has already kept His promise to give you life and light, but there is one promise which He has yet to keep. Do you want to know what it is? God promised, "I will come again, and receive you to Myself; that where I am, *there* you may be also" (John 14:3*b*). When can you look for His promise to come true? Any day now; and when He comes, you will see Him, not just His star. I can hardly wait for that day! How about you?

And, what about you? What if you have not believed in Him as yet? Would you like to be real wise, as wise as those wise men who went out to find Him? Would you like to have life and light, those heavenly gifts which only Jesus can give? Would you like to have Christmas every day from now on? "God has sent His only begotten Son into the world so that we [all of us] might live through Him" (1 John 4:9*b*). How about it? Will you believe in Him today?

> ***Memory Verse***
> "God has sent His only begotten Son into the world so that we might live through Him." (1 John 4:9*b*)

Chapter Twenty-Four

Easter Holiday Lesson

OVERVIEW

A. Subject: Easter Holiday Lesson—Matthew 28

B. Lesson Title: The Risen Savior

C. Story Objective:
　The resurrection of the Lord Jesus was unique in that He was the first human being to come back to life with a changed and glorified body, eternal and immortal in nature (1 Cor. 15:20; 1 Tim. 6:16). All three members of the Trinity had a part in the resurrection of Jesus Christ: God the Father (Rom. 6:4; Gal. 1:1); God the Son (John 10:18); God the Holy Spirit (Rom. 8:11; 1 Pet. 3:18).
　Because He rose, we, too, shall be raised and have bodies like that of the Son of God (1 Cor. 15:52–53; Phil. 3:20–21).

D. Vocabulary and Doctrinal Concepts:
　1. Vocabulary: earthquake, manger, prophecy, tomb
　2. Doctrinal Concepts:
　　a. The Resurrection prophesied:
　　　1) In the Old Testament (Ps. 16:8–10; 118:22)
　　　2) By Christ Himself (Matt. 12:39–41; 16:21; John 2:19–21)
　　b. Resurrection narrative (Matt. 28; Mark 16:1–9; Luke 24; John 20)
　　c. Appearances after the Resurrection (John 20:14—21:25; Luke 24:15–51; Acts 1:3, 8–11; 1 Cor. 15:5–8)
　　d. Importance of the Resurrection (1 Cor. 15)

E. *Source Book* Keywords: cross, John, Peter, Resurrection

F. Activities:
　1. Suggested Visuals: none
　2. Games, Songs, Worksheets
　3. Memory Verse: "Because I live, you shall live also." (John 14:19*b*)
　4. Opening and Closing Prayer

Lesson
The Risen Savior

What kind of life does God have? Right, eternal life, life that has neither beginning nor ending. God cannot die. So when God the Son decided to come down to earth to be our Savior, He had to have our kind of life, human life, with a beginning and an end. Otherwise, He could never have died for our sins. His life on earth began like your life and mine, as a baby. He was born in Bethlehem, the Baby in the manger. Do you know how His human life ended? Yes, when He died for our sins on that cruel, wooden cross on Calvary.

The Lord Jesus had always known that the Father had sent Him to be our Savior (Luke 2:49; John 3:14–16; 9:4; Heb. 10:5–9). He was trying to tell His friends about His death and how important His death was to them and to us. Let's hear what He said to them one day: "Unless a grain of wheat falls into the earth and dies, it remains by itself alone; but if it dies, it bears much fruit" (John 12:24).

I wonder if the disciples understood what the Lord Jesus meant. Perhaps they didn't try hard enough because they did not want the Lord to die. They did not see that He was telling them He would rise from the dead.

But even though they didn't get it, we will make sure that you do. Have you ever seen a tiny seed of wheat? What is it good for? Is it a pretty decoration? Is it good to eat? Oh! It must grow first, you say. Well, let me put it in my pocket and wait for it to grow. Of course, nothing will happen there. It must be put into the ground and buried. The Lord Jesus, who Himself created the seed this way, used it to show us what would surely happen after He died and was buried.

When a grain of wheat is planted, the little dead seed lies buried in the ground, but in it is a germ of life. After a few days, a beautiful green plant springs up out of the ground. How the seed has changed! It is no longer the plain, little brown-seed body we planted; it has a new and greater body—a 'glorified' body. As we will see later in our lesson, after Jesus died for our sins and was buried in the grave, He, too, came forth in a new and changed body—a glorified body.

Jesus is both God and man. His human body had died on the cross, but God had not died. God has eternal life and omnipotence. As man, Jesus was dead and could not help Himself. God has power to raise that dead body to new life.

Now look at our plant again. Some time has passed, and at last the new plant has burst first into flower and then into fruit. There had been only one grain of wheat planted, and see how much fruit it has borne! Just as the Lord Jesus died and rose again for us, we who have believed in Him have become God's children (Gal. 3:26). God had one Son; now He has many, many children. Had the Lord Jesus not died and risen, there would have been no fruit. No one could have been saved. But now, we all have His promise: "Because I live, you shall live also" (John 14:19b). Yes, some day all of God's children will be given new and glorified bodies, exactly like that of the Lord Jesus. But now, let's hear how it all happened.

The Resurrection

One, two, three days had passed since the Lord Jesus had been nailed to the cross for the sins of the world, and one, two, three nights since He was buried in the tomb. All that time the door of the tomb had been sealed, and soldiers stood guarding the place where the Lord Jesus was buried. Why was that? Well, I can tell you: While Jesus' friends had forgotten His promise that He would rise after three days and nights, His enemies remembered it only too well. They thought they would make sure that He would not get out of that tomb, and that none of His disciples could steal the body to pretend that He had risen (Matt. 27:63–66). Now it was early Sunday morning, the first day of the new week. It had just barely begun to get light, when suddenly there was an awful earthquake.

In the great earthquake, an angel, bright as lightning, came down from heaven and frightened the guards so that they fainted (Matt. 28:2–4). The angel then rolled away the large stone which covered the entrance to the tomb where the Lord Jesus had been buried. There were the linen strips that had been wrapped tightly around and around His body, as was the custom in those days. But the Lord Jesus was not there! How long had it been since He was buried in that tomb? Yes, three days and three nights. The Lord Jesus Christ had risen! He was not dead any longer. He had already left the tomb before the stone was rolled away. The guards had not even seen Him leave. No grave could hold the risen Christ, for He was and always is God, and God is eternal life!

So it was by God's omnipotence that life came back into the human body of the Lord Jesus. Was it the same kind of life He had while He lived on the earth before He died? No! Think of our little seed. Jesus Christ had new life, resurrection life, and His body was changed. He did something in His resurrection body which you and I could never do—He walked right through the stone and rock without breaking the seal.

The Women at the Tomb

The sun was beginning to come up in the east when three women came to the tomb of the Lord Jesus. They were bringing spices and perfumes to put on the body of Jesus. Something was troubling them. "Who shall roll away the stone from the door of the tomb?" they kept wondering, for the stone was far too heavy for three women to roll away. Besides, as you will remember, the tomb was tightly sealed. But imagine their surprise when they got close enough to see that the stone was rolled aside, and the tomb was open (Mark 16:1–4).

"Oh, no," thought Mary Magdeline, "they have stolen the Lord's body; I must run quickly and tell Peter and John about this" (John 20:1–2). As fast as she could, she turned and made her way back to the city. But the other two women came closer to the tomb. They trembled as they looked inside. Who was that, sitting on the right side (Mark 16:5)? He didn't look like a thief. Why, he looked like an angel, which indeed he was! And, now the angel was speaking to them: "Do not be afraid; for I know that you are looking for Jesus who has been crucified [put on the cross]. He is not here, for He is risen, just as He said. Come, see the place where He was lying" (Matt. 28:5–6; cf., Mark 16:6).

What was the angel saying? Risen? What did it all mean? The women looked again. Yes, the tomb was empty! Only the linen strips were left. Oh, what wonderful, wonderful news! How sad they had all been after the Lord's death and burial! Now all that was changed. The Lord was alive! They listened carefully, for the angel was speaking again. "Go quickly and tell His disciples that He has risen from the dead; and behold, He is going before you into Galilee, there you will see Him," the angel said (Matt. 28:7a). The two women ran to tell the wonderful news to the disciples (Matt. 28:8).

The Race between Peter and John

In the meantime, Mary Magdalene had found Peter and John. She was all out of breath as she reported to them: "They have taken away the Lord out of the tomb, and we do not know where they have laid Him," she cried (John 20:2b). Peter and John jumped to their feet at once. They raced to the tomb, their feet fairly flying. John was there first, for he was younger and quicker than Peter (John 20:3–4).

It was true! There were the linen strips, still tightly wrapped, but Jesus was not in them. No one could have stolen the body and left the mummy-like wrappings like that! Peter went away, wondering about that (Luke 24:12). But John knew differently; the body of Jesus had not been stolen. John was convinced that Jesus had really risen from the dead (John 20:8).

A Surprise for Mary Magdalene

By now, Mary Magdalene arrived back at the tomb. She had not stopped crying since early that morning. This time she, too, decided to look in and see for herself the empty tomb. Oh, that was a morning full of surprises! First, the stone had been rolled away mysteriously; then the body of Jesus had disappeared. And now, Mary Magdalene must have blinked her eyes; was she seeing right? Two angels in dazzling white robes sat at the head and feet where Jesus' body had lain. "Why are you weeping?" they asked her, "and for whom are you looking?"

Suddenly, Jesus stood beside her and asked her the same question. Poor Mary Magdalene, her eyes were all puffy from weeping and full of tears. She could not see clearly through her tears and thought He was the gardener. She begged Him to tell her where the body of Jesus was. Then came the biggest surprise of all! The Lord Jesus said simply, "Mary!" She knew that voice—why, it was the Lord Jesus! She fell at His feet. "Teacher!" she exclaimed in joyous wonder (John 20:11–16).

What God Wants Me to Know

Do you wonder why Mary Magdalene did not recognize the Lord? Didn't she know Him? Of course she did, but you must remember that she did not expect Him to be alive. If you had seen a friend die, and watched him being put into a grave, you probably would not recognize him if you saw him walking around three days later. You would be sure it was someone else. Yet, I believe there was also another reason. You see, Jesus now had a resurrection body, a new and changed body, a body that was made over for heaven. We don't know exactly what it looked like. We know that it had flesh and bones, yet it could go right through a wall, even a closed steel door.

Because Jesus rose with a changed body, glorified and eternal, we, too, have the promise that our bodies will be changed and made just like His own. (Phil. 3:21). Aren't you glad you believed in Him?

"Because I live, you shall live also" (John 14:19b). What a wonderful promise! Jesus made that promise come true when He rose to live forevermore. "Jesus is risen!" What wonderful news! If Jesus had not risen, we would still be dead in our sins. But He did rise from the dead!

When Jesus Christ came out of the grave, that was God's promise that our sins will be forgiven if we will believe in God's Son. When we put our trust in Him, God gives us His perfect righteousness. More than that, He gives us His eternal life. Would you like God's promise to come true for you? Then believe in Christ right now!

Memory Verse

"Because I live, you shall live also." (John 14:19b)

Visual Aids

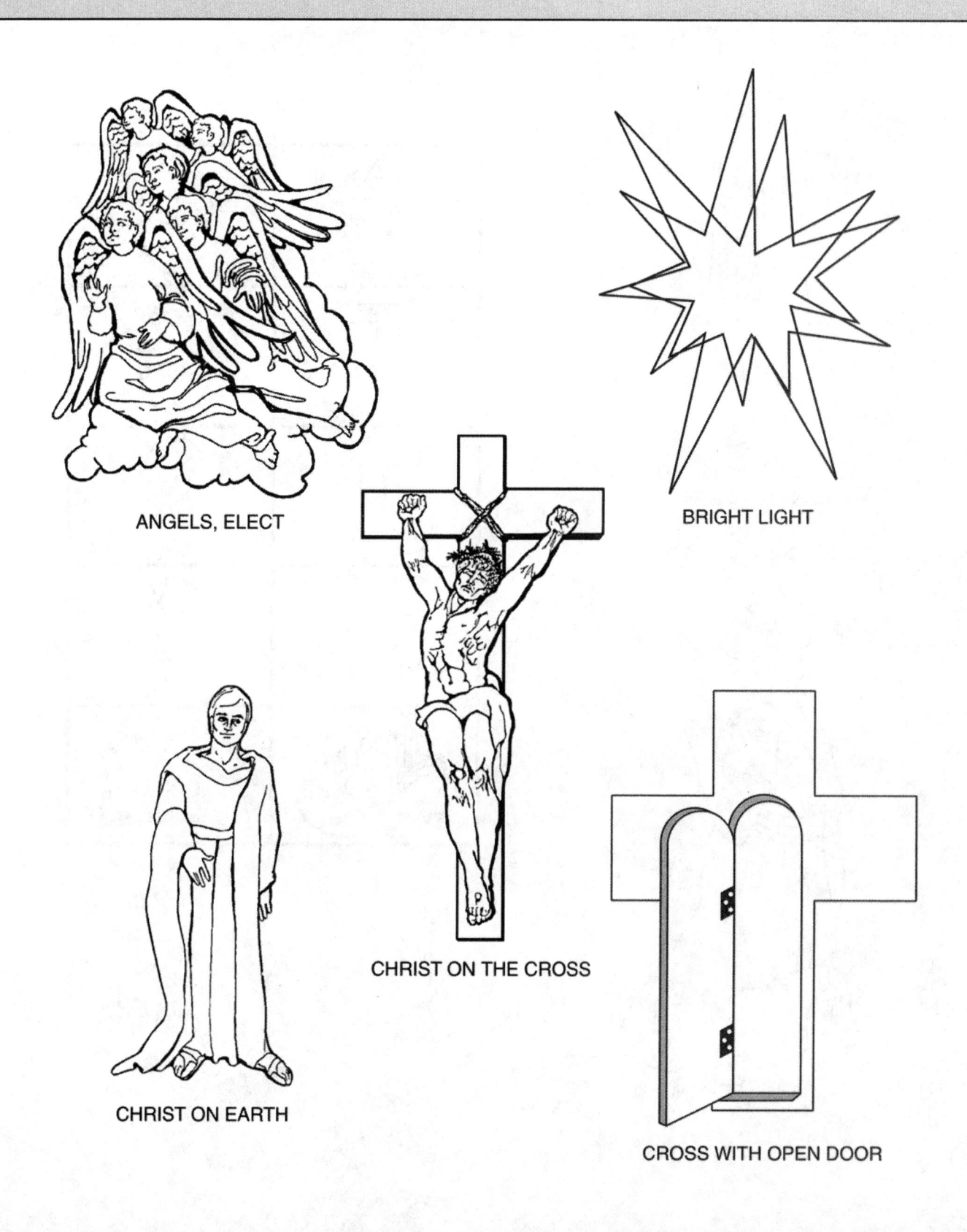

ANGELS, ELECT

BRIGHT LIGHT

CHRIST ON THE CROSS

CHRIST ON EARTH

CROSS WITH OPEN DOOR

138 CHILDREN'S BIBLE STUDIES: WHAT IS GOD LIKE?

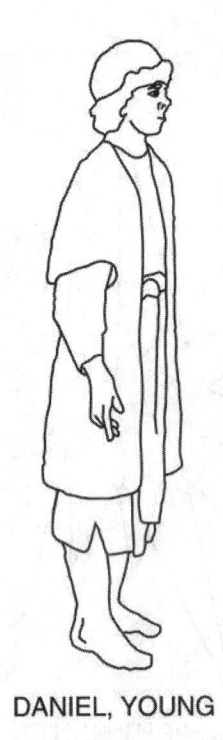

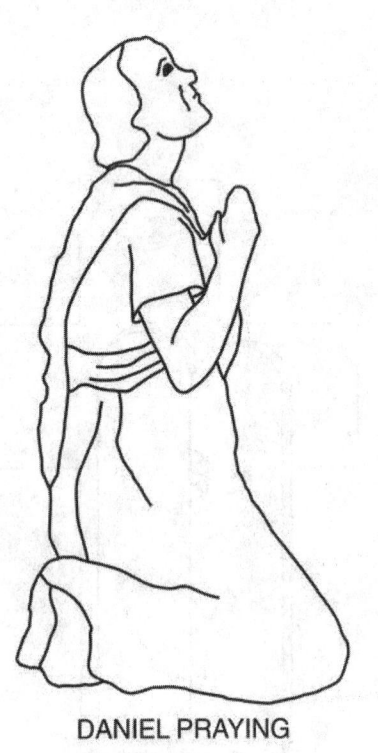

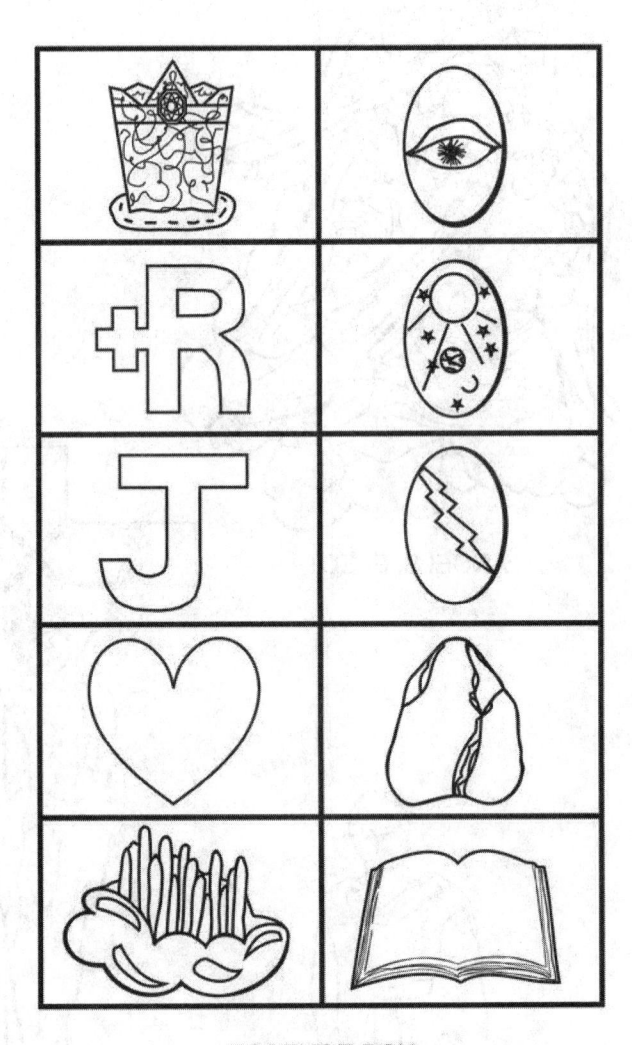

DANIEL, YOUNG

DANIEL PRAYING

ESSENCE BOX

Visual Aids 139

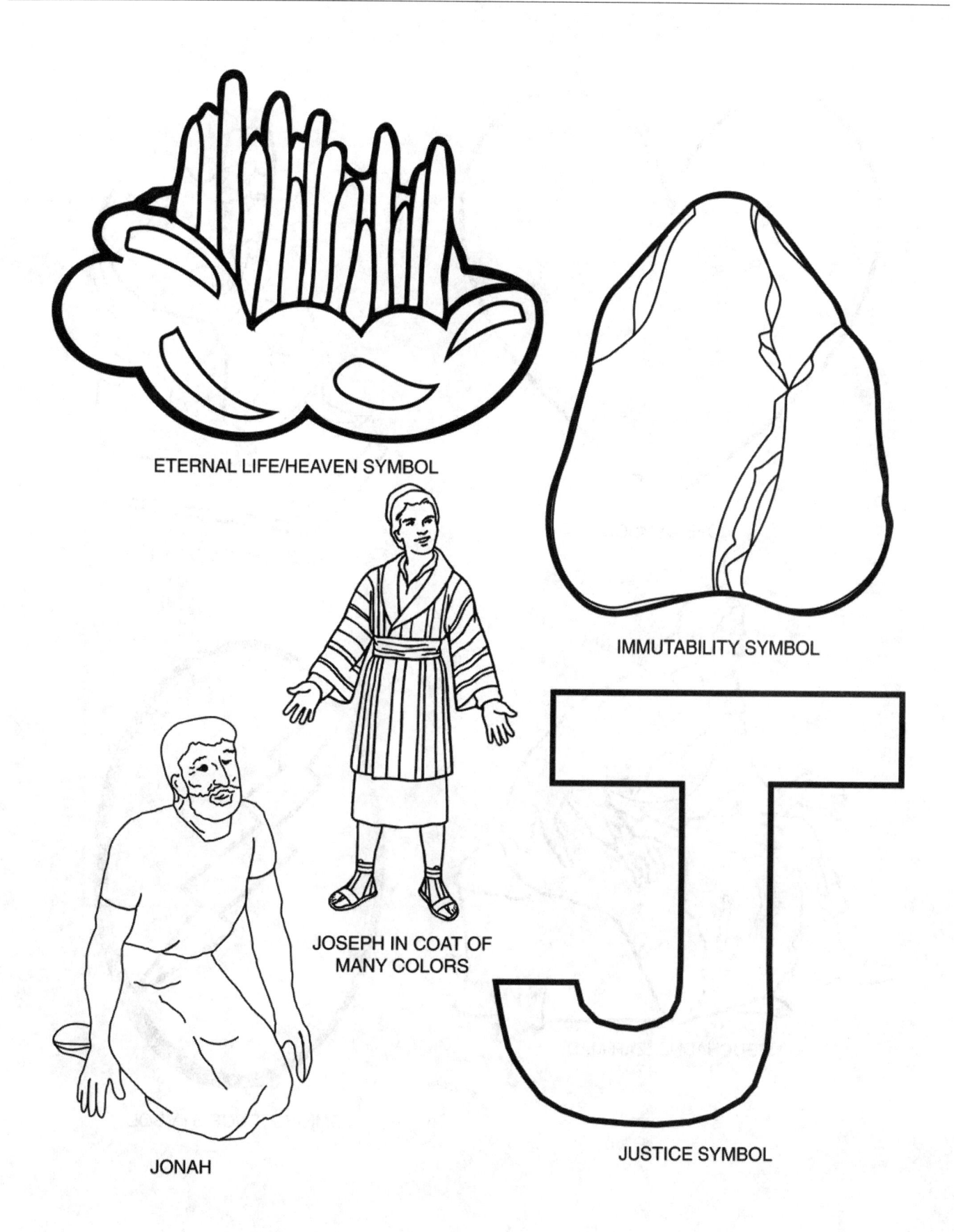

ETERNAL LIFE/HEAVEN SYMBOL

IMMUTABILITY SYMBOL

JOSEPH IN COAT OF
MANY COLORS

JONAH

JUSTICE SYMBOL

140   CHILDREN'S BIBLE STUDIES: WHAT IS GOD LIKE?

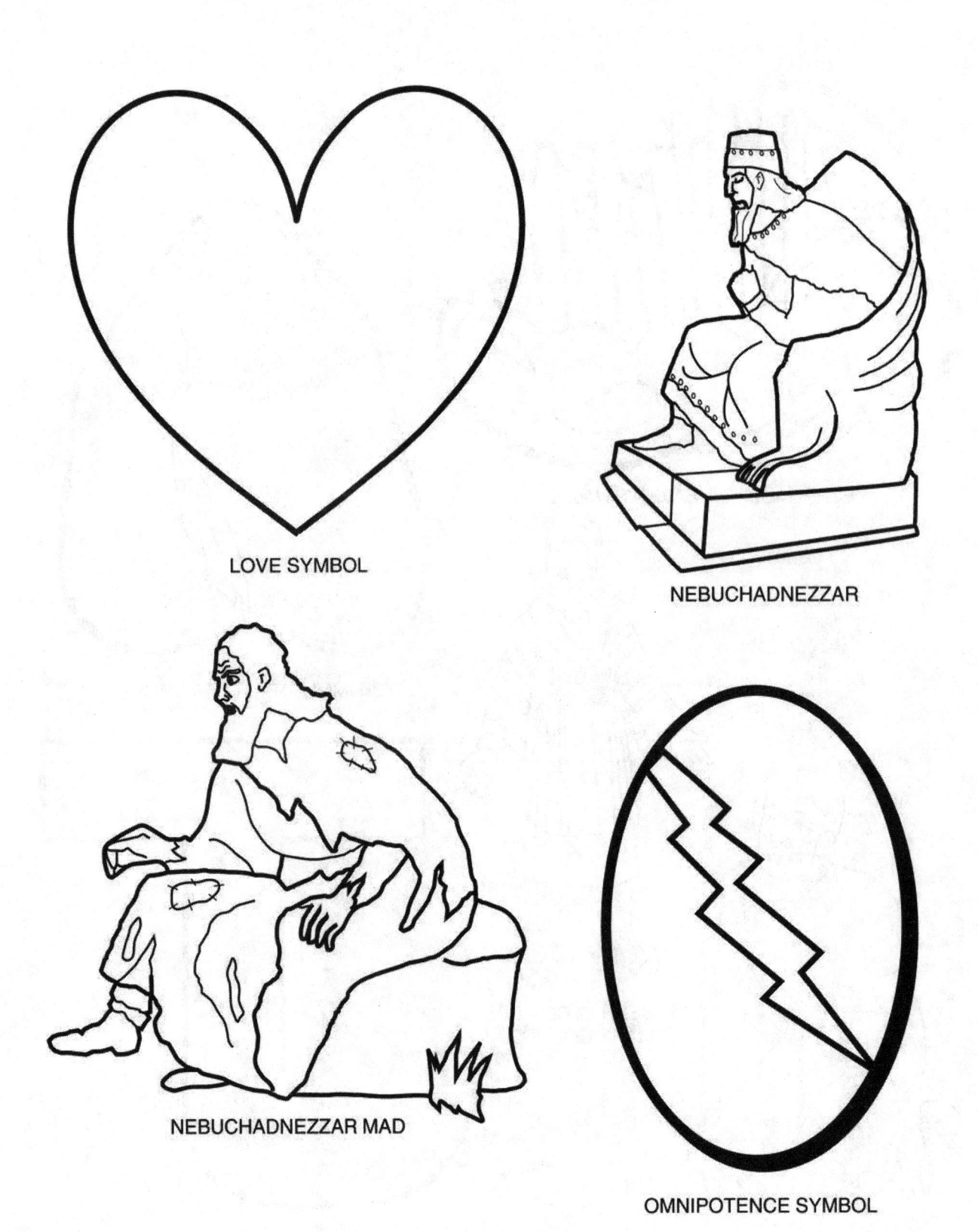

LOVE SYMBOL

NEBUCHADNEZZAR

NEBUCHADNEZZAR MAD

OMNIPOTENCE SYMBOL

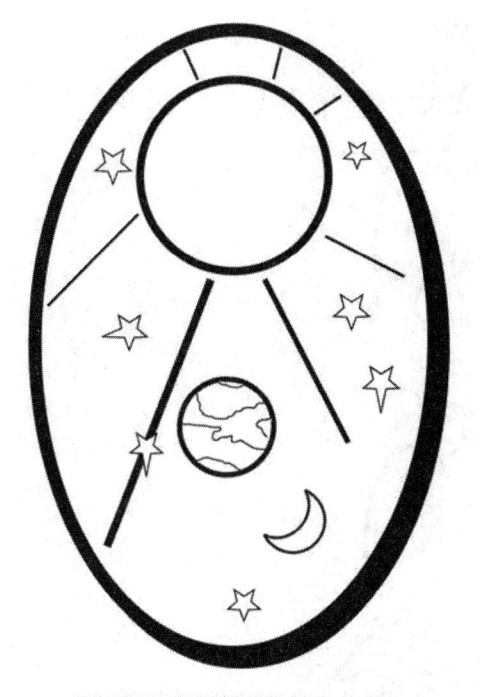

Visual Aids

OMNIPRESENCE SYMBOL

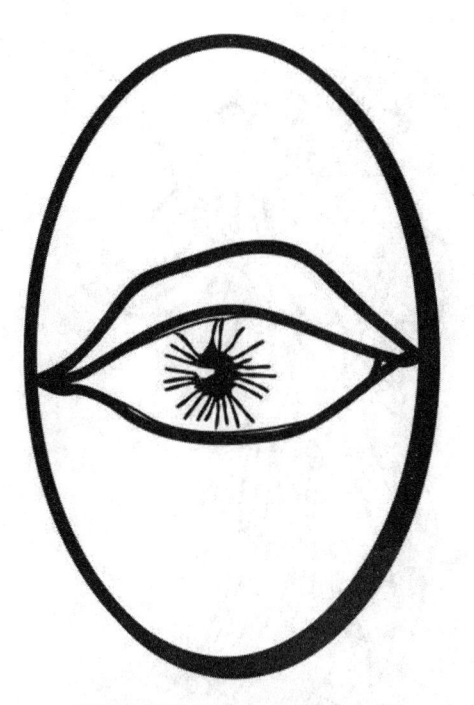

OMNISCIENCE SYMBOL

RIGHTEOUSNESS SYMBOL

SAMUEL ANOINTING DAVID

142 CHILDREN'S BIBLE STUDIES: WHAT IS GOD LIKE?

SATAN

SAUL BLINDED

SIN CIRCLE

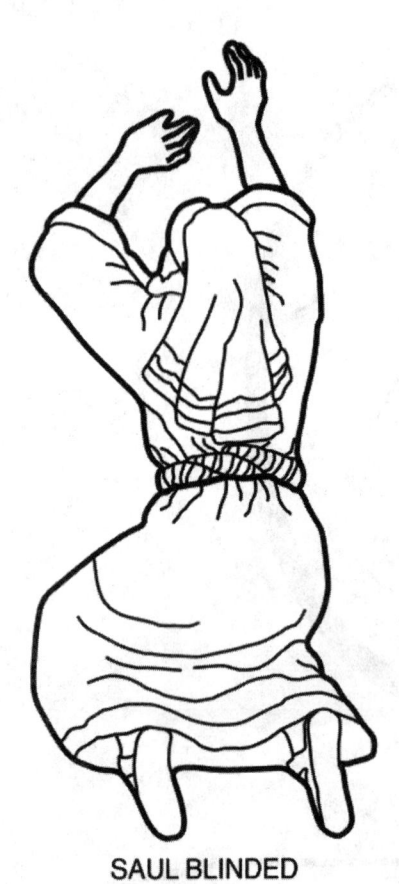

SOVEREIGNTY SYMBOL

Visual Aids

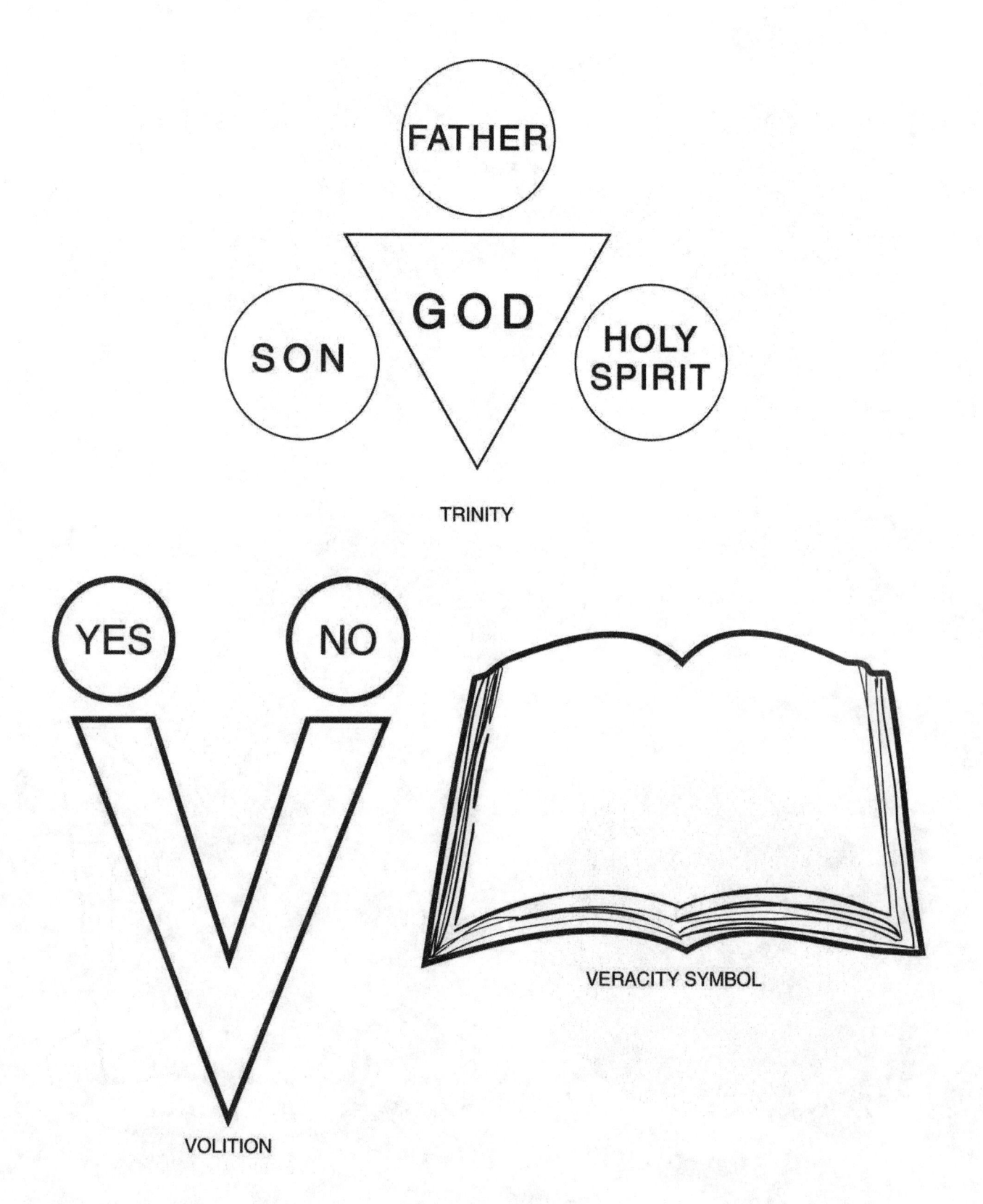

TRINITY

VOLITION

VERACITY SYMBOL